TEACH YOUR CHILDREN WELL

TEACH YOUR CHILDREN WELL

*A Parent's Guide to the Stories, Poems, Fables, and
Tales That Instill Traditional Values*

EDITED BY
CHRISTINE ALLISON

A John Boswell & Associates Book

Delacorte **Press**

Published by
Delacorte Press
Bantam Doubleday Dell Publishing Group, Inc.
1540 Broadway
New York, New York 10036

Library of Congress Cataloging in Publication Data

Allison, Christine.
Teach your children well: a parent's guide to the stories, poems,
fables, and tales that instill traditional values / Christine Allison.
p.   cm.
Summary: Presents readings from classical and modern literature
to emphasize good values for children ages six to ten.
ISBN 0-385-30290-8: $22.95
1. Children's literature.   [1. Literature—Collections.]
I. Title.
PZ5.A48Te   1993
808.8'99282—dc20   92-42762 CIP   AC

Manufactured in the United States of America
Published simultaneously in Canada

August 1993
10 9 8 7 6 5 4 3 2 1
RRH

v

For Maisie Moonbeams,
with love

CONTENTS

CONTENTS

CONTENTS

CONTENTS

Acknowledgments

It was a challenge, indeed, to look at the vast universe of children's literature and say yes to a very few stories for inclusion in this volume. To accomplish this task, I relied not only on my own childhood reading experience, but on the experience of some very gifted individuals, whom I would like to thank.

Thank you especially to Camilla Corcoran of Eeyore's Bookstore in New York City. Camilla's enthusiasm and genuine understanding of what excites and inspires children is unsurpassed. So also is the dedication of the staff who care for the children's books at the Larchmont Public Library. Nancy Manion, Bernadette McGuire, and Ray Messing patiently pointed me this way and that over the course of several months. We acknowledge national treasures; I think intelligent, generous librarians are community treasures and I am particularly grateful for those in Larchmont.

Emily Reichert, my editor, falls into the treasure category in a major way. I hope we grow old together, making lots of books along the way. Thank you to Patty Brown for keeping me on course, and of course, thank you very much to John Boswell. Mom and Dad, I could not have created this book without your extraordinary support. It was you who taught me what I know, and taught me well. Debbie Trumpet, thank you so much for the peace you bring to our home, and for your knowing sense of humor. Thank you to Wick, for love. And to Gillea, Maisie, Chrissie, and Loddie: take these stories and fly.

A Song of Greatness

Mary Austin

When I hear the old men
Telling of heroes,
Telling of great deeds
Of ancient days,

When I hear that telling
Then I think within me
I too am one of these.

When I hear the people
Praising great ones,
Then I know that I too
Shall be esteemed,
I too when my time comes
Shall do mightily.

CHAPTER ONE

Teaching Your Child with Stories

Not long ago my daughter Maisie came walking down the stairs in an outfit that gave new meaning to the word "colorful." We were about to have dinner with friends, and her ensemble was not exactly what I had in mind. Using my best diplomatic skills, I asked her to change into something else. She was not enthusiastic. After a few minutes of getting nowhere, her big sister Gillea passed by and asked, "Mom, why does everything always have to be perfect?"

In a very real way, that question was a turning point in my life as a parent, and the ripples of that moment still affect me. Obviously, everything doesn't have to be perfect. Like many parents, I had been caught up in the external, the trivial. I was making a major flap about . . . a skirt and a blouse!

These days, it's not surprising to find my children wearing odd clothes, but I am no longer concerned. When my children and yours reach old age, it probably won't matter what they wore or how fabulous their sixth birthday party was. If you think about it, a good portion of our efforts are devoted to external matters that may not really matter at all. What will be important is the content of our children's hearts and minds, or what is often described as character. When we say, "It's what's inside that counts," we speak a simple but profound truth.

1

You and I have growing, amorphic agendas for raising our children. But while we are feverish about providing our children every opportunity from tennis lessons to a college degree, it seems that our most important task is much simpler—and that is to raise a decent human being.

Decency might sound like a modest ambition, but in today's culture it's not so easy to achieve as we might think. Every parent I know lives with the uneasy sense that our children are growing up too fast, without clear values or a real code to live by. While we spin our wheels worrying about reading, writing, and arithmetic, our children are missing the real basics like respect, loyalty, and a sense of fair play. Survey after survey shows that our children, who will be the best educated and most privileged in human history, are too willing to do anything it takes to "get ahead."

Teach Your Children Well evolved from my need as a parent to have *tools* for teaching values. Once I realized that collecting for UNICEF in a Halloween costume once a year was not going to add up to moral development, I started looking seriously for ways to help my children learn right from wrong, and to know that sometimes there is a decision to be made in the middle. My children were facing tough choices and complicated situations that couldn't be addressed with simple lectures on the value of kindness or isolated chats about standing up for one's beliefs. I wanted to surround my children with a sturdy sensibility, a world view, and I wanted it to be different from the "Me" mentality of modern culture.

Television was not part of the solution. Though my children watch very little of it, what is presented mostly falls under the heading of inappropriate or just plain stupefying. In families where television viewing is an ongoing part of daily life, it has even become the moral authority for children, with mostly bad results. Yet even if television offered twenty-four hours of uplifting, intelligent fare each day, a sound bite on moral courage just doesn't penetrate. The medium delivers information in a flash—and then it's gone.

Stories found in books, by contrast, seep into our very being. We all have books that lifted the fog for us, caused the Great Aha!, and literally changed our lives. The printed word is pondered, and it is received only when the mind is fully engaged. *Like no other medium, it has the power to stay with us.* In my own case, I remembered learning from the biographies of Nellie Bly and Clara Barton and Elizabeth Blackwell that even great individuals start out as everyday children—letting all children know that life's possibilities are without limit. Then there were the role models in fairy tales and legends and historical tales. Cinderella enchanted not because she got the prince but because she was cheerful and dignified even in unbearable circumstances. King Arthur showed what a noble deed looks like—and that there is such a thing as duty and sacrifice. And historical figures like Pocahontas revealed daring—her unconventional approach to life inspires us all.

These images and impressions form a child's view of life and the higher, more ennobling range of responses to the inevitable trials that come with it. They are lessons delivered by highly moral characters, who—unlike a parent—do not preach and cannot be disappointed. *Teach Your Children Well* is about the lessons and the values that have animated our civilization for centuries: respect, fair play, persistence, daring, gratitude, generosity, wisdom, the love of truth—as well as the characters and stories that personify them.

Teaching values to children has probably never been more difficult. Not only are the influences many, varied, and not so pretty, but parents have less time to fend them off. In many families both parents work; often a mother is trying to raise her children alone. When we do have time to spend with our children, we fall into the temptation of yet another outing, as if childhood were one extended summer vacation. But my guess is that most children don't need another outing as much as they need . . . us. This is why even a quarter of an hour of reading aloud every day can add an extraordinary dimension of intimacy and cohesiveness to your family life. It doesn't always have to be classical literature; the comics or a magazine article read aloud can bring a parent and a tense ten-year-old together on neutral ground, and relaxed. Sometimes, reading aloud is even better than talking.

Teach Your Children Well is geared to parents of children who are about six to ten years old. At this age children are intellectually able to conceptualize values and have to a great extent moved out into the world. It is a complicated time for them—and for us. It is also a tremendous opportunity to help our children form their moral and spiritual foundations.

And, despite the complexities and contradictions of the modern world, helping our children to develop a moral sensibility is not a difficult proposition. Children are innately moral and spiritual creatures. They are also innately cruel and contemptuous! But two factors will influence them now and for a lifetime: parental example and powerful literature.

It's kind of spooky, but the cues children receive from us regarding right and wrong behavior are profound. And children hear and see *everything*. This is why if Daddy is rude to waiters, you can bet Junior will be too. It is why at some point you will always lose the argument that something is okay for *you* to do, and not okay for *them* to do.

Parental example is up to us, and the best evidence shows that this does not mean being perfect. It means trying—struggling—to do the right thing, and making your children aware of both the right thing and your struggle. My children will get a stronger message from my husband's tortured attempts to quit smoking than they will from me simply not smoking.

So it is good to show our children our struggles and to be explicit about our aims. And to let them know that none of this is easy.

Another favor we might do for our children is not to be timid about right and wrong behavior. Many in our generation are still trying to shake off the "whatever" mentality; we operate as if right and wrong behavior were simply a matter of opinion, and we have a fear about laying something "heavy" on our kids. Someday—at the appropriate moments in their lives—our children will make their own choices. But while they are children—and until they are ready—it is overwhelming and unfair to allow them to make decisions they are unqualified to make.

Be clear with your children. You've figured out a lot along the way; share your values and beliefs enthusiastically. They are the grand harvest of your intellectual and spiritual life.

On to the Stories

So what does this have to do with *Ivanhoe*? If parental example is what the eyes and ears behold, literary example is what the heart and soul behold. The lessons in a great children's story are not loaded. They don't come to us in an anxious moment from an authority figure, but in a dreamy intellectual state where we are free and without defenses.

The stories in this book are your great allies. Whether it is the price of friendship or respect for the elderly or the sturdiness to stand up for a lost but righteous cause, these tales cry out unabashedly that *words and deeds matter* and, in fact, give life itself meaning. They are not all stories with happy endings. And even those for the youngest of your children are not, really, simple.

The stories are wonderful to read aloud. If it feels right, talk about the story a little. If your child loves the story, he may well want you to get the whole book. But these stories ought not to be used like medicine. If a friend was cheating on her husband, you probably wouldn't hand her a copy of *Anna Karenina*. These stories aren't a ruler on the hand; they are revelations, not remedies.

When my first child was born, a friend called to congratulate me. "There are two kinds of people in the world," he said with uncustomary drama, "parents and everyone else." It did not take more than a day or two to understand well what my friend was telling me. Parenthood is the club of clubs: it is a terrifying, exhilarating, and gorgeous experience that only those who have had a child will ever understand.

These stories are really for you.

CHAPTER TWO

Stories You Won't Find Here

Like most parents, I spent the first five years of my children's lives diligently preparing them to read. Now it seems that I spend a great amount of time hiding things I don't want them to read, tucking copies of the *New York Post* under seat cushions, veering them away from vulgar headlines at the newsstands.

These are difficult times for parents who, shall we say, like to *control* things. Other solar systems begin to have their appeal when you realize that your child is just as likely to find a condom as an acorn at the park. And then there's that day when you discover that even the library contains questionable material. Only they call it children's literature.

I found out in a phone call. It was my seven-year-old, calling from our faraway country retreat. She and her father had spent a special weekend together and she phoned to tell me about the "great book" she checked out from the little country library. "And in the book, Alice and her boyfriend French kiss!" she said excitedly.

"French kiss?" I said, dumbfounded. "Gosh, honey, uh, what's that?" She then explained how special a French kiss is. Special indeed! My husband, naively thinking a children's book is a children's book, didn't vet Gillea's trip to the library, and this is what we got.

But this is what everyone is getting, if they have a six- to ten-year-old who likes to read, and it is in many ways an unavoidable aspect of our cultural landscape. Isaac Bashevis Singer, who respected the minds of children enormously, put the consequences in harsh terms: "A lot of the evil taking place today, I often feel, is the result of the rotten stuff this modern generation read in its school days."

Some of it is simply banal. For example, there is a boatload of children's books that are often categorized as "problem books." In these books magic is out, reality is in, and the result is perky, sometimes naughty, sometimes terribly depressing episodes that somehow pass for children's literature.

In many cases the stories are not expansive odes to the human condition but puny tales about social conditions or family life; the facts of life instead of the truth about life. Issues like divorce, death, homosexuality, abortion, racism, and disabilities become the main characters of the books. One observer described them as "kiddie pop psych"— and for the child who has no other recourse, they do provide a flash of comfort. But mostly, they are experiments by good writers who feel compelled to play the role of social worker. ("Writers can be guilty of every kind of human conceit but one, the conceit of the social worker," W. H. Auden once wrote.) Great literature is not didactic, though it almost always instructs. Literature that *strains* to instruct almost always fails.

This is not to damn all books that are written in the realistic mode; a vast number of realistic books are written without a social agenda or the need to be explicit or titillating, and they are marvelous, humorous, powerful, disturbing, illuminating: everything one might want in a good read.

Some of them are a hundred years old. For instance, *The Adventures of Tom Sawyer* is a realistic book, and when it made its debut in 1876 it was wild fare for the young readers, most of whom were spending their waking hours trying to avoid eternal damnation (while Tom was merrily swindling, lying, and stealing!). *Tom Sawyer* does not contain an ounce of preachiness, yet it is as much about wisdom as it is about wisecracks. It teaches about friendship and sincerity and playing fair, without being pat. It is an encyclopedia of virtues and vices.

Little Women is realism, too, and still is beloved by young female readers who don't need Valley Girl dialogue to enjoy a book. While she might seem tame now, the tomboy character Jo is a determined, scrappy, independent woman; she probably ruffled a few feathers in her time. But Louisa May Alcott didn't create her to assert women's rights, just as Mark Twain didn't create Tom Sawyer as a cog in some campaign; neither of these writers was a propagandist for this cause or that. They were not moralists, yet their writing *is* moral.

When they work, realistic books become classics, like *Sounder* by William Armstrong or *Harriet the Spy* by Louise Fitzhugh. When they fail, they are literary pests. But they are not the only pests. A couple of years ago my daughter came home from first grade bursting to show me the fantasy book she had checked out from the school library. With great expectation, I watched as *She-Ra* emerged from Gillea's backpack—a Mattel book. A *toy* book? From the school library? As it happens, *She-Ra* left me humorless. The message basically was "scanty togs = female success." It was not a message I wanted conveyed to the eldest of my four daughters. To top it off, the writing was atrocious.

When I mentioned that the book should be removed from the school library, the response was "We don't believe in censorship." Gosh, now we call throwing out junk . . . censorship?

The librarian did pull the book for reasons of her own, good ones I am sure. But one cannot really expect to purge the world of lesser reads for children, nor is that the point. What one can do is funnel excellent material to one's children, keep the mush level low and the level of enchantment high.

This will require some vigilance and humor, but it is entirely worth it. You don't need to wear a uniform and a badge, but it makes sense to be aware of what your children are reading, and to make sure that the best books—classics old and new—are available to them.

If you are fortunate, as I am, your local librarian will direct your children to books that are age appropriate and geared to their interests. Indeed, I think a close relationship with a good librarian is one of the most important a parent can establish. In addition, I recommend a book called *Choosing Books for Children* (Delacorte Press, 1981; rev. 1990) by Betsy Hearne. It's an extremely well written discussion of children's literature, with listings. I differ a little on some points with Ms. Hearne, but I respect her completely.

In another wonderful book for parents and teachers called *Choosing Books for Kids* (Ballantine, 1986), authors Joanne Oppenheim, Barbara Brenner, and Betty D. Boegehold underscore the importance of proper book selection this way: "Books are still the most memorable artifact of childhood. They are not only good for the child; they are a family resource beyond anything that any medium has to offer. And children's books remain what the best of them have always been . . . a powerful transmitter of the culture and the values of a civilization."

Your role is not to protect your children from the truth but to protect them from something *less* than the truth. And the truth is that French kissing can be wonderful. But love is even better.

CHAPTER THREE

Tell the Truth

"Did you have any fun?
Tell me. What did you do?"

And Sally and I did not know
What to say. Should we tell her
The things that went on there that day?

Should we tell her about it?
Now, what SHOULD *we do?*

Well . . .
What would YOU *do*
If your mother asked YOU?

From *The Cat in the Hat*
by DR. SEUSS

11

It was April 1. Our five-year-old crawled into our bed for a hug and some whispered conversation. Though the hour was early, I had my wits about me and began to describe in a sweet voice the breakfast menu, which consisted of all of her most hated foods.

Almost anyone can be convincing at 6 A.M., and as I ended my recitation with a big, tall glass of tomato juice, her face started to cloud up. My little joke had gone too far, so I cried out, "April Fool!" hoping for a laugh or an "Oh, Mom." Instead, she began sobbing uncontrollably. Whoops.

I compared notes that day and found that a lot of parents, like me, learned the hard way that it is inappropriate to deceive your children, even with a silly joke. Little children, especially, cannot sort out the difference between fantasy and reality, and what might seem like kidding to you could be a monstrous betrayal to Junior. Obviously, silly jokes rank pretty low in the vice department, but insincerity as a general approach ranks almost at the top. While a gag is just a gag, insincerity destroys trust, which is the foundation of human relationships. It also drains the soul.

This chapter is about sincerity, honesty inside and out, as a virtue. It is odd that the word *sincere* sounds kind of wimpy or trite to most of us; we sign our correspondence "all the best" as if it were a yearbook, rather than "sincerely," which connotes a message from the heart.

However passé the word has become, its meaning is profound. Sincerity is the all-encompassing virtue of people who love the truth. A sincere person has integrity, respects and searches for the truth, and abhors fakery. You can trust a sincere person. You can work for him or marry him or invest in him, and feel secure. Sincerity is the mark of a person who is truly at peace and truly free.

Before a child is seven, sincerity is not a real option. The child cannot reasonably be expected to detect or provide the truth because he is still prone to compelling journeys into his fantasy world. As he enters the age of reason, though, he is ready to learn the difference between facts and opinions, and to grasp that there are distinctions in life, some of them very subtle. Children need to learn to seek truth and befriend it, even when it makes them uncomfortable. This can range from confessions: "Who stole the cookie from the cookie jar?" to the much more complicated matter of maintaining one's integrity. Like all virtues, sincerity is the quest of a lifetime.

David Isaacs, in his marvelous book *Character Building*, discusses the virtue of sincerity, which he explains in part by listing its opposites: slander, lying, hypocrisy, flattery, and self-deception. As it happens, in much of children's literature adults are portrayed as having all of these negative qualities: they are pompous, shallow, and stupid. Remember the parents in *Mary Poppins*? Selfish jerks! The father in *Peter Pan*? A dolt! The portrayal of the insincere adult resonates with the child reader. The child views himself as purveyor of simple truth and sincerity, forced to operate in a world of giant manipulators. I don't know that we all fit that description, but I can see how a child might view it so. It is purity pitted against false complexity.

Here are some highs in children's literature discussing some lows in human behavior.

From The Adventures of Tom Sawyer
by Mark Twain

Having agreed that there are some "conspicuous advantages to a life of crime," three of the best known buddies in literature agree to become pirates: Tom Sawyer, the Black Avenger of the Spanish Main; Joe Harper, the Terror of the Seas; and Huck Finn, the Red-Handed. Taking a raft down the river, they hole up at Jackson's Island, three miles below St. Petersburg, telling no one of their whereabouts.

This excerpt carries the reader in and out of Tom Sawyer's extraordinary conscience. While the entire town, including dear Aunt Polly, is deceived into believing the three "pirates" are dead, Tom's emotions run the gambit. He even feels a sense of remorse. Sort of.

Tom stirred up the other pirates and they all clattered away with a shout, and in a minute or two were stripped and chasing after and tumbling over each other in the shallow limpid water of the white sandbar. They felt no longing for the little village sleeping in the distance beyond the majestic waste of water. A vagrant current or a slight rise in the river had carried off their raft, but this only gratified them, since its going was something like burning the bridge between them and civilization.

They came back to camp wonderfully refreshed, glad-hearted, and ravenous; and they soon had the campfire blazing again. Huck found a spring of clear cold water close by, and the boys made cups of broad oak or hickory leaves, and felt that water, sweetened with such a wildwood charm as that, would be a good enough substitute for coffee. While Joe was slicing bacon for breakfast, Tom and Huck asked him to hold on a minute; they stepped to a promising nook in the riverbank and threw in their lines; almost immediately they had reward. Joe had not had time to get impatient before they were back again with some handsome bass, a couple of sun-perch and a small catfish—provisions enough for quite a family. They fried the fish with the bacon, and were astonished; for no fish had ever seemed so delicious before. They did not know that the quicker a freshwater fish is on the fire after he is caught the better he is; and they reflected little upon what a sauce open-air sleeping, open-air exercise, bathing and a large ingredient of hunger make, too.

They lay around in the shade, after breakfast, while Huck had a smoke, and then went off through the woods on an exploring expedition. They tramped gaily along, over decaying logs, through tangled underbrush, among solemn monarchs of the forest, hung from their crowns to the ground with a drooping regalia of grapevines. Now and then they came upon snug nooks carpeted with grass and jeweled with flowers.

They found plenty of things to be delighted with, but nothing to be astonished at. They discovered that the island was about three miles long and a quarter of a mile wide, and that the shore it lay closest to was only separated from it by a narrow channel hardly two hundred yards wide. They took a swim about every hour, so it was close upon the middle of the afternoon when they got back to camp. They were too hungry to stop to fish, but they fared sumptuously upon cold ham, and then threw themselves down in the shade to talk. But the talk soon began to drag, and then died. The stillness, the solemnity that brooded in the woods, and the sense of loneliness began to tell upon the spirits of the boys. They fell to thinking. A sort of undefined longing crept upon them. This took dim shape, presently—it was budding homesickness. Even Finn the Red-Handed was dreaming of his doorsteps and empty hogsheads. But they were all ashamed of their weakness, and none was brave enough to speak his thought.

For some time, now, the boys had been dully conscious of a peculiar sound in the distance, just as one sometimes is of the ticking of a clock which he takes no distinct note of. But now this mysterious sound became more pronounced, and forced a recognition. The boys started, glanced at each other, and then each assumed a listening attitude. There was a long silence, profound and unbroken; then a deep, sullen boom came floating down out of the distance.

"What is it!" exclaimed Joe, under his breath.

"I wonder," said Tom in a whisper.

" 'Tain't thunder," said Huckleberry, in an awed tone. "Becuz thunder—"

They waited a time that seemed an age, and then the same muffled boom troubled the solemn hush.

"Let's go and see."

They sprang to their feet and hurried to the shore toward the town. They parted the bushes on the bank and peered out over the water. The little steam ferryboat was about a mile below the village, drifting with the current. Her broad deck seemed crowded with people. There were a great many skiffs rowing about or floating with the stream in the neighborhood of the ferryboat, but the boys could not determine what the men in them were doing. Presently a great jet of white smoke burst from the ferryboat's side, and as it expanded and rose in a lazy cloud, that same dull throb of sound was borne to the listeners again.

"I know now!" exclaimed Tom; "somebody's drownded!"

"That's it!" said Huck; "they done that last summer, when Bill Turner got drownded; they shoot a cannon over the water, and that makes him come up to the top. Yes, and they take loaves of bread and put quicksilver in 'em and set 'em afloat, and wherever there's anybody that's drownded, they'll float right there and stop."

"Yes, I've heard about that," said Joe. "I wonder what makes the bread do that."

"Oh, it ain't the bread, so much," said Tom; "I reckon it's mostly what they say over it before they start it out."

"But they don't say anything over it," said Huck. "I've seen 'em and they don't."

"Well, that's funny," said Tom. "But maybe they say it to themselves. Of course they do. Anybody might know that."

The other boys agreed that there was reason in what Tom said, because an ignorant lump of bread, uninstructed by an incantation, could not be expected to act very intelligently when sent upon an errand of such gravity.

"By jings, I wish I was over there now," said Joe.

"I do too," said Huck. "I'd give heaps to know who it is."

The boys still listened and watched. Presently a revealing thought flashed through Tom's mind, and he exclaimed, "Boys, I know who's drownded—it's us!"

They felt like heroes in an instant. Here was a gorgeous triumph; they were missed; they were mourned; hearts were breaking on their account; tears were being shed; accusing memories of unkindnesses to these poor lost lads were rising up, and unavailing regrets and remorse were being indulged; and best of all, the departed were the talk of the whole town, and the envy of all the boys, as far as this dazzling notoriety was concerned. This was fine. It was worthwhile to be a pirate, after all.

As twilight drew on, the ferryboat went back to her accustomed business and the skiffs disappeared. The pirates returned to camp. They were jubilant with vanity over their new grandeur and the illustrious trouble they were making. They caught fish, cooked supper and ate it, and then fell to guessing at what the village was thinking and saying about them; and the pictures they drew of the public distress on their account were gratifying to look upon—from their point of view. But when the shadows of night closed them in, they gradually ceased to talk, and sat gazing into the fire, with their minds evidently wandering elsewhere. The excitement was gone now, and Tom and Joe could not keep back thoughts of certain persons at home who were not enjoying this fine frolic as much as they were. Misgivings came; they grew troubled and unhappy; a sigh or two escaped, unawares. By and by Joe timidly ventured upon a roundabout "feeler" as to how the others might look upon a return to civilization—not right now, but—

Tom withered him with derision! Huck, being uncommitted as yet, joined in with Tom, and the waverer quickly "explained," and was glad to get out of the scrape with as little taint of chickenhearted homesickness clinging to his garments as he could. Mutiny was effectually laid to rest for the moment.

As the night deepened, Huck began to nod, and presently to snore. Joe followed next. Tom lay upon his elbow motionless, for some time, watching the two intently. At last he got up cautiously, on his knees, and went searching among the grass and the flickering reflections flung by the campfire. He picked up and inspected several large semi-cylinders of the thin white bark of a sycamore, and finally chose two which seemed to suit him. Then he knelt by the fire and painfully wrote something upon each of these with his "red keel"; one he rolled up and put in his jacket pocket, and the other he put in Joe's hat and removed it to a little distance from the owner. And he also put into the hat certain schoolboy treasures of almost inestimable value—among them a lump of chalk, an India-rubber ball, three fishhooks, and one of that kind of marbles known as a "sure 'nuff crystal." Then he tiptoed his way cautiously among the trees till he felt that he was out of hearing, and straightaway broke into a keen run in the direction of the sandbar.

A few minutes later Tom was in the shoal water of the bar, wading toward the Illinois shore. Before the depth reached his middle he was halfway over; the current would permit no more wading, now, so he struck out confidently to swim the remaining hundred yards. He swam quartering upstream, but still was swept downward rather faster than he had expected. However, he reached the shore finally, and drifted along till he found a low place and drew himself out. He put his hand on his jacket pocket, found his piece of bark safe, and then struck through the woods, following the shore, with streaming garments. Shortly before ten o'clock he came out into an open place opposite the village, and saw the ferryboat lying in the shadow of the trees and the high bank. Everything was quiet under the blinking stars. He crept down the bank, watching with all his eyes, slipped into the water, swam three or four strokes and climbed into the skiff that did yawl duty at the boat's stern. He laid himself down under the thwarts and waited, panting.

Presently the cracked bell tapped and a voice gave the order to cast off. A minute or two later the skiff's head was standing high up, against the boat's swell, and the voyage was begun. Tom felt happy in his success, for he knew it was the boat's last trip for the night. At the end of a long twelve or fifteen minutes the wheels stopped, and Tom slipped overboard and swam ashore in the dusk, landing fifty yards downstream, out of danger of possible stragglers.

He flew along unfrequented alleys, and shortly found himself at his aunt's back fence. He climbed over, approached the "ell," and looked in at the sitting room window, for a light was burning there. There sat Aunt Polly, Sid, Mary, and Joe Harper's mother, grouped together, talking. They were by the bed, and the bed was between them and the door. Tom went to the door and began to softly lift the latch; then he pressed gently and the door yielded a crack; he continued pushing cautiously, and quaking every time it creaked, till he judged he might squeeze through on his knees; so he put his head through and began, warily.

"What makes the candle blow so?" said Aunt Polly. Tom hurried up. "Why, that door's open, I believe. Why, of course it is. No end of strange things now. Go 'long and shut it, Sid."

Tom disappeared under the bed just in time. He lay and "breathed" himself for a time, and then crept to where he could almost touch his aunt's foot.

"But as I was saying," said Aunt Polly, "he warn't *bad*, so to say— only misch*ee*vous. Only just giddy, and harum-scarum, you know. He warn't any more responsible than a colt. He never meant any harm, and he was the best-hearted boy that ever was"—and she began to cry.

"It was just so with my Joe—always full of his devilment, and up to every kind of mischief, but he was just as unselfish and kind as he could be—and laws bless me, to think I went and whipped him for taking that cream, never once recollecting that I threw it out myself because it was sour, and I never to see him again in this world, never, never, never, poor abused boy!" And Mrs. Harper sobbed as if her heart would break.

"I hope Tom's better off where he is," said Sid, "but if he'd been better in some ways—"

"Sid!" Tom felt the glare of the old lady's eye, though he could not see it. "Not a word against my Tom, now that he's gone! God'll take care of him—never you trouble, yourself, sir! Oh, Mrs. Harper, I don't know how to give him up! I don't know how to give him up! He was such a comfort to me, although he tormented my old heart out of me, 'most."

"The Lord giveth and the Lord hath taken away—blessed be the name of the Lord! But it's *so* hard—oh, it's so hard! Only last Saturday my Joe busted a firecracker right under my nose and I knocked him sprawling. Little did I know then, how soon—oh, if it was to do over again I'd hug him and bless him for it."

"Yes, yes, yes, I know just how you feel, Mrs. Harper, I know just exactly how you feel. No longer ago than yesterday noon, my Tom took and filled the cat full of painkiller, and I did think the cretur would tear the house down. And God forgive me, I cracked Tom's head with my thimble, poor boy, poor dead boy. But he's out of all his troubles now. And the last words I ever heard him say was to reproach—"

But this memory was too much for the old lady, and she broke entirely down. Tom was snuffling, now, himself—and more in pity of himself than anybody else. He could hear Mary crying, and putting in a kindly word for him from time to time. He began to have a nobler opinion of himself than ever before. Still, he was sufficiently touched by his aunt's grief to long to rush out from under the bed and overwhelm her with joy—and the theatrical gorgeousness of the thing appealed strongly to his nature, too, but he resisted and lay still.

He went on listening, and gathered by odds and ends that it was conjectured at first that the boys had got drowned while taking a swim; then the small raft had been missed; next, certain boys said the missing lads had promised that the village should "hear something" soon; and wise heads had "put this and that together" and decided that the lads had gone off on that raft and would turn up at the next town below, presently; but toward noon the raft had been found, lodged against the Missouri shore some five or six miles below the village—and then hope perished; they must be drowned, else hunger would have driven them home by nightfall if not sooner. It was believed that the search for the bodies had been a fruitless effort merely because the drowning must have occurred in midchannel, since the boys, being good swimmers, would otherwise have escaped to shore. This was Wednesday night. If the bodies continued missing until Sunday, all hope would be given over, and the funerals would be preached on that morning. Tom shuddered.

Mrs. Harper gave a sobbing good night and turned to go. Then with a mutual impulse the two bereaved women flung themselves into each other's arms and had a good, consoling cry, and then parted. Aunt Polly was tender far beyond her wont, in her good night to Sid and Mary. Sid snuffled a bit and Mary went off crying with all her heart.

Aunt Polly knelt down and prayed for Tom so touchingly, so appealingly, and with such measureless love in her words and her old trembling voice, that he was weltering in tears again, long before she was through.

He had to keep still long after she went to bed, for she kept making brokenhearted ejaculations from time to time, tossing unrestfully, and turning over. But at last she was still, only moaning a little in her sleep. Now the boy stole out, rose gradually by the bedside, shaded the candlelight with his hand, and stood regarding her. His heart was full of pity for her. He took out his sycamore scroll and placed it by the candle. But something occurred to him, and he lingered, considering. His face lighted with a happy solution to his thought; he put the bark hastily in his pocket. Then he bent over and kissed the faded lips, and straightway made his stealthy exit, latching the door behind him.

He threaded his way back to the ferry landing, found nobody at large there, and walked boldly on board the boat, for he knew she was tenantless except that there was a watchman, who always turned in and slept like a graven image. He untied the skiff at the stern, slipped into it, and was soon rowing cautiously upstream. When he had pulled a mile above the village, he started quartering across and bent himself stoutly to his work. He hit the landing on the other side neatly, for this was a familiar bit of work to him. He was moving to capture the skiff, arguing that it might be considered a ship and therefore legitimate prey for a pirate, but he knew a thorough search would be made for it and that might end in revelations. So he stepped ashore and entered the wood.

He sat down and took a long rest, torturing himself meantime to keep awake, and then started warily down the homestretch. The night was far spent. It was broad daylight before he found himself fairly abreast the island bar. He rested again until the sun was well up and gliding the great river with its splendor, and then he plunged into the stream. A little later he paused, dripping, upon the threshold of the camp, and heard Joe say, "No, Tom's true-blue, Huck, and he'll come back. He won't desert. He knows that would be a disgrace to a pirate, and Tom's too proud for that sort of thing. He's up to something or other. Now, I wonder what?"

"Well, the things is ours, anyway, ain't they?"

"Pretty near, but not yet, Huck. The writing says they are if he ain't back here to breakfast."

"Which he is!" exclaimed Tom, with fine dramatic effect, stepping grandly into camp.

A sumptuous breakfast of bacon and fish was shortly provided, and as the boys set to work upon it, Tom recounted (and adorned) his adventures. They were a vain and boastful company of heroes when the tale was done. Then Tom hid himself away in a shady nook to sleep till noon, and the other pirates got ready to fish and explore.

There was no hilarity in the little town on Saturday afternoon. The Harpers, and Aunt Polly's family, were being put into mourning, with great grief and many tears. An unusual quiet possessed the village, although it was ordinarily quiet enough, in all conscience. The villagers conducted their concerns with an absent air, and talked little; but they sighed often. The Saturday holiday seemed a burden to the children. They had not heart in their sports, and gradually gave them up.

In the afternoon Becky Thatcher found herself moping around the deserted schoolhouse yard, and feeling very melancholy. But she found nothing there to comfort her. She soliloquized, "Oh, if I only had a brass and iron knob again! But I haven't got anything now to remember him by." And she choked back a little sob.

Presently she stopped, and said to herself, "It was right here. Oh, if it was to do over again, I wouldn't say that—I wouldn't say it for the whole world. But he's gone now; I'll never, never, never see him anymore."

This thought broke her down, and she wandered away, with tears rolling down her cheeks. Then quite a group of boys and girls— playmates of Tom's and Joe's—came by, and stood looking over the paling fence and talking in reverent tones of how Tom did so-and-so the last time they saw him, and how Joe said this and that small trifle (pregnant with awful prophecy, as they could easily see now!)—and each speaker pointed out the exact spot where the lost lads stood at the time, and then added something like, "and I was a-standing just so— just as I am now, and as if you was him—I was as close as that—and he smiled, just this way—and then something seemed to go all over me, like—awful, you know—and I never thought what it meant, of course, but I can see now!"

Then there was a dispute about who saw the dead boys last in life, and many claimed that dismal distinction, and offered evidences, more or less tampered with by the witness; and when it was ultimately decided who did see the departed last, and exchanged the last words with them, the lucky parties took upon themselves a sort of sacred importance, and were gaped at and envied by all the rest. One poor chap, who had no other grandeur to offer, said with tolerably manifest pride in the remembrance, "Well, Tom Sawyer, he licked me once."

But that bid for glory was a failure. Most of the boys could say that, and so that cheapened the distinction too much. The group loitered away, still recalling memories of the lost heroes, in awed voices.

When the Sunday-school hour was finished, the next morning, the bell began to toll, instead of ringing in the usual way. It was a very still Sabbath, and the mournful sound seemed in keeping with the musing hush that lay upon nature. The villagers began to gather, loitering a moment in the vestibule to converse in whispers about the sad event. But there was no whispering in the house; only the funereal rustling of dresses as the women gathered to their seats disturbed the silence there. None could remember when the little church had been so full before. There was finally a waiting pause, an expectant dumbness, and then Aunt Polly entered, followed by Sid and Mary, and they by the Harper family, all in deep black, and the whole congregation, the old minister as well, rose reverently and stood until the mourners were seated in the front pew. There was another communing silence, broken at intervals by muffled sobs, and then the minister spread his hands abroad and prayed. A moving hymn was sung, and the text followed: "I am the Resurrection and the Life."

As the service proceeded, the clergyman drew such pictures of the graces, the winning ways, and the rare promise of the lost lads that every soul there, thinking he recognized those pictures, felt a pang in remembering that he had persistently blinded himself to them always before, and had as persistently seen only faults and flaws in the poor boys. The minister related many a touching incident in the lives of the departed, too, which illustrated their sweet, generous natures, and the people could easily see, now, how noble and beautiful those episodes were, and remembered with grief that at the time they occurred they had seemed rank rascalities, well deserving of the cowhide. The congregation became more and more moved, as the pathetic tale went on, till at last the whole company broke down and joined the weeping mourners in a chorus of anguished sobs, the preacher himself giving way to his feelings, and crying in the pulpit.

There was a rustle in the gallery, which nobody noticed; a moment later the church door creaked; the minister raised his streaming eyes above his handkerchief, and stood transfixed! First one and then another pair of eyes followed the minister's, and then almost with one impulse the congregation rose and stared while the three dead boys came marching up the aisle, Tom in the lead, Joe next, and Huck, a ruin of drooping rags, sneaking sheepishly in the rear! They had been hid in the unused gallery listening to their own funeral sermon!

Aunt Polly, Mary, and the Harpers threw themselves upon their restored ones, smothered them with kisses and poured out thanksgivings, while poor Huck stood abashed and uncomfortable, not knowing exactly what to do or where to hide from so many unwelcoming eyes. He wavered, and started to slink away, but Tom seized him and said, "Aunt Polly, it ain't fair. Somebody's got to be glad to see Huck."

"And so they shall. I'm glad to see him, poor motherless thing!" And the loving attentions Aunt Polly lavished upon him were the one thing capable of making him more uncomfortable than he was before.

Suddenly the minister shouted at the top of his voice, "Praise God from whom all blessings flow—SING!—and put your hearts in it!"

And they did. "Old Hundred" swelled up with a triumphant

burst, and while it shook the rafters Tom Sawyer the pirate looked around upon the envying juveniles about him and confessed in his heart that this was the proudest moment of his life.

As the "sold" congregation trooped out they said they would almost be willing to be made ridiculous again to hear "Old Hundred" sung like that once more.

Tom got more cuffs and kisses that day—according to Aunt Polly's varying moods—than he had earned before in a year; and he hardly knew which expressed the most gratefulness to God and affection for himself.

That was Tom's great secret—the scheme to return home with his brother pirates and attend their own funerals. They had paddled over to the Missouri shore on a log, at dusk on Saturday, landing five or six miles below the village; they had slept in the woods at the edge of the town till nearly daylight, and had then crept through back lanes and alleys and finished their sleep in the gallery of the church among a chaos of invalided benches.

At breakfast, Monday morning, Aunt Polly and Mary were very loving to Tom, and very attentive to his wants. There was an unusual amount of talk. In the course of it Aunt Polly said, "Well, I don't say it wasn't a fine joke, Tom, to keep everybody suffering 'most a week so you boys had a good time, but it is a pity you could be so hardhearted as to let me suffer so. If you could come over on a log to go to your funeral, you could have come over and give me a hint some way that you warn't dead, but only run off."

"Yes, you could have done that, Tom," said Mary; "and I believe you would if you had thought of it."

"Would you, Tom?" said Aunt Polly, her face lighting wistfully. "Say, now, would you, if you'd thought of it?"

"I—well, I don't know. 'Twould 'a' spoiled everything."

"Tom, I hoped you loved me that much," said Aunt Polly, with a grieved tone that discomforted the boy. "It would have been something if you'd cared enough to think of it, even if you didn't do it."

"Now, Auntie, that ain't any harm," pleaded Mary; "it's only Tom's giddy way—he is always in such a rush that he never thinks of anything."

"More's the pity. Sid would have thought. And Sid would have come and done it too. Tom, you'll look back, some day, when it's too late, and wish you'd care a little more for me when it would have cost you so little."

"Now, Auntie, you know I do care for you," said Tom.

"I'd know it better if you acted more like it."

"I wish now I'd thought," said Tom, with a repentant tone; "but I dreamt about you, anyway. That's something, ain't it?"

"It ain't much—a cat does that much—but it's better than nothing. What did you dream?"

"Why, Wednesday night I dreamt that you was sitting over there by the bed, and Sid was sitting by the woodbox, and Mary next to him."

"Well, so we did. So we always do. I'm glad your dreams could take even that much trouble about us."

"And I dreamt that Joe Harper's mother was here."

"Why, she was here! Did you dream any more?"

"Oh, lots. But it's so dim now."

"Well, try to recollect—can't you?"

"Somehow it seems to me that the wind—the wind blowed the—the—"

"Try harder, Tom! The wind did blow something. Come!"

Tom pressed his fingers on his forehead an anxious moment, and then said, "I've got it now! I've got it now! It blowed the candle!"

"Mercy on us! Go on, Tom—go on!"

"And it seems to me that you said, 'Why, I believe that the door—' "

"Go on, Tom!"

"Just let me study a moment—just a moment. Oh, yes—you said you believed the door was open."

"As I'm sitting here, I did! Didn't I, Mary! Go on!"

"And then—and then—well, I won't be certain, but it seems like as if you made Sid go and—and—"

"Well, for the land's sake! I never heard the beat of that in all my days! Don't tell me there ain't anything in dreams, anymore. Sereny Harper shall know of this before I'm an hour older. I'd like to see her get around this with her rubbage 'bout superstition. Go on, Tom!"

"Oh, it's all getting just as bright as day now. Next you said I warn't *bad*, only misch*ee*vous and harum-scarum, and not any more responsible than—than—I think it was a colt, or something."

"And so it was! Well, goodness gracious! Go on, Tom!"

"And then you began to cry."

"So I did. So I did. Not the first time, neither. And then—"

"Then Mrs. Harper, she began to cry, and said Joe was just the same, and she wished she hadn't whipped him for taking cream when she'd throwed it out her own self—"

"Tom! The sperrit was upon you! You was a prophesying—that's what you was doing! Land alive, go on, Tom!"

"Then Sid, he said—he said—"

"I don't think I said anything," said Sid.

"Yes, you did, Sid," said Mary.

"Shut your heads and let Tom go on! What did he say, Tom?"

"He said—I think he said he hoped I was better off where I was gone to, but if I'd been better sometimes—"

"There, d'you hear that! It was his very words!"

"And you shut him up sharp."

"I lay I did! There must 'a' been an angel there. There was an angel there, somewheres!"

"And Mrs. Harper told about Joe scaring her with a firecracker, and you told about Peter and the painkiller—"

"Just as true as I live!"

"And then there was a whole lot of talk 'bout dragging the river for us, and 'bout having the funeral Sunday, and then you and old Mrs. Harper hugged and cried, and she went."

"It happened just so! It happened just so, as sure as I'm a-sitting in these very tracks. Tom, you couldn't 'a' told it more like if you'd 'a' seen it! And then what? Go on, Tom!"

"Then I thought you prayed for me—and I could see you and hear every word you said. And you went to bed, and I was so sorry that I took and wrote on a piece of sycamore bark, 'We ain't dead—we are only off being pirates,' and put it on the table by the candle; and then you looked so good, laying there asleep, that I thought I went and leaned over and kissed you on the lips."

"Did you, Tom, did you! I just forgive you everything for that!" And she seized the boy in a crushing embrace that made him feel like the guiltiest of villains.

"The Discovery of Oz, the Terrible"
from The Wizard of Oz
by L. Frank Baum

*All of us, at one time or another, feel like the little man behind
the screen. We have overstated our powers to ourself or to others,
and we have gotten caught. This is the confrontation between
Dorothy, the Scarecrow, the Lion, the Tin Man, and the Wizard.
The brave foursome have completed their mission and killed the
Wicked Witch, and have come to collect their respective rewards.
The Wizard must confess that he is not who he seems to be.*

The soldiers had the news carried straight to Oz that Dorothy and
the other travelers had come back again, after destroying the Wicked
Witch; but Oz made no reply. They thought the Great Wizard would
send for them at once, but he did not. They had no word from him the
next day, nor the next, nor the next. The waiting was tiresome and
wearing, and at last they grew vexed that Oz should treat them in so
poor a fashion, after sending them to undergo hardships and slavery.
So the Scarecrow at last asked the green girl to take another message to
Oz, saying if he did not let them in to see him at once they would call the
Winged Monkeys to help them, and find out whether he kept his
promises or not. When the Wizard was given this message he was so
frightened that he sent word for them to come to the Throne Room at
four minutes after nine o'clock the next morning. He had once met the
Winged Monkeys in the Land of the West, and he did not wish to meet
them again.

The four travelers passed a sleepless night, each thinking of the gift
Oz had promised to bestow upon him. Dorothy fell asleep only once,
and then she dreamed she was in Kansas, where Aunt Em was telling
her how glad she was to have her little girl at home again.

Promptly at nine o'clock the next morning the green-whiskered
soldier came to them, and four minutes later they all went into the
Throne Room of the Great Oz.

Of course each one of them expected to see the Wizard in the shape he had taken before, and all were greatly surprised when they looked about and saw no one at all in the room. They kept close to the door and closer to one another, for the stillness of the empty room was more dreadful than any of the forms they had seen Oz take.

Presently they heard a Voice, seeming to come from somewhere near the top of the great dome, and it said solemnly, "I am Oz, the Great and Terrible. Why do you seek me?"

They looked again in every part of the room, and then, seeing no one, Dorothy asked, "Where are you?"

"I am everywhere," answered the voice. "But to the eyes of common mortals I am invisible. I will now seat myself upon my throne, that you may converse with me." Indeed, the Voice seemed just then to come straight from the throne itself; so they walked toward it and stood in a row while Dorothy said, "We have come to claim our promise, O Oz."

"What promise?" asked Oz.

"You promised to send me back to Kansas when the Wicked Witch was destroyed," said the girl.

"You promised to give me brains," said the Scarecrow.

"And you promised to give me a heart," said the Tin Woodman.

"And you promised to give me courage," said the Cowardly Lion.

"Is the Wicked Witch really destroyed?" asked the Voice, and Dorothy thought it trembled a little.

"Yes," she answered, "I melted her with a bucket of water."

"Dear me," said the Voice; "how sudden! Well, come to me tomorrow, for I must have time to think it over."

"You've had plenty of time already," said the Tin Woodman angrily.

"We shan't wait a day longer," said the Scarecrow.

"You must keep your promises to us!" exclaimed Dorothy.

The Lion thought it might be as well to frighten the Wizard, so he gave a large, loud roar, which was so fierce and dreadful that Toto jumped away from him in alarm and tipped over the screen that stood in a corner. As it fell with a crash they looked that way, and the next moment all of them were filled with wonder. For they saw, standing in just the spot the screen had hidden, a little, old man, with a bald head and a wrinkled face, who seemed to be as much surprised as they were. The Tin Woodman raised his ax, rushed toward the little man, and cried out, "Who are you?"

"I am Oz, the Great and Terrible," said the little man, in a trembling voice. "But don't strike me—please don't!—and I'll do anything you want me to."

Our friends looked at him in surprise and dismay.

"I thought Oz was a Great Head," said Dorothy.

"I thought Oz was a Lovely Lady," said the Scarecrow.

"And I thought Oz was a Terrible Beast," said the Tin Woodman.

"And I thought Oz was a Ball of Fire," exclaimed the Lion.

"No; you are all wrong," said the little man meekly. "I have been making believe."

"Making believe!" cried Dorothy. "Are you not a Great Wizard?"

"Hush, my dear," he said; "don't speak so loud, or you will be overheard—and I should be ruined. I'm supposed to be a Great Wizard."

"And aren't you?"

"Not a bit of it, my dear; I'm just a common man."

"You're more than that," said the Scarecrow, in a grieved tone; "you're a humbug."

"Exactly so!" declared the little man, rubbing his hands together as if it pleased him; "I am a humbug."

"But this is terrible," said the Tin Woodman; "how shall I ever get my heart?"

"Or I my courage?" asked the Lion.

"Or I my brains?" wailed the Scarecrow, wiping the tears from his eyes with his coat sleeve.

"My dear friends," said Oz, "I pray you not to speak of these little things. Think of me, and the terrible trouble I'm in at being found out."

"Doesn't anyone else know you're a humbug?" asked Dorothy.

"No one knows it but you four—and myself," replied Oz. "I have fooled everyone so long that I thought I should never be found out. It was a great mistake my ever letting you into the Throne Room. Usually I will not see even my subjects, and so they believe I am something terrible."

"But I don't understand," said Dorothy in bewilderment. "How was it that you appeared to me as a Great Head?"

"That was one of my tricks," answered Oz. "Step this way, please, and I will tell you all about it."

He led the way to a small chamber in the rear of the Throne Room, and they all followed him. He pointed to one corner, in which lay the Great Head, made out of many thicknesses of paper, and with a carefully painted face.

"This I hung from the ceiling by a wire," said Oz; "I stood behind the screen and pulled a thread to make the eyes move and the mouth open."

"But how about the Voice?" she inquired.

"Oh, I am a ventriloquist," said the little man, "and I can throw the sound of my voice wherever I wish; so that you thought it was coming out of the Head. Here are the other things I used to deceive you." He showed Scarecrow the dress and the mask he had worn when he seemed to be the Lovely Lady; and the Tin Woodman saw that his Terrible Beast was nothing but a lot of skins, sewn together, with slats to keep their sides out. As for the Ball of Fire, the False Wizard had hung that also from the ceiling. It was really a ball of cotton, but when oil was poured upon it the ball burned fiercely.

"Really," said the Scarecrow, "you ought to be ashamed of yourself for being such a humbug."

"I am—I certainly am," answered the little man sorrowfully; "but it was the only thing I could do. Sit down, please; there are plenty of chairs, and I will tell you my story."

So they sat down and listened while he told the following tale:

"I was born in Omaha—"

"Why, that isn't very far from Kansas!" cried Dorothy.

"No, but it's farther from here," he said, shaking his head at her sadly. "When I grew up I became a ventriloquist, and at that I was very well trained by a great master. I can imitate any kind of a bird or beast." Here he mewed so like a kitten that Toto pricked up his ears and looked everywhere to see where she was. "After a time," continued Oz, "I tired of that, and became a balloonist."

"What is that?" asked Dorothy.

"A man who goes up in a balloon on circus day, so as to draw a crowd of people together and get them to pay to see the circus," he explained.

"Oh," she said; "I know."

"Well, one day I went up in a balloon and the ropes got twisted, so that I couldn't come down again. It went way up above the clouds, so far that a current of air struck it and carried it many, many miles away. For a day and a night I traveled through the air, and on the morning of the second day I awoke and found the balloon floating over a strange and beautiful country.

"It came down gradually, and I was not hurt a bit. But I found myself in the midst of a strange people, who, seeing me come from the clouds, thought I was a Great Wizard. Of course I let them think so, because they were afraid of me, and promised to do anything I wished them to.

"Just to amuse myself, and keep the good people busy, I ordered them to build this City, and my Palace, and they did it all willingly and well. Then I thought, as the country was so green and beautiful, I would call it the Emerald City, and to make the name fit better I put green spectacles on all the people, so that everything they saw was green."

"But isn't everything here green?" asked Dorothy.

"No more than in any other city," replied Oz; "but when you wear green spectacles, why, of course everything you see looks green to you. The Emerald City was built a great many years ago, for I was a young man when the balloon brought me here, and I am a very old man now. But my people have worn green glasses on their eyes so long that most of them think it really is an Emerald City, and it certainly is a beautiful place, abounding in jewels and precious metals, and every good thing that is needed to make one happy. I have been good to the people, and they like me; but ever since this Palace was built I have shut myself up and would not see any of them.

"One of my greatest fears was the Witches, for while I had no magical powers at all I soon found out that the Witches were really able to do wonderful things. There were four of them in this country, and they ruled the people who live in the North and South and East and West. Fortunately, the Witches of the North and South were good, and I knew they would do me no harm; but the Witches of the East and West were terribly wicked, and had they not thought I was more powerful than they themselves, they would surely have destroyed me. As it was, I lived in deadly fear of them for many years; so you can imagine how pleased I was when I heard your house had fallen on the Wicked Witch of the East. When you came to me I was willing to promise anything if you would only do away with the other Witch, but, now that you have melted her, I am ashamed to say that I cannot keep my promises."

"I think you are a very bad man," said Dorothy.

"Oh, no, my dear; I'm really a very good man; but I'm a very bad Wizard, I must admit."

"Can't you give me brains?" asked the Scarecrow.

"You don't need them. You are learning something every day. A baby has brains, but it doesn't know much. Experience is the only thing that brings knowledge, and the longer you are on Earth the more experience you are sure to get."

"That may all be true," said the Scarecrow, "but I shall be very unhappy unless you give me brains."

The false Wizard looked at him carefully.

"Well," he said with a sigh, "I'm not much of a magician, as I said; but if you will come to me tomorrow morning, I will stuff your head with brains. I cannot tell you how to use them, however, you must find that out for yourself."

"Oh, thank you—thank you!" cried the Scarecrow. "I'll find a way to use them, never fear!"

"But how about my courage?" asked the Lion anxiously.

"You have plenty of courage, I am sure," answered Oz. "All you need is confidence in yourself. There is no living thing that is not afraid when it faces danger. True courage is in facing danger when you are afraid, and that kind of courage you have in plenty."

"Perhaps I have, but I'm scared just the same," said the Lion. "I shall really be very unhappy unless you give me the sort of courage that makes one forget he is afraid."

"Very well; I will give you that sort of courage tomorrow," replied Oz.

"How about my heart?" asked the Tin Woodman.

"Why, as for that," answered Oz, "I think you are wrong to want a heart. It makes most people unhappy. If you only knew it, you are in luck not to have a heart."

"That must be a matter of opinion," said the Tin Woodman. "For my part, I will bear all the unhappiness without a murmur, if you will give me the heart."

"Very well," answered Oz meekly. "Come to me tomorrow and you shall have a heart. I have played Wizard for so many years that I may as well continue the part a little longer."

"And now," said Dorothy, "how am I going to get back to Kansas?"

"We shall have to think about that," replied the little man. "Give me two or three days to consider the matter and I'll try to find a way to carry you over the desert. In the meantime you shall all be treated as my guests, and while you live in the Palace my people will wait upon you and obey your slightest wish. There is only one thing I ask in return for my help—such as it is. You must keep my secret and tell no one I am a humbug."

They agreed to say nothing of what they had learned, and went back to their rooms in high spirits. Even Dorothy had hope that "The Great and Terrible Humbug," as she called him, would find a way to send her back to Kansas, and if he did that she was willing to forgive him everything.

"George Washington and the Cherry-Tree"
from The Life and Memorable Actions of George Washington

by Mason Locke ("Parson") Weems

We've all heard this one. Here is the passage that details one of the best-known American legends.

The following anecdote is a case in point. It is too valuable to be lost, and too true to be doubted; for it was communicated to me by the same excellent lady to whom I am indebted for the last.

"When George," said she, "was about six years old, he was made the wealthy master of a hatchet! of which, like most little boys, he was immoderately fond, and was constantly going about chopping every thing that came in his way. One day, in the garden, where he often amused himself hacking his mother's pea-sticks, he unluckily tried the edge of his hatchet on the body of a beautiful young cherry-tree, which he barked so terribly that I don't believe the tree ever got the better of it. The next morning the old gentleman, finding out what had befallen his tree, which, by the by, was a great favorite, came into the house; and with much warmth asked for the mischievous author, declaring at the same time that he would not have taken five guineas for his tree. Nobody could tell him anything about it. Presently George and his hatchet made their appearance. 'George,' said his father, 'do you know who killed that beautiful little cherry-tree yonder in the garden?' This was a tough question; and George staggered under it for a moment; but quickly recovered himself; and looking at his father, with the sweet face of youth brightened with the inexpressible charm of all-conquering truth, he bravely cried out, 'I can't tell a lie. I did cut it with my hatchet.' 'Run to my arms, you dearest boy,' cried his father in transports, 'run to my arms; glad am I, George, that you killed my tree; for you have paid me for it a thousand-fold. Such an act of heroism in my son is more worth than a thousand trees, though blossomed with silver, and their fruits of purest gold.'"

"The Shepherd Boy"

by Aesop

A childhood education is not complete without this story.

There was once a young shepherd boy who tended his sheep at the foot of a mountain near a dark forest. It was rather lonely for him all day, so he thought upon a plan by which he could get a little company and some excitement. He rushed down toward the village calling out, "Wolf, wolf," and the villagers came out to meet him, and some of them stopped with him for a considerable time. This pleased the boy so much that a few days afterward he tried the same trick, and again the villagers came to his help. But shortly after this a wolf actually did come out from the forest, and began to worry the sheep, and the boy of course cried out, "Wolf, wolf," still louder than before. But this time the villagers, who had been fooled twice before, thought the boy was again deceiving them, and nobody stirred to come to his help. So the wolf made a good meal off the boy's flock, and when the boy complained, the wise man of the village said, "A liar will not be believed, even when he speaks the truth."

CHAPTER FOUR

Be a Friend

"Oh, Bear!" said Christopher Robin.
"How I do love you!"

"So do I," said Pooh.

From *Winnie-the-Pooh*
by A. A. MILNE

A good friendship is a vitamin for the soul. Childhood friendships have a special place in our lives because they teach us so much about love and loyalty, and of course, their opposites. Take a moment to contemplate your childhood friends: they are great ghosts. Your senses still carry an impression of that glorious other person, the little Ann or Sam or Cindy who helped you find out who you were, who reflected something about you that no one else could. There is probably no lovelier union than a childhood friendship.

Almost every virtue can be applied to friendship, but essentially it requires *empathy*, *loyalty*, and *generosity*. These three elements keep all relationships alive and powerful; they are the cornerstones of love. Children begin cultivating these habits when they are about seven or eight years old. At this age the pain also begins, with cliques and fights and constantly shifting alliances and power plays. The strange phenomenon of socialization among small humans (can you imagine squirrels having three different best friends in one day?) unfolds on playgrounds all over the world. One year he is the victim, the next year he becomes the bully. For the parent, it is a difficult process indeed.

Contemporary children's literature examines this process in detail, especially female "relationships." Many of the works on childhood friendships are lyrical and well written. Some are pedestrian but entertaining. The Babysitters' Club, for instance, is a beloved series for girls that has some fifty million copies in print, and has been translated into twelve languages. But there are others, many of them listed in my list of recommended books on page 287, which take on the anguish and pleasure of childhood friendships in an even deeper way so that the child learns about human nature, and the forces that propel us all. They are truly insightful works that deserve your child's reading time.

Children watch how we behave as friends to our community, to our neighbors, and to those special few we actually call friends. When we cheerfully do favors for our friends, when we open our house to our friends, when we remember our friends with little notes and small gifts, and when we truly listen to our friends, we show our children our best.

One of life's great luxuries is to have a friend, and while we cannot choose our children's friends, we can show them what it is to be one. The stories that follow paint word pictures of empathy, loyalty, and generosity, and should serve your children well.

"The Dog of Pompeii"
by Louis Untermeyer

*Dog stories are a marvelous lesson in friendship, especially as
they display the virtue of loyalty. This is one of my favorites by an
author you will remember from your own childhood.*

Tito and his dog Bimbo lived (if you could call it living) under the city
wall where it joined the inner gate. They really didn't live there; they
just slept there. They lived anywhere. Pompeii was one of the gayest of
the old Roman towns, but although Tito was never an unhappy boy, he
was not exactly a merry one. The streets were always lively with shining
chariots and bright-red trappings; the open-air theaters rocked with
laughing crowds; sham battles and athletic sports were free for the
asking in the great stadium. Once a year the emperor visited the
pleasure city, and the fireworks and other forms of entertainment lasted
for days.

But Tito saw none of these things, for he was blind—had been
blind from birth. He was known to everyone in the poorer quarters. But
no one could say how old he was; no one remembered his parents; no
one could tell where he came from. Bimbo was another mystery. As
long as people could remember seeing Tito—several years at least—
they had seen Bimbo. The dog never left his side. He was not only a
watchdog, but mother and father to Tito.

Did I say Bimbo never left his master? (Perhaps I had better say
"comrade," for if anyone was the master, it was Bimbo.) I was wrong.
Bimbo did trust Tito alone exactly three times a day. It was a custom
understood between boy and dog since the beginning of their friendship, and the way it worked was this:

Early in the morning, shortly after dawn, while Tito was still
dreaming, Bimbo would disappear. When Tito awoke, Bimbo would be
sitting quietly at his side, his ears cocked, his stump of a tail tapping
the ground, and a fresh-baked loaf of bread—more like a large round

roll—at his feet. Tito would stretch himself, Bimbo would yawn, and they would breakfast.

At noon, no matter where they happened to be, Bimbo would put his paw on Tito's knee, and the two of them would return to the inner gate. Tito would curl up in the corner (almost like a dog) and go to sleep, while Bimbo, looking quite important (almost like a boy), would disappear again. In a half hour he would be back with their lunch. Sometimes it would be a piece of fruit or a scrap of meat; often it was nothing but a dry crust. But sometimes there would be one of those flat, rich cakes, sprinkled with raisins and sugar, that Tito liked so much.

At suppertime the same thing happened, although there was a little less of everything, for things were hard to snatch in the evening with the streets full of people.

But whether there was much or little, hot or cold, fresh or dry, food was always there. Tito never asked where it came from, and Bimbo never told him. There was plenty of rain water in the hollows of soft stones; the old egg-woman at the corner sometimes gave him a cupful of strong goat's milk; in the grape season the fat wine-maker let him having drippings of the mild juice. So there was no danger of going hungry or thirsty. There was plenty of everything in Pompeii if you knew where to find it—and if you had a dog like Bimbo.

As I said before, Tito was not the merriest boy in Pompeii. He could not romp with the other youngsters or play hare-and-hounds and I-spy and follow-your-master and ball-against-the-building and jackstone and kings-and-robbers with them. But that did not make him sorry for himself. If he could not see the sights that delighted the lads of Pompeii, he could hear and smell things they never noticed. When he and Bimbo went out walking, he knew just where they were going and exactly what was happening.

As they passed a handsome villa, he'd sniff and say, "Ah, Glaucus Pansa is giving a grand dinner here tonight. They're going to have three kinds of bread and roast pigling and stuffed goose and a great stew—I think bear stew—and a fig pie." And Bimbo would note that this would be a good place to visit tomorrow.

Or "Hmm," Tito would murmur, half through his lips, half

through his nostrils. "The wife of Marcus Lucretius is expecting her mother. She's airing all the linens; she's going to use the best clothes, the ones she's been keeping in pine needles and camphor, and she's got an extra servant cleaning the kitchen. Come, Bimbo, let's get out of the dust!"

Or, as they neared the forum, "Mmm! What good things they have in the marketplace today! Dates from Africa and salt oysters from sea caves and cuttlefish and new honey and sweet onions and—ugh!— water-buffalo steaks. Come, let's see what's what in the forum." And Bimbo, just as curious as his comrade, hurried on. Being a dog, he, too, trusted his ears and nose more than his eyes, and so the two of them entered the center of Pompeii.

The forum was the part of town to which everybody came at least once during each day. Everything happened there. There were no private houses; all was public—the chief temples, the gold and red bazaars, the silk shops, the town hall, the booths belonging to the weavers and the jewel merchants, the wealthy woolen market. Everything gleamed brightly here; the buildings looked new. The earthquake of twelve years ago had brought down all the old structures; and since the citizens of Pompeii were ambitious to rival Naples and even Rome, they had seized the opportunity to rebuild the whole town. Hence there was scarcely a building that was older than Tito.

Tito had heard a great deal about the earthquake, although, since he was only about a year old at the time, he could hardly remember it. This particular quake had been a light one, as earthquakes go. The crude houses had been shaken down, and parts of the outworn wall had been wrecked, but there had been little loss of life. No one knew what caused these earthquakes. Records showed they had happened in the neighborhood since the beginning of time. Sailors said that it was to teach the lazy cityfolk a lesson and make them appreciate those who risked the dangers of the sea to bring them luxuries and to protect their town from invaders. The priests said that the gods took this way of showing their anger to those who refused to worship properly or failed to bring enough sacrifices to the altars. The tradesmen said that the foreign merchants had corrupted the ground and it was no longer safe to traffic in imported goods that came from strange places and carried a curse upon them. Everyone had a different explanation, and everyone's explanation was louder and sillier than his neighbor's.

People were talking about it this afternoon as Tito and Bimbo came out of the side street into the public square. The forum was crowded. Tito's ears, as well as his nose, guided them to the place where the talk was loudest.

"I tell you," rumbled a voice which Tito recognized as that of the bath-master, Rufus, "there won't be another earthquake in my lifetime or yours. There may be a tremble or two, but earthquakes, like lightning, never strike twice in the same place."

"Don't they?" asked a thin voice Tito had never heard before. It had a high, sharp ring to it, and Tito knew it as the accent of a stranger. "How about the two towns in Sicily that have been ruined three times within fifteen years by the eruptions of Mount Etna? And were they not warned? And does that column of smoke above Vesuvius mean nothing?"

"That?" Tito could hear the grunt with which one question answered another. "That's always there. We use it for our weather guide. When the smoke stands up straight, we know we'll have fair weather, when it flattens out, it's sure to be foggy; when it drifts to the east—"

"Very well, my confident friend," cut in the thin voice, which now sounded curiously flat. "We have a proverb: 'Those who will not listen to man must be taught by the gods.' I say no more. But I leave a last warning. Remember the holy ones. Look to your temples. And when the smoke tree above Vesuvius grows to the shape of an umbrella pine, look to your lives!"

Tito could hear the air whistle as the speaker drew his toga about him, and the quick shuffle of feet told him that the stranger had gone.

"Now what," said Attilio, the cameo-cutter, "did he mean by that?"

"I wonder," grunted Rufus. "I wonder."

Tito wondered too. And Bimbo, his head at a thoughtful angle, looked as if he were doing a heavy bit of pondering. By nightfall the argument had been forgotten. If the smoke had increased, no one saw it in the dark. Besides, it was Caesar's birthday, and the town was in a holiday mood. Tito and Bimbo were among the merrymakers, dodging the charioteers, who shouted at them. But Tito never missed his footing. He was thankful for his keen ears and quick instinct—most thankful of all for Bimbo.

They visited the open-air theater; then went to the city walls, where the people of Pompeii watched a sham naval battle in which the city, attacked from the sea, was saved after thousands of flaming arrows had been burned. Though the thrill of flaring ships and lighted skies was lost to Tito, the shouts and cheers excited him as much as anyone.

The next morning there were two of the beloved raisin cakes for his breakfast. Bimbo was unusually active and thumped his bit of a tail until Tito was afraid he would wear it out. Tito couldn't imagine whether Bimbo was urging him to some sort of game or was trying to tell him something. After a while he ceased to notice Bimbo. He felt drowsy. Last night's late hours had tired him. Besides, there was a heavy mist in the air—no, a thick fog rather than a mist—a fog that got into his throat and made him cough. He walked as far as the marine gate to get a breath of the sea. But even the salt air seemed smoky.

Tito went to bed before dusk, but he did not sleep well. . . .

He awoke early. Or rather, he was pulled awake, Bimbo doing the pulling. The dog had dragged Tito to his feet and was urging the boy along. Where, Tito did not know. His feet stumbled uncertainly; he was still half asleep. For a while he noticed nothing except the fact that it was hard to breathe. The air was hot and heavy, so heavy that he could taste it. The air, it seemed, had turned to powder, a warm powder that stung his nostrils and burned his sightless eyes.

Then he began to hear sounds, peculiar sounds. Like animals under the earth. Hissings and groanings and muffled cries. There was no doubt of it now. The noises came from underneath. He not only heard them—he could feel them. The earth twitched; the twitching changed to an uneven shrugging of the soil. Then, as Bimbo half pulled, half coaxed him along, the ground jerked away from his feet and he was thrown against a stone fountain.

The water—hot water!—splashing in his face revived him. He got to his feet, Bimbo steadying him, helping him on again. The noises grew louder; they came closer. The cries were even more animallike than before, but now they came from human throats. A few people began to rush by; a family or two, then a group, then, it seemed, the whole city of people. Tito, bewildered though he was, could recognize Rufus's voice as he bellowed like a water buffalo gone mad.

It was then the crashing began. First a sharp crackling, like a monstrous snapping of twigs; then an explosion that tore earth and sky. The heavens, though Tito could not see them, were shot through with continual flickerings of fire. Lightning above was answered by thunder beneath. A house fell. Then another. By a miracle the two companions had escaped the dangerous side streets and were in a more open space. It was the forum. They rested here awhile; how long, the boy did not know.

Tito had no idea of the time of day. He could feel it was black—an unnatural blackness. Something inside, perhaps the lack of breakfast and lunch, told him it was past noon. But it didn't matter. Nothing seemed to matter. He was getting drowsy, too drowsy to walk. But walk he must. He knew it. And Bimbo knew it; the sharp tugs told him so. Nor was it a moment too soon. The sacred ground of the forum was safe no longer. It began to rock, then to pitch, then to split. As they stumbled out of the square, the earth wriggled like a caught snake, and all the columns of the Temple of Jupiter came down. It was the end of the world, or so it seemed.

To walk was not enough now. They must run. Tito, too frightened to know what to do or where to go, had lost all sense of direction. He started to go back to the inner gate; but Bimbo, straining his back to the last inch, almost pulled his clothes from him. What did the dog want? Had he gone mad?

Then suddenly he understood. Bimbo was telling him the way out. The sea gate, of course. The sea gate—and then the sea, far from falling buildings, heaving ground. He turned, Bimbo guiding him across open pits and dangerous pools of bubbling mud, away from buildings that had caught fire and were dropping their burning beams.

New dangers threatened. All Pompeii seemed to be thronging toward the marine gate, and there was the chance of being trampled to death. But the chance had to be taken. It was growing harder and harder to breathe. What air there was choked him. It was all dust now, dust and pebbles as large as beans. They fell on his head, his hands— pumice stones from the black heart of Vesuvius! The mountain was turning itself inside out. Tito remembered what the stranger had said in the forum two days ago: "Those who will not listen to man must be taught by the gods." The people of Pompeii had refused to heed the warnings; they were being taught now, if it was not too late.

Suddenly it seemed too late for Tito. The red-hot ashes blistered his skin; the stinging vapors tore his throat. He could not go on. He staggered toward a small tree at the side of the road and fell. In a moment Bimbo was beside him. He coaxed, but there was no answer. He licked Tito's hands, his feet, his face. The boy did not stir. Then Bimbo did the thing he least wanted to do. He bit his comrade, bit him deep in the arm. With a cry of pain, Tito jumped to his feet, Bimbo after him. Tito was in despair, but Bimbo was determined. He drove the boy on, snapping at his heels, worrying his way through the crowd, barking, baring his teeth, heedless of kicks or falling stones.

Sick with hunger, half dead with fear and sulfur fumes, Tito plodded on, pursued by Bimbo. How long, he never knew. At last he staggered through the marine gate and felt soft sand under him. Then Tito fainted.

Someone was dashing sea water over him. Someone was carrying him toward a boat.

"Bimbo!" he called. And then louder, "Bimbo!" But Bimbo had disappeared.

Voices jarred against each other. "Hurry! Hurry!" "To the boats!" "Can't you see the child's frightened and starving?" "He keeps calling for someone!" "Poor child, he's out of his mind." "Here, boy, take this!"

They tucked him in among them. The oarlocks creaked; the oars splashed; the boat rode over the toppling waves. Tito was safe. But he wept continually. "Bimbo!" he wailed. "Bimbo! Bimbo!"

He could not be comforted.

*   *   *

Eighteen hundred years passed. Scientists were restoring the ancient city; excavators were working their way through the stones and trash that had buried the entire town. Much had already been brought to light—statues, bronze instruments, bright mosaics, household articles, even delicate paintings, which had been preserved by the ashes that had taken over two thousand lives. Columns were dug up, and the forum was beginning to emerge.

It was at a place where the ruins lay deepest that the director paused.

"Come here," he called to his assistant. "I think we've discovered the remains of a building in good shape. Here are four huge millstones that were most likely turned by slaves or mules, and here is a whole wall standing, with shelves inside it. Why, it must have been a bakery! And here's a curious thing—the skeleton of a dog!"

"Amazing!" gasped his assistant. "You'd think a dog would have had sense enough to run away at that time. What is that flat thing he's holding between his teeth? It can't be a stone."

"No. It must have come from this bakery. Do you know, it looks to me like some sort of cake, hardened with the years. And bless me, if those little black pebbles aren't raisins! A raisin cake almost two thousand years old! I wonder what made him want it at such a moment?"

"I wonder," murmured his assistant.

"Damon and Pythias"

by Frederick Hoppin

Here is a grand lesson about loyalty from two of the most famous friends in mythology.

We are told about many pairs of friends in history and in stories, like David and Jonathan in the Old Testament, who were famous for their love and devotion to each other, but when we want to say that two men are the finest and truest of friends we say that they are like Damon and Pythias.

These two boys grew up in the city of Syracuse at a time when it was ruled by the tyrant Dionysius. He was a very able man who had gained his power by leading the army of Syracuse to victory. At first Dionysius had ruled well and justly, but gradually he became more and more tyrannical. The people murmured so much against him and his harsh laws that he began to be afraid some of them would try to kill him. He lived in constant fear of this, and he did not trust anybody.

At that time Damon and Pythias were about twenty years old. They were both brave and fearless, and Damon had dared to speak openly against one of the tyrant's laws. Dionysius therefore shut him up in prison and declared that he would have his head cut off on a certain day.

When Damon knew that he was to be killed, he asked Dionysius to let him be free for a month first so that he could go and say good-bye to his father and mother, who lived in another town far away from Syracuse. He promised faithfully that, if Dionysius would let him do this, he would come back at the end of the month and have his head cut off.

Dionysius laughed loud and long at this request.

"You would never come back," he said to Damon. "What pledge could you possibly give me that would make me feel sure that you would return here to be killed? No, you will have to stay in prison till the day you are to die."

When Pythias heard of this he did not wait a minute. He went

50

straight to Dionysius and said to him, "I will stay in prison in place of Damon, if you will let him go. I know that he will come back on the day he says. If he does not return, then you can kill me instead."

Dionysius was filled with astonishment, and at first he thought that Pythias was not in earnest. When he was convinced that Pythias meant exactly what he said and was ready to stay in prison while Damon was away, he declared that Damon could go free for the month on condition that he would return and be killed on the day fixed for his execution.

So Pythias went into the prison and waited there patiently while Damon took a ship and sailed away to see his father and mother once more before he died.

The time passed by until it came to the last day before that fixed for Damon's execution. There was no sign of Damon, but Pythias still had perfect confidence in him and felt sure that he would come back as he had promised.

"The winds have been against him," he said, "or he has been held back for some other reason which he could not help. He will keep his word."

The day of the execution dawned. The jailer came to the prison cell to lead Pythias out to die in place of Damon.

Just as they reached the prison door Damon came rushing up. His ship had been held back by a storm, and he had only reached the harbor of Syracuse that morning, just in time.

Dionysius was so struck by the trust of these two friends and their love for each other that he pardoned Damon, and let them both go free.

"I would give all my power," he said, "to know that I had one friend who cared for me as Damon does for Pythias and Pythias for Damon."

The Velveteen Rabbit
or
How Toys Become Real
by Margery Williams

I have shed many a tear over this story, which can be read over and over again to young children. It is one of the great love stories in children's literature.

There was once a velveteen rabbit, and in the beginning he was really splendid. He was fat and bunchy, as a rabbit should be; his coat was spotted brown and white, he had real thread whiskers, and his ears were lined with pink sateen. On Christmas morning, when he sat wedged in the top of the Boy's stocking, with a sprig of holly between his paws, the effect was charming.

There were other things in the stocking, nuts and oranges and a toy engine, and chocolate almonds and a clockwork mouse, but the Rabbit was quite the best of all. For at least two hours the Boy loved him, and then Aunts and Uncles came to dinner, and there was a great rustling of tissue paper and unwrapping of parcels, and in the excitement of looking at all the new presents the Velveteen Rabbit was forgotten.

For a long time he lived in the toy cupboard or on the nursery floor, and no one thought very much about him. He was naturally shy, and being only made of velveteen, some of the more expensive toys quite snubbed him. The mechanical toys were very superior, and looked down upon every one else; they were full of modern ideas, and pretended they were real. The model boat, who had lived through two seasons and lost most of his paint, caught the tone from them and never missed an opportunity of referring to his rigging in technical terms. The Rabbit could not claim to be a model of anything, for he didn't know that real rabbits existed; he thought they were all stuffed with sawdust like himself, and he understood that sawdust was quite out-of-date and should never be mentioned in modern circles. Even

Timothy, the jointed wooden lion, who was made by the disabled soldiers and should have had broader views, put on airs and pretended he was connected with Government. Between them all the poor little Rabbit was made to feel himself very insignificant and commonplace, and the only person who was kind to him at all was the Skin Horse.

The Skin Horse had lived longer in the nursery than any of the others. He was so old that his brown coat was bald in patches and showed the seams underneath, and most of the hairs in his tail had been pulled out to string bead necklaces. He was wise, for he had seen a long succession of mechanical toys arrive to boast and swagger, and by-and-by break their mainsprings and pass away, and he knew that they were only toys, and would never turn into anything else. For nursery magic is very strange and wonderful, and only those playthings that are old and wise and experienced like the Skin Horse understand all about it.

"What is REAL?" asked the Rabbit one day, when they were lying side by side near the nursery fender, before Nana came to tidy the room. "Does it mean having things that buzz inside you and a stick-out handle?"

"Real isn't how you are made," said the Skin Horse. "It's a thing that happens to you. When a child loves you for a long, long time, not just to play with, but REALLY loves you, then you become Real."

"Does it hurt?" asked the Rabbit.

"Sometimes," said the Skin Horse, for he was always truthful. "When you are Real you don't mind being hurt."

"Does it happen all at once, like being wound up," he asked, "or bit by bit?"

"It doesn't happen all at once," said the Skin Horse. "You become. It takes a long time. That's why it doesn't often happen to people who break easily, or have sharp edges, or who have to be carefully kept. Generally, by the time you are Real, most of your hair has been loved off, and your eyes drop out and you get loose in the joints and very shabby. But these things don't matter at all, because once you are Real you can't be ugly, except to people who don't understand."

"I suppose you are Real?" said the Rabbit. And then he wished he had not said it, for he thought the Skin Horse might be sensitive. But the Skin Horse only smiled.

"The Boy's Uncle made me Real," he said. "That was a great many years ago; but once you are Real you can't become unreal again. It lasts for always."

The Rabbit sighed. He thought it would be a long time before this magic called Real happened to him. He longed to become Real, to know what it felt like; and yet the idea of growing shabby and losing his eyes and whiskers was rather sad. He wished that he could become it without these uncomfortable things happening to him.

There was a person called Nana who ruled the nursery. Sometimes she took no notice of the playthings lying about, and sometimes, for no reason whatever, she went swooping about like a great wind and hustled them away in cupboards. She called this "tidying up," and the playthings all hated it, especially the tin ones. The Rabbit didn't mind it so much, for wherever he was thrown he came down soft.

One evening, when the Boy was going to bed, he couldn't find the china dog that always slept with him. Nana was in a hurry, and it was too much trouble to hunt for china dogs at bedtime, so she simply looked about her, and seeing that the toy cupboard door stood open, she made a swoop.

"Here," she said, "take your old Bunny! He'll do to sleep with you!" And she dragged the Rabbit out by one ear, and put him into the Boy's arms.

That night, and for many nights after, the Velveteen Rabbit slept in the Boy's bed. At first he found it rather uncomfortable, for the Boy hugged him very tight, and sometimes he rolled over on him, and sometimes he pushed him so far under the pillow that the Rabbit could scarcely breathe. And he missed, too, those long moonlight hours in the nursery, when all the house was silent, and his talks with the Skin Horse. But very soon he grew to like it, for the Boy used to talk to him, and made nice tunnels for him under the bedclothes that he said were like the burrows the real rabbits lived in. And they had splendid games together, in whispers, when Nana had gone away to her supper and left the night-light burning on the mantelpiece. And when the Boy dropped off to sleep, the Rabbit would snuggle down close under his little warm chin and dream, with the Boy's hands clasped close around him all night long.

And so time went on, and the little Rabbit was very happy—so happy that he never noticed how his beautiful velveteen fur was getting shabbier and shabbier, and his tail coming unsewn, and all the pink rubbed off his nose where the Boy had kissed him.

Spring came, and they had long days in the garden, for wherever the Boy went the Rabbit went too. He had rides in the wheelbarrow, and picnics on the grass, and lovely fairy huts built for him under the raspberry canes behind the flower border. And once, when the Boy was called away suddenly to go out to tea, the Rabbit was left out on the lawn until long after dusk, and Nana had to come and look for him with the candle because the Boy couldn't go to sleep unless he was there. He was wet through with the dew and quite earthy from diving into the burrows the Boy had made for him in the flower bed, and Nana grumbled as she rubbed him off with a corner of her apron.

"You must have your old Bunny!" she said. "Fancy all that fuss for a toy!"

The Boy sat up in bed and stretched out his hands.

"Give me my Bunny!" he said. "You mustn't say that. He isn't a toy. He's REAL!"

When the little Rabbit heard that, he was happy, for he knew that what the Skin Horse had said was true at last. The nursery magic had happened to him, and he was a toy no longer. He was Real. The Boy himself had said it.

That night he was almost too happy to sleep, and so much love stirred in his little sawdust heart that it almost burst. And into his boot-button eyes, that had long ago lost their polish, there came a look of wisdom and beauty, so that even Nana noticed it next morning when she picked him up, and said, "I declare if that old Bunny hasn't got quite a knowing expression!"

That was a wonderful Summer!

Near the house where they lived there was a wood, and in the long June evenings the Boy liked to go there after tea to play. He took the Velveteen Rabbit with him, and before he wandered off to pick flowers, or play at brigands among the trees, he always made the Rabbit a little nest somewhere among the bracken, where he would be quite cozy, for he was a kind-hearted little boy and he liked Bunny to be comfortable. One evening, while the Rabbit was lying there alone, watching the ants that ran to and fro between his velvet paws in the grass, he saw two strange beings creep out of the tall bracken near him.

They were rabbits like himself, but quite furry and brand-new. They must have been very well made, for their seams didn't show at all, and they changed shape in a queer way when they moved; one minute they were long and thin and the next minute fat and bunchy, instead of always staying the same like he did. Their feet padded softly on the ground, and they crept quite close to him, twitching their noses, while the Rabbit stared hard to see which side the clockwork stuck out, for he knew that people who jump generally have something to wind them up. But he couldn't see it. They were evidently a new kind of rabbit altogether.

They stared at him, and the little Rabbit stared back. And all the time their noses twitched.

"Why don't you get up and play with us?" one of them asked.

"I don't feel like it," said the Rabbit, for he didn't want to explain that he had no clockwork.

"Ho!" said the furry rabbit. "It's as easy as anything." And he gave a big hop sideways and stood on his hind legs.

"I don't believe you can!" he said.

"I can!" said the little Rabbit. "I can jump higher than anything!" He meant when the Boy threw him, but of course he didn't want to say so.

"Can you hop on your hind legs?" asked the furry rabbit.

That was a dreadful question, for the Velveteen Rabbit had no hind legs at all! The back of him was made all in one piece, like a pincushion. He sat still in the bracken, and hoped that the other rabbits wouldn't notice.

"I don't want to!" he said again.

But the wild rabbits had very sharp eyes. And this one stretched out his neck and looked.

"He hasn't got any hind legs!" he called out. "Fancy a rabbit without any hind legs!" And he began to laugh.

"I have!" cried the little Rabbit. "I have got hind legs! I am sitting on them!"

"Then stretch them out and show me, like this!" said the wild rabbit. And he began to whirl around and dance, till the little Rabbit got quite dizzy.

"I don't like dancing," he said. "I'd rather sit still!"

But all the while he was longing to dance, for a funny new tickly feeling ran through him, and he felt he would give anything in the world to be able to jump about like these rabbits did.

The strange rabbit stopped dancing, and came quite close. He came so close this time that his long whiskers brushed the Velveteen Rabbit's ear, and then he wrinkled his nose suddenly and flattened his ears and jumped backward.

"He doesn't smell right!" he exclaimed. "He isn't a rabbit at all! He isn't real!"

"I *am* Real!" said the little Rabbit. "I am Real! The Boy said so!" And he nearly began to cry.

Just then there was a sound of footsteps, and the Boy ran past near them, and with a stamp of feet and a flash of white tails the two strange rabbits disappeared.

"Come back and play with me!" called the little Rabbit. "Oh, do come back! I know I am Real!"

But there was no answer, only the little ants ran to and fro, and the bracken swayed gently where the two strangers had passed. The Velveteen Rabbit was all alone.

"Oh, dear!" he thought. "Why did they run away like that? Why couldn't they stop and talk to me?"

For a long time he lay very still, watching the bracken, and hoping that they would come back. But they never returned, and presently the sun sank lower and the little white moths fluttered out, and the Boy came and carried him home.

Weeks passed, and the little Rabbit grew very old and shabby, but the Boy loved him just as much. He loved him so hard that he loved all his whiskers off, and the pink lining to his ears turned gray, and his brown spots faded. He even began to lose his shape, and he scarcely looked like a rabbit anymore, except to the Boy. To him he was always beautiful, and that was all that the little Rabbit cared about. He didn't mind how he looked to other people, because the nursery magic had made him Real, and when you are Real, shabbiness doesn't matter.

And then, one day, the Boy was ill.

His face grew very flushed, and he talked in his sleep, and his little body was so hot that it burned the Rabbit when he held him close. Strange people came and went in the nursery, and a light burned all night and through it all the little Velveteen Rabbit lay there, hidden from sight under the bedclothes, and he never stirred, for he was afraid that if they found him someone might take him away, and he knew that the Boy needed him.

It was a long, weary time, for the Boy was too ill to play, and the little Rabbit found it rather dull with nothing to do all day long. But he snuggled down patiently, and looked forward to the time when the Boy should be well again, and they would go out in the garden among the flowers and the butterflies and play splendid games in the raspberry thicket like they used to. All sorts of delightful things he planned, and while the Boy lay half asleep he crept up close to the pillow and whispered them in his ear. And presently the fever turned, and the Boy got better. He was able to sit up in bed and look at picture books, while the little Rabbit cuddled close at his side. And one day, they let him get up and dress.

It was a bright, sunny morning, and the windows stood wide open. They had carried the Boy out onto the balcony, wrapped in a shawl, and the little Rabbit lay tangled up among the bedclothes, thinking.

The Boy was going to the seaside tomorrow. Everything was arranged, and now it only remained to carry out the doctor's orders. They talked about it all, while the little Rabbit lay under the bedclothes, with just his head peeping out, and listened. The room was to be disinfected, and all the books and toys that the Boy had played with in bed must be burnt.

"Hurrah!" thought the little Rabbit. "Tomorrow we shall go to the seaside!" For the Boy had often talked of the seaside, and he wanted very much to see the big waves coming in, and the tiny crabs, and the sand castles.

Just then Nana caught sight of him.

"How about his old Bunny?" she asked.

"*That?*" said the doctor. "Why, it's a mass of scarlet fever germs! Burn it at once. What? Nonsense! Get him a new one. He mustn't have that anymore!"

And so the little Rabbit was put into a sack with the old picture books and a lot of rubbish, and carried out to the end of the garden behind the fowl-house. That was a fine place to make a bonfire, only the gardener was too busy just then to attend to it. He had the potatoes to dig and the green peas to gather, but next morning he promised to come quite early and burn the whole lot.

That night the Boy slept in a different bedroom, and he had a new bunny to sleep with him. It was a splendid bunny, all white plush with real glass eyes, but the Boy was too excited to care very much about it. For tomorrow he was going to the seaside, and that in itself was such a wonderful thing that he could think of nothing else.

And while the Boy was asleep, dreaming of the seaside, the little Rabbit lay among the old picture books in the corner behind the fowl-house, and he felt very lonely. The sack had been left untied, and so by wriggling a bit he was able to get his head through the opening and look out. He was shivering a little, for he had always been used to sleeping in a proper bed, and by this time his coat had worn so thin and threadbare from hugging that it was no longer any protection to him. Nearby he could see the thicket of raspberry canes, growing tall and close like a tropical jungle, in whose shadow he had played with the Boy on bygone mornings. He thought of those long sunlit hours in the garden—how happy they were—and a great sadness came over him. He seemed to see them all pass before him, each more beautiful than the other, the fairy huts in the flower bed, the quiet evenings in the wood when he lay in the bracken and the little ants ran over his paws; the wonderful day when he first knew that he was Real. He thought of the Skin Horse, so wise and gentle, and all that he had told him. Of what use was it to be loved and lose one's beauty and become Real if it all ended like this? And a tear, a real tear, trickled down his shabby velvet nose and fell to the ground.

And then a strange thing happened. For where the tear had fallen a flower grew out of the ground, a mysterious flower, not at all like any that grew in the garden. It had slender green leaves the color of emeralds, and in the center of the leaves a blossom like a golden cup. It was so beautiful that the little Rabbit forgot to cry, and just lay there watching it. And presently the blossom opened, and out of it there stepped a fairy.

She was quite the loveliest fairy in the whole world. Her dress was of pearl and dewdrops, and there were flowers around her neck and in her hair, and her face was like the most perfect flower of all. And she came close to the little Rabbit and gathered him up in her arms and kissed him on his velveteen nose that was all damp from crying.

"Little Rabbit," she said, "don't you know who I am?"

The Rabbit looked up at her, and it seemed to him that he had seen her face before, but he couldn't think where.

"I am the nursery magic Fairy," she said. "I take care of all the playthings that the children have loved. When they are old and worn out and the children don't need them anymore, then I come and take them away with me and turn them into Real."

"Wasn't I Real before?" asked the little Rabbit.

"You were Real to the Boy," the Fairy said, "because he loved you. Now you shall be Real to everyone."

And she held the little Rabbit close in her arms and flew with him into the wood.

It was light now, for the moon had risen. All the forest was beautiful, and the fronds of the bracken shone like frosted silver. In the open glade between the tree trunks the wild rabbits danced with their shadows on the velvet grass, but when they saw the Fairy they all stopped dancing and stood around in a ring to stare at her.

"I've brought you a new playfellow," the Fairy said. "You must be very kind to him and teach him all he needs to know in Rabbitland, for he is going to live with you forever and ever!"

And she kissed the little Rabbit again and put him down on the grass.

"Run and play, little Rabbit!" she said.

But the little Rabbit sat quite still for a moment and never moved. For when he saw all the wild rabbits dancing around him he suddenly remembered about his hind legs, and he didn't want them to see that he was made in all one piece. He did not know that when the Fairy kissed him that last time she had changed him altogether. And he might have sat there a long time, too shy to move, if just then something hadn't tickled his nose, and before he thought what he was doing he lifted his hind toe to scratch it.

And he found that he actually had hind legs! Instead of dingy velveteen he had brown fur, soft and shiny, his ears twitched by themselves, and his whiskers were so long that they brushed the grass. He gave one leap and the joy of using those hind legs was so great that he went springing about the turf on them, jumping sideways and whirling around as the others did, and he grew so excited that when at last he did stop to look for the Fairy she had gone.

He was a Real Rabbit at last, at home with the other rabbits.

Autumn passed and Winter, and in the Spring, when the days grew warm and sunny, the Boy went out to play in the wood behind the house. And while he was playing, two rabbits crept out from the bracken and peeped at him. One of them was brown all over, but the other had strange markings under his fur, as though long ago he had been spotted, and the spots still showed through. About his little soft nose and his round black eyes there was something familiar, so that the Boy thought to himself: "Why, he looks just like my old Bunny that was lost when I had scarlet fever!"

But he never knew that it really was his own Bunny, come back to look at the child who had first helped him to be Real.

"Lucy Looks into the Wardrobe; What Lucy Found There"
from The Lion, the Witch and the Wardrobe
by C. S. Lewis

This is from the first book in the Narnia Chronicles, and my deepest hope is that it gets you started on the entire series, which is one of the most unforgettable literary experiences you and your child can have. (Other books are Prince Caspian, The Voyage of the Dawn Treader, The Silver Chair, The Horse and His Boy, The Magician's Nephew, *and* The Last Battle.) *These tales tell of mighty conflicts between good and evil, and are fabulous adventures, whether you grasp their theological content or not. Here you go, to Narnia.*

Once there were four children whose names were Peter, Susan, Edmund, and Lucy. This story is about something that happened to them when they were sent away from London during the war because of the air raids. They were sent to the house of an old professor who lived in the heart of the country, ten miles from the nearest railway station and two miles from the nearest post office. He had no wife and he lived in a very large house with a housekeeper called Mrs. Macready and three servants. (Their names were Ivy, Margaret, and Betty, but they do not come into the story much.) He himself was a very old man with shaggy white hair, which grew over most of his face as well as on his head, and they liked him almost at once; but on the first evening when he came out to meet them at the front door he was so odd-looking that Lucy (who was the youngest) was a little afraid of him, and Edmund (who was the next youngest) wanted to laugh and had to keep on pretending he was blowing his nose to hide it.

As soon as they had said good night to the professor and had gone upstairs on the first night, the boys came into the girls' room and they talked it all over.

"We've fallen on our feet and no mistake," said Peter. "This is going to be perfectly splendid. That old chap will let us do anything we like."

"I think he's an old dear," said Susan.

"Oh, come off it!" said Edmund, who was tired and pretending not to be tired, which always made him bad-tempered. "Don't go on talking like that."

"Like what?" said Susan; "and anyway, it's time you were in bed."

"Trying to talk like Mother," said Edmund. "And who are you to say when I'm to go to bed? Go to bed yourself."

"Hadn't we all better go to bed?" said Lucy. "There's sure to be a row if we're heard talking here."

"No, there won't," said Peter. "I tell you, this is the sort of house where no one's going to mind what we do. Anyway, they won't hear us. It's about ten minutes' walk from here down to that dining room, and any amount of stairs and passages in between."

"What's that noise?" said Lucy suddenly. It was a far larger house than she had ever been in before and the thought of all those long passages and rows of doors leading into empty rooms was beginning to make her feel a little creepy.

"It's only a bird, silly," said Edmund.

"It's an owl," said Peter. "This is going to be a wonderful place for birds. I shall go to bed now. I say, let's go and explore tomorrow. You might find anything in a place like this. Did you see those mountains as we came along? And the woods? There might be eagles. There might be stags. There'll be hawks."

"Badgers!" said Lucy.

"Snakes!" said Edmund.

"Foxes!" said Susan.

But when next morning came, there was a steady rain falling so thick that when you looked out of the window you could see neither the mountains nor the woods nor even the stream in the garden.

"Of course it *would* be raining!" said Edmund. They had just finished breakfast with the professor and were upstairs in the room he had set apart for them—a long, low room with two windows looking out in one direction and two in another.

"Do stop grumbling, Ed," said Susan. "Ten to one it'll clear up in an hour or so. And in the meantime we're pretty well off. There's a wireless and lots of books."

"Not for me," said Peter. "I'm going to explore in the house."

Everyone agreed to this and that was how the adventure began. It was the sort of house that you never seem to come to the end of, and it was full of unexpected places. The first few doors they tried led only into spare bedrooms, as everyone had expected that they would; but soon they came to a very long room full of pictures and there they found a suit of armor; and after that was a room all hung with green, with a harp in one corner; and then came three steps down and five steps up, and then a kind of little upstairs hall and a door that led out onto a balcony, and then a whole series of rooms that led into each other and were lined with books—most of them very old books and some bigger than a Bible in a church. And shortly after that they looked into a room that was quite empty except for one big wardrobe; the sort that has a looking glass in the door. There was nothing else in the room at all except a dead bluebottle on the windowsill.

"Nothing there!" said Peter, and they all trooped out again—all except Lucy. She stayed behind because she thought it would be worthwhile trying the door of the wardrobe, even though she felt almost sure that it would be locked. To her surprise it opened quite easily, and two mothballs dropped out.

Looking into the inside, she saw several coats hanging up—mostly fur coats. There was nothing Lucy liked so much as the smell and feel of fur. She immediately stepped into the wardrobe and got in among the coats and rubbed her face against them; leaving the door open, of course, because she knew that it is very foolish to shut oneself inside any wardrobe. Soon she went further in and found that there was a second row of coats hanging up behind the first one. It was almost quite dark in there and she kept her arms stretched out in front of her so as not to bump her face into the back of the wardrobe. She took a step further in—then two or three steps—always expecting to feel woodwork against the tips of her fingers. But she could not feel it.

"This must be a simply enormous wardrobe!" thought Lucy, going still further in and pushing the soft folds of the coats aside to make room for herself. Then she noticed that there was something crunching under her feet. "I wonder is that more mothballs?" she thought, stooping down to feel it with her hands. But instead of feeling the hard, smooth wood of the floor of the wardrobe, she felt something soft and powdery and extremely cold. "This is very queer," she said, and went on a step or two further.

Next moment she found that what was rubbing against her face and hands was no longer soft fur but something hard and rough and even prickly. "Why, it is just like branches of trees!" exclaimed Lucy. And then she saw that there was a light ahead of her; not a few inches away where the back of the wardrobe ought to have been, but a long way off. Something cold and soft was falling on her. A moment later she found that she was standing in the middle of a wood at nighttime with snow under her feet and snowflakes falling through the air.

Lucy felt a little frightened, but she felt very inquisitive and excited as well. She looked back over her shoulder and there, between the dark tree trunks, she could still see the open doorway of the wardrobe and even catch a glimpse of the empty room from which she had set out. (She had, of course, left the door open, for she knew that it is a very silly thing to shut oneself up in a wardrobe.) It seemed to be still daylight there. "I can always get back if anything goes wrong," thought Lucy. She began to walk forward, *crunch-crunch,* over the snow and through the wood toward the other light.

In about ten minutes she reached it and found that it was a lamppost. As she stood looking at it, wondering why there was a lamppost in the middle of a wood and wondering what to do next, she heard a pitter-patter of feet coming toward her. And soon after that a very strange person stepped out from among the trees into the light of the lamppost.

He was only a little taller than Lucy herself and he carried over his head an umbrella, white with snow. From the waist upward he was like a man, but his legs were shaped like a goat's (the hair on them was glossy black) and instead of feet he had goats' hooves. He also had a tail, but Lucy did not notice this at first because it was neatly caught up over the arm that held the umbrella so as to keep it from trailing in the snow. He had a red woolen muffler around his neck and his skin was rather reddish too. He had a strange but pleasant little face with a short pointed beard and curly hair, and out of the hair there stuck two horns, one on each side of his forehead. One of his hands, as I have said, held the umbrella: in the other arm he carried several brown paper parcels. What with the parcels and the snow it looked just as if he had been doing his Christmas shopping. He was a Faun. And when he saw Lucy he gave such a start of surprise that he dropped all his parcels.

"Goodness gracious me!" exclaimed the Faun.

"Good evening," said Lucy. But the Faun was so busy picking up his parcels that at first he did not reply. When he had finished he made her a little bow.

"Good evening, good evening," said the Faun. "Excuse me—I don't want to be inquisitive—but should I be right in thinking that you are a Daughter of Eve?"

"My name's Lucy," said she, not quite understanding him.

"But you are—forgive me—you are what they call a girl?" asked the Faun.

"Of course I'm a girl," said Lucy.

"You are in fact Human?"

"Of course I'm human," said Lucy, still a little puzzled.

"To be sure, to be sure," said the Faun. "How stupid of me! But I've never seen a Son of Adam or a Daughter of Eve before. I am delighted. That is to say—" and then he stopped as if he had been going to say something he had not intended but had remembered in time. "De-lighted, delighted," he went on. "Allow me to introduce myself. My name is Tumnus."

"I am very pleased to meet you, Mr. Tumnus," said Lucy.

"And may I ask, O Lucy, Daughter of Eve," said Mr. Tumnus, "how you have come into Narnia?"

"Narnia? What's that?" said Lucy.

"This is the land of Narnia," said the Faun, "where we are now; all that lies between the lamppost and the great castle of Cair Paravel on the eastern sea. And you—you have come from the wild woods of the west?"

"I—I got in through the wardrobe in the spare room," said Lucy.

"Ah!" said Mr. Tumnus in a rather melancholy voice. "If only I had worked harder at geography when I was a little Faun, I should no doubt know all about those strange countries. It is too late now."

"But they aren't countries at all," said Lucy, almost laughing. "It's only just back there—at least—I'm not sure. It is summer there."

"Meanwhile," said Mr. Tumnus, "it is winter in Narnia, and has been for ever so long, and we shall both catch cold if we stand here talking in the snow. Daughter of Eve from the far land of Spare Oom where eternal summer reigns around the bright city of War Drobe, how would it be if you came and had tea with me?"

"Thank you very much, Mr. Tumnus," said Lucy. "But I was wondering whether I ought to be getting back."

"It's only just around the corner," said the Faun, "and there'll be a roaring fire—and toast—and sardines—and cake."

"Well, it's very kind of you," said Lucy. "But I shan't be able to stay long."

"If you will take my arm, Daughter of Eve," said Mr. Tumnus, "I shall be able to hold the umbrella over both of us. That's the way. Now—off we go."

And so Lucy found herself walking through the wood arm in arm with this strange creature as if they had known one another all their lives.

They had not gone far before they came to a place where the ground became rough and there were rocks all about and little hills up and little hills down. At the bottom of one small valley Mr. Tumnus turned suddenly aside as if he were going to walk straight into an unusually large rock, but at the last moment Lucy found he was leading her into the entrance of a cave. As soon as they were inside she found herself blinking in the light of a wood fire. Then Mr. Tumnus stooped and took a flaming piece of wood out of the fire with a neat little pair of tongs, and lit a lamp. "Now we shan't be long," he said, and immediately put a kettle on.

Lucy thought she had never been in a nicer place. It was a little, dry, clean cave of reddish stone with a carpet on the floor and two little chairs ("one for me and one for a friend," said Mr. Tumnus) and a table and a dresser and a mantelpiece over the fire and above that a picture of an old Faun with a gray beard. In one corner there was a door, which Lucy thought must lead to Mr. Tumnus's bedroom, and on one wall was a shelf full of books. Lucy looked at these while he was setting out the tea things. They had titles like *The Life and Letters of Silenus* or *Nymphs and Their Ways* or *Men, Monks, and Gamekeepers; a Study in Popular Legend* or *Is Man a Myth?*

"Now, Daughter of Eve!" said the Faun.

And really it was a wonderful tea. There was a nice brown egg, lightly boiled, for each of them, and then sardines on toast, and then buttered toast, and then toast with honey, and then a sugar-topped cake. And when Lucy was tired of eating, the Faun began to talk. He had wonderful tales to tell of life in the forest. He told about the midnight dances and how the Nymphs who lived in the wells and the Dryads who lived in the trees came out to dance with the Fauns; about long hunting parties after the milk-white Stag who could give you wishes if you caught him; about feasting and treasure-seeking with the wild Red Dwarfs in deep mines and caverns far beneath the forest floor; and then about summer when the woods were green and old Silenus on his fat donkey would come to visit them, and sometimes Bacchus himself, and then the streams would run with wine instead of water and the whole forest would give itself up to jollification for weeks on end. "Not that it isn't always winter now," he added gloomily. Then to cheer himself up he took out from its case on the dresser a strange little flute that looked as if it were made of straw and began to play. And the tune he played made Lucy want to cry and laugh and go to sleep all at the same time. It must have been hours later when she shook herself and said, "Oh, Mr. Tumnus—I'm so sorry to stop you, and I do love that tune—but really, I must go home. I only meant to stay for a few minutes."

"It's no good now, you know," said the Faun, laying down his flute and shaking his head at her very sorrowfully.

"No good?" said Lucy, jumping up and feeling rather frightened. "What do you mean? I've got to go home at once. The others will be wondering what has happened to me." But a moment later she asked, "Mr. Tumnus! Whatever is the matter?" for the Faun's brown eyes had filled with tears and then the tears began trickling off the end of his nose; and at last he covered his face with his hands and began to howl.

"Mr. Tumnus! Mr. Tumnus!" said Lucy in great distress. "Don't! Don't! What is the matter? Aren't you well? Dear Mr. Tumnus, do tell me what is wrong." But the Faun continued sobbing as if his heart would break. And even when Lucy went over and put her arms around him and lent him her handkerchief, he did not stop. He merely took the handkerchief and kept on using it, wringing it out with both hands whenever it got too wet to be any more use, so that presently Lucy was standing in a damp patch.

"Mr. Tumnus!" bawled Lucy in his ear, shaking him. "Do stop. Stop at once! You ought to be ashamed of yourself, a great big Faun like you. What on earth are you crying about?"

"Oh-oh-oh!" sobbed Mr. Tumnus. "I'm crying because I'm such a bad Faun."

"I don't think you're a bad Faun at all," said Lucy. "I think you are a very good Faun. You are the nicest Faun I've ever met."

"Oh—oh—you wouldn't say that if you knew," replied Mr. Tumnus between his sobs. "No, I'm a bad Faun. I don't suppose there ever was a worse Faun since the beginning of the world."

"But what have you done?" asked Lucy.

"My old father, now," said Mr. Tumnus, "that's his picture over the mantelpiece. He would never have done a thing like this."

"A thing like what?" said Lucy.

"Like what I've done," said the Faun. "Taken service under the White Witch. That's what I am. I'm in the pay of the White Witch."

"The White Witch? Who is she?"

"Why, it is she that has got all Narnia under her thumb. It's she that makes it always winter. Always winter and never Christmas; think of that!"

"How awful!" said Lucy. "But what does she pay you for?"

"That's the worst of it," said Mr. Tumnus with a deep groan. "I'm a kidnapper for her, that's what I am. Look at me, Daughter of Eve. Would you believe that I'm the sort of Faun to meet a poor innocent child in the wood, one that had never done me any harm, and pretend to be friendly with it, and invite it home to my cave, all for the sake of lulling it asleep and then handing it over to the White Witch?"

"No," said Lucy. "I'm sure you wouldn't do anything of the sort."

"But I have," said the Faun.

"Well," said Lucy rather slowly (for she wanted to be truthful and yet not to be too hard on him). "Well, that was pretty bad. But you're so sorry for it that I'm sure you will never do it again."

"Daughter of Eve, don't you understand?" said the Faun. "It isn't something I have done. I'm doing it now, this very moment."

"What do you mean?" cried Lucy, turning very white.

"You are the child," said Mr. Tumnus. "I had orders from the White Witch that if ever I saw a Son of Adam or a Daughter of Eve in the wood, I was to catch them and hand them over to her. And you are the first I ever met. And I've pretended to be your friend and asked you to tea, and all the time I've been meaning to wait till you were asleep and then go and tell her."

"Oh, but you won't, Mr. Tumnus," said Lucy. "You won't, will you? Indeed, indeed you really mustn't."

"And if I don't," said he, beginning to cry again, "she's sure to find out. And she'll have my tail cut off, and my horns sawn off, and my beard plucked out, and she'll wave her wand over my beautiful cloven hooves and turn them into horrid solid hooves like a wretched horse's. And if she is extra and specially angry she'll turn me into stone and I shall be only a statue of a Faun in her horrible house until the four thrones at Cair Paravel are filled—and goodness knows when that will happen, or whether it will ever happen at all."

"I'm very sorry, Mr. Tumnus," said Lucy. "But please let me go home."

"Of course I will," said the Faun. "Of course I've got to. I see that now. I hadn't known what Humans were like before I met you. Of course I can't give you up to the Witch; not now that I know you. But we must be off at once. I'll see you back to the lamppost. I suppose you can find your own way from there back to Spare Oom and War Drobe?"

"I'm sure I can," said Lucy.

"We must go as quietly as we can," said Mr. Tumnus. "The whole wood is full of her spies. Even some of the trees are on her side."

They both got up and left the tea things on the table, and Mr. Tumnus once more put up his umbrella and gave Lucy his arm, and they went out into the snow. The journey back was not at all like the journey to the Faun's cave; they stole along as quickly as they could, without speaking a word, and Mr. Tumnus kept to the darkest places. Lucy was relieved when they reached the lamppost again.

"So you know your way from here, Daughter of Eve?" said Tumnus.

Lucy looked very hard between the trees and could just see in the distance a patch of light that looked like daylight. "Yes," she said, "I can see the wardrobe door."

"Then be off home as quick as you can," said the Faun, "and— c-can you ever forgive me for what I meant to do?"

"Why, of course I can," said Lucy, shaking him heartily by the hand. "And I do hope you won't get into dreadful trouble on my account."

"Farewell, Daughter of Eve," said he. "Perhaps I may keep the handkerchief?"

"Rather!" said Lucy, and then ran toward the far-off patch of daylight as quickly as her legs would carry her. And presently instead of rough branches brushing past her she felt coats, and instead of crunching snow under her feet she felt wooden boards, and all at once she found herself jumping out of the wardrobe into the same empty room from which the whole adventure had started. She shut the wardrobe door tightly behind her and looked around, panting for breath. It was still raining and she could hear the voices of the others in the passage.

"I'm here," she shouted. "I'm here. I've come back, I'm all right."

"The Wind and the Sun"

by Aesop

A classic fable that speaks well of the kind friend.

The wind and the sun were disputing which was the stronger. Suddenly they saw a traveler coming down the road, and the sun said, "I see a way to decide our dispute. Whichever of us can cause that traveler to take off his cloak shall be regarded as the stronger. You begin." So the sun retired behind a cloud, and the wind began to blow as hard as it could upon the traveler. But the harder he blew, the more closely did the traveler wrap his cloak around him, till at last the wind had to give up in despair. Then the sun came out and shone in all his glory upon the traveler, who soon found it too hot to walk with his cloak on.

Kindness effects more than Severity.

"Zlateh the Goat"

by Isaac Bashevis Singer

A boy and a goat face a terrifying snowstorm together and experience the kind of love only hardship can create. Master storyteller Isaac Bashevis Singer tells this simple tale with perfection.

At Hanukkah time the road from the village to the town is usually covered with snow, but this year the winter had been a mild one. Hanukkah had almost come, yet little snow had fallen. The sun shone most of the time. The peasants complained that because of the dry weather there would be a poor harvest of winter grain. New grass sprouted, and the peasants sent their cattle out to pasture.

For Reuven the furrier it was a bad year, and after long hesitation he decided to sell Zlateh the goat. She was old and gave little milk. Feivel the town butcher had offered eight guldens for her. Such a sum would buy Hanukkah candles, potatoes and oil for pancakes, gifts for the children, and other holiday necessaries for the house. Reuven told his oldest boy Aaron to take the goat to town.

Aaron understood what taking the goat to Feivel meant, but he had to obey his father. Leah, his mother, wiped the tears from her eyes when she heard the news. Aaron's younger sisters, Anna and Miriam, cried loudly. Aaron put on his quilted jacket and a cap with earmuffs, bound a rope around Zlateh's neck, and took along two slices of bread with cheese to eat on the road. Aaron was supposed to deliver the goat by evening, spend the night at the butcher's, and return the next day with the money.

While the family said good-bye to the goat, and Aaron placed the rope around her neck, Zlateh stood as patiently and good-naturedly as ever. She licked Reuven's hand. She shook her small white beard. Zlateh trusted human beings. She knew that they always fed her and never did her any harm.

When Aaron brought her out on the road to town, she seemed

73

somewhat astonished. She'd never been led in that direction before. She looked back at him questioningly, as if to say, "Where are you taking me?" But after a while she seemed to come to the conclusion that a goat shouldn't ask questions. Still, the road was different. They passed new fields, pastures, and huts with thatched roofs. Here and there a dog barked and came running after them, but Aaron chased it away with his stick.

The sun was shining when Aaron left the village. Suddenly the weather changed. A large black cloud with a bluish center appeared in the east and spread itself rapidly over the sky. A cold wind blew in with it. The crows flew low, croaking. At first it looked as if it would rain, but instead it began to hail as in summer. It was early in the day, but it became dark as dusk. After a while the hail turned to snow.

In his twelve years Aaron had seen all kinds of weather, but had never experienced a snow like this one. It was so dense it shut out the light of the day. In a short time their path was completely covered. The wind became as cold as ice. The road to town was narrow and winding. Aaron no longer knew where he was. He could not see through the snow. The cold soon penetrated his quilted jacket.

At first Zlateh didn't seem to mind the change in weather. She, too, was twelve years old and knew what winter meant. But when her legs sank deeper and deeper into the snow she began to turn her head and look at Aaron in wonderment. Her mild eyes seemed to ask, "Why are we out in such a storm?" Aaron hoped that a peasant would come along with his cart, but no one passed by.

The snow grew thicker, falling to the ground in large, whirling flakes. Beneath it Aaron's boots touched the softness of a plowed field. He realized that he was no longer on the road. He had gone astray. He could no longer figure out which was east or west, which was the village or the town. The wind whistled, howled, whirled the snow about in eddies. It looked as if white imps were playing tag on the fields. A white dust rose above the ground. Zlateh stopped. She could walk no longer. Stubbornly she anchored her cleft hooves in the earth and bleated as if pleading to be taken home. Icicles hung from her white beard, and her horns were glazed with frost.

Aaron did not want to admit the danger, but he knew just the same that if they did not find shelter they would freeze to death. This was no ordinary storm. It was a mighty blizzard. The snowfall had reached his knees. His hands were numb, and he could no longer feel his toes. He choked when he breathed. His nose felt like wood and he rubbed it with snow. Zlateh's bleating began to sound like crying. Those humans in whom she had so much confidence had dragged her into a trap. Aaron began to pray to God for himself and for the innocent animal.

Suddenly he made out the shape of a hill. He wondered what it could be. Who had piled snow into such a huge heap? He moved toward it, dragging Zlateh after him. When he came near it, he realized that it was a large haystack which the snow had blanketed.

Aaron realized immediately that they were saved. With great effort he dug his way through the snow. He was a village boy and knew what to do. When he reached the hay, he hollowed out a nest for himself and the goat. No matter how cold it may be outside, in the hay it is always warm. And hay was food for Zlateh. The moment she smelled it she became contented and began to eat. Outside, the snow continued to fall. It quickly covered the passageway Aaron had dug. But a boy and an animal need to breathe, and there was hardly any air in their hideout. Aaron bored a kind of window through the hay and snow and carefully kept the passage clear.

Zlateh, having eaten her fill, sat down on her hind legs and seemed to have regained her confidence in man. Aaron ate his two slices of bread and cheese, but after the difficult journey he was still hungry. He looked at Zlateh and noticed her udders were full. He lay down next to her, placing himself so that when he milked her he could squirt the milk into his mouth. It was rich and sweet. Zlateh was not accustomed to being milked that way, but she did not resist. On the contrary, she seemed eager to reward Aaron for bringing her to a shelter whose very walls, floor, and ceiling were made of food.

Through the window Aaron could catch a glimpse of the chaos outside. The wind carried before it whole drifts of snow. It was completely dark, and he did not know whether night had already come or

75

whether it was the darkness of the storm. Thank God that in the hay it was not cold. The dried hay, grass, and field flowers exuded the warmth of the summer sun. Zlateh ate frequently; she nibbled from above, below, from the right and left. Her body gave forth an animal warmth, and Aaron cuddled up to her. He had always loved Zlateh, but now she was like a sister. He was alone, cut off from his family, and wanted to talk. He began to talk to Zlateh. "Zlateh, what do you think about what has happened to us?" he asked.

"Maaaa," Zlateh answered.

"If we hadn't found this stack of hay, we would both be frozen stiffly by now," Aaron said.

"Maaaa," was the goat's reply.

"If the snow keeps on falling like this, we may have to stay here for days," Aaron explained.

"Maaaa," Zlateh bleated.

"What does 'maaaa' mean?" Aaron asked. "You'd better speak up clearly."

"Maaaa, maaaa," Zlateh tried.

"Well, let it be 'maaaa' then," Aaron said patiently. "You can't speak, but I know you understand. I need you and you need me. Isn't that right?"

"Maaaa."

Aaron became sleepy. He made a pillow out of some hay, leaned his head on it, and dozed off. Zlateh, too, fell asleep.

When Aaron opened his eyes, he didn't know whether it was morning or night. The snow blocked up his window. He tried to clear it, but when he had bored through to the length of his arm, he still hadn't reached the outside. Luckily he had his stick with him and was able to break through to the open air. It was still dark outside. The snow continued to fall and the wind wailed, first with one voice and then with many. Sometimes it had the sound of devilish laughter. Zlateh, too, awoke and when Aaron greeted her, she answered, "Maaaa." Yes, Zlateh's language consisted of only one word, but it meant many things. Now she was saying, "We must accept all that God gives us— heat, cold, hunger, satisfaction, light, and darkness."

Aaron had awakened hungry. He had eaten up his food, but Zlateh had plenty of milk.

For three days Aaron and Zlateh stayed in the haystack. Aaron had always loved Zlateh, but in these three days he loved her more and more. She fed him with her milk and helped him keep warm. She comforted him with her patience. He told her many stories, and she always cocked her ear and listened. When he patted her, she licked his hand and his face. Then she said, "Maaaa," and he knew it meant, I love you, too.

The snow fell for three days, though after the first day it was not as thick and the wind quieted down. Sometimes Aaron felt that there could never have been a summer, that the snow had always fallen, ever since he could remember. He, Aaron, never had a father or mother or sisters. He was a snow child, born of snow, and so was Zlateh. It was so quiet in the hay that his ears rang in the stillness. Aaron and Zlateh slept all night and a good part of the day. As for Aaron's dreams, they were all about warm weather. He dreamed of green fields, trees covered with blossoms, clear brooks, and singing birds. By the third night the snow had stopped, but Aaron did not dare to find his way home in the darkness. The sky became clear and the moon shone, casting silvery nets on the snow. Aaron dug his way out and looked at the world. It was all white, quiet, dreaming dreams of heavenly splendor. The stars were quite large and close. The moon swam in the sky as in a sea.

On the morning of the fourth day Aaron heard the ringing of sleigh bells. The haystack was not far from the road. The peasant who drove the sleigh pointed out the way to him—not to the town and Feivel the butcher, but home to the village. Aaron had decided in the haystack that he would never part with Zlateh.

Aaron's family and their neighbors had searched for the boy and the goat but had found no trace of them during the storm. They feared they were lost. Aaron's mother and sisters cried for him; his father remained silent and gloomy. Suddenly one of the neighbors came running to their house with the news that Aaron and Zlateh were coming up the road.

There was great joy in the family. Aaron told them how he had found the stack of hay and how Zlateh had fed him with her milk. Aaron's sisters kissed and hugged Zlateh and gave her a special treat of chopped carrots and potato peels, which Zlateh gobbled up hungrily.

Nobody ever again thought of selling Zlateh, and now that the cold weather had finally set in, the villagers needed the services of Reuven the furrier once more. When Hanukkah came, Aaron's mother was able to fry pancakes every evening, and Zlateh got her portion, too. Even though Zlateh had her own pen, she often came to the kitchen, knocking on the door with her horns to indicate she was ready to visit, and she was always admitted. In the evening Aaron, Miriam, and Anna played dreidel. Zlateh sat near the stove watching the children and the flickering of the Hanukkah candles.

Once in a while Aaron would ask her, "Zlateh, do you remember the three days we spent together?"

And Zlateh would scratch her neck with a horn, shake her white bearded head, and come out with the single sound which expressed all her thoughts, and all her love.

From Thank You, Jackie Robinson
by Barbara Cohen

It is hard to resist a book that begins this way: "Listen. When I was a kid, I was crazy. Nuttier than a fruitcake. Madder than a hatter. Out of my head. You see, I had this obsession. This hang-up. It was all that mattered to me. I was in love with the Brooklyn Dodgers."

The story is about Sammy, a sheltered young boy who loves the Dodgers, and Davy, an elderly cook who works for the boy's mother. The two love the Brooklyn Dodgers and eventually each other. In this scene, Davy is dying. Sammy has gone to enormous lengths to get his friend a prize: a ball autographed by their beloved Jackie Robinson. Sammy has just arrived at the hospital, and he is a little nervous. Davy is in bed, being tended by his sister Henrietta.

I tiptoed quietly into the room. It was hot and sunny in there. White curtains hung limply at the once open window. There were four beds with men in all of them, but I hardly noticed them as I went softly by.

I could see Henrietta sitting in a wooden armchair with green plastic cushions next to the bed by the window. Davy lay in the bed. His eyes were shut. For a second I thought maybe he was dead already, but when I got closer I could see the white sheet moving with his shallow breath.

Maybe he wasn't dead, but he sure didn't look like Davy. He made such a small lump under that white sheet for a man who a few weeks before must have weighed more than two hundred pounds. And his face was kind of sunken and dull-looking, not round and shiny the way I was used to seeing it.

There was a smell in that room I didn't like. I had smelled that smell the day my father died, the day they had let us come into his hospital room to see him. All I could remember of that visit was the smell. I'd forgotten all the rest.

I really couldn't believe the man in the bed was Davy, even though I knew it was. He was not my Davy. He was not the Davy I wanted to know.

I was overcome with an almost irresistible desire to turn and run out of that room. I wanted to run as fast as my legs would carry me. It took the most tremendous effort of will to prevent my body from doing what it wanted to do. Luckily, my will had gotten some good training in the past couple of days. I had come this far, I had come through so much, I knew I couldn't go back again. So I just kind of looked at Henrietta, and she smiled at me and said, "It's okay, Sammy, you can talk to him. He isn't really asleep—just dozing." I was shocked to hear her voice. She talked right out loud—she didn't even whisper, and her voice didn't even sound sad, the way it had in her house earlier that morning. It didn't sound particularly happy either—just normal. "Go ahead," she went on. "Go stand up there by the head of the bed and talk to him."

I did as she said. The top of the bed had been cranked up a little bit and I bent over the pillow. "Davy," I said softly. "Davy." My voice kind of cracked, so I repeated his name again, louder. "Davy, it's me, Sammy. I've brought you a present."

Even before his eyes opened—it seemed to cost him a great effort to open his eyes—his lips formed a little smile. I knew he had heard me. Then his eyes did open and the smile got broader. He looked more like himself. His cheeks were still sunken and his skin still dull and loose, but his eyes and his smile were the same.

He spoke softly, in a kind of whisper, and very slowly, but with perfect clarity. "Why, boy, I am glad to see you. I sure am glad to see you."

I put my hand on his. "How do you feel?" I asked.

"Lots better," he said. "Nothing hurts me anymore. I'm just kinda tired. Once I have a little more energy they're going to let me go home."

"You been following the games okay?" I asked.

"Henrietta gives me the report every afternoon," Davy replied. "Sometimes I can even read the paper a little. They won't let me have a radio, you know. The doctor said it might disturb the other guys in the room."

"We been doing all right," I said.

"All right?" he said. "Just all right?" His voice got a little stronger. "My God, Sammy," he said, "this is the year we've been waiting for. This is next year! They won't blow it now."

"Don't get your hopes up," I said. Now I was talking to him like he usually talked to me. Now I was the old man and he was the boy. "You never can tell with the Dodgers. You can't count on the pennant until it's actually flying over the field."

"Nah," he said. "They won't blow it. This time they won't blow it."

"Well," I agreed carefully, "Jackie is sure having some season. I guess nothing can change that. It's already happened. He's so far ahead in batting he'd have to go into a terrible slump for anyone to catch up."

"It isn't just the hitting though," Davy said. We were going over the old ground again. "He can do everything. How many bases has he stolen this year so far?"

"Twenty-nine," I said. "And four times he stole home!"

"That's what I mean. And RBI's? How many RBI's?"

"A hundred and one," I said with a little laugh.

Davy almost crowed, even though he could speak only in that hoarse kind of whisper. "He can do anything," Davy said. "That boy can do anything."

"He sent you a present," I said.

Davy lifted his head and shoulders up sharply. "What are you talking about?" he said, almost in his old way. "Who sent me a present?"

"Jackie Robinson," I replied with a smile that came right up out of the inside of me. "Jackie Robinson himself, and all the Dodgers."

I put the box on the bed next to him.

"Crank me up a little more," he said. "I gotta see what you've got here."

Henrietta did it, and when he was comfortable he said, "Now, give me that there box." I did, and he opened it. He took out the ball. "Hand me my glasses," he ordered. "They're over there on the night stand." I obeyed, and then waited while he examined the ball for many minutes without saying a word. The men in the other beds were talking to their visitors, and I could hear the murmur of their voices, but it seemed to me as if Davy and Henrietta and I were floating on our own island of silence, far away from anyone else.

Finally he looked away from the ball, which he had been turning and turning in his hands, and looked at me. "How'd you come by this ball, Sammy?" he asked. "Did you finally catch an Old Gold Special?"

"Well, not exactly," I admitted. "But it turned out even better than that. That's a ball that Jackie Robinson himself hit. He hit a double with it." And then I told him the whole story of the day before.

Davy shook his head in wonder. "You went and did all that?" he said.

"Does your mama know?" Henrietta asked. "Does your mama know where you were and what you were doing yesterday?"

"Not yet," I admitted, "but don't worry, I'll tell her. Don't you tell her, Henrietta. Let me."

Henrietta nodded. "Well, you make sure you do that now, hear? You should have told her before."

"I know."

"She's going to have to think of some good punishment for doing all of that without telling her," Henrietta said.

I shrugged. I didn't want to say "So what?" but that's what I felt. I had given the ball to Davy and Davy loved it. That was all that mattered.

"This isn't my ball, though," Davy said.

"What do you mean?" I asked. "Of course it's your ball. It says right on it, 'For Davy.' "

"It's our ball," Davy said. "We'll share it. Six months in my house and six months in yours. Like we said. Only I keep it first."

"It's your ball, Davy," I said. "It's your ball all the time. Jackie Robinson meant it for you."

"Well, if he meant it for me, I can do what I want with it, and I want you to keep it for me six months out of the year. And Henrietta, you listen to me. When I die, that ball goes to Sam. You're not to let Elliot have it."

"Oh, go put it in your will, Pops," she said. "Take care of it yourself, when you come home. I don't want no truck with no balls."

"You heard me, Henrietta," Davy said in a stern voice. He was still kind of whispering, but even so, he could make his voice stern. There was a twinkle in his eye though, and I knew laughter lay right behind the sternness. "It's a sin to disobey the wishes of the dead," he teased, "and if you do I'll come back to haunt you. Every time the Dodgers lose I'll haunt you."

"If the Dodgers lose, it sure won't be my fault," Henrietta said.

"You just see to it that my wishes are followed," Davy said, "and you got nothing to worry about."

The nurse who had been coming down the room bed by bed got to Davy now. She looked at me and then she looked at Henrietta. "Immediate family?" she asked Henrietta, raising her eyebrows.

"You better run along now, Sammy," Henrietta said. "The nurse has got to do all her fussing with Pops and then he'll probably sleep for a while."

Davy sunk back into his pillows. The little spurt of energy he had exhibited when I had given him the ball seemed to have faded. He shut his eyes for a moment, and then he opened them again and looked at me. "I am sure glad you came, Sammy. I sure am glad you came. Who they playing today?"

He didn't even know. He was really sick. "The Pirates," I said.

"Root hard," he said. "Root hard enough for both of us."

"I will," I promised.

"I'll be home in time for the Series," he said. "You'll come down and listen to it with me on the radio."

"Right," I said. It was about all I could say. I wasn't good at making my voice normal, like Henrietta.

"Go along now," the nurse said.

"Good-bye, Davy."

"Good-bye, Sam." He lifted his hand up off the bed. I took it. He closed his fingers around mine. "See you soon," he whispered. Then he let go and shut his eyes.

"So long," I whispered back, and then I left as quickly as I could.

Elliot was waiting for me in the sunroom at the end of the corridor, where patients who could walk around went to sit. He drove me back to his house, where I got my bike and rode home. I ran up to my room fast as I could, because I didn't want to meet my mother or my sisters or anyone else.

There was no magic in the ball. He loved it, but there was no magic in it. It was not going to cure him, the way deep down in my heart I had somehow thought it would. I knew that. My whole self knew that now.

I threw myself on my bed and cried and cried. I cried and cried as if I would never stop. After a while there was a knock on my door. I didn't answer, but my mother came in anyway. My face was buried in my pillow and she couldn't see it.

"Where have you been?" she asked.

"To see Davy," I answered, my voice muffled by my sobs and the pillow.

She put her hand on my shoulder and gently turned me over, and looked into my face. She touched my forehead with her hand, and then she went to the sink in the corner of the room. With cool water she wet a washcloth, which she put across my face. After a while, I stopped crying and fell asleep.

I guess I cried myself out that Sunday, because a week or so later, when Mother told me that Davy had died, I didn't cry at all. It was no surprise to me.

I was listening to the game in my room when she came up to tell me. She didn't say much, and I didn't say much. After she left, I turned off the radio.

"Of Giving"

by Arthur Guiterman

Not what you Get, but what you Give
Is that which proves your Right to Live.

CHAPTER FIVE

Play Fair

But when the Frog came knocking at the door to claim an evening with the Princess, she pooh-poohed him. "I refuse to let that slimy little creature dine at my table or sleep in my bed!" she said in a huff.

Her father, hearing that she had made a promise to the Frog, cautioned the Princess. "You made a promise, and now you must keep it," he told her. Reluctantly, she opened the door, and the creature hopped in.

From "The Frog Prince"
by the BROTHERS GRIMM

Maisie was playing with some friends in the backyard when a dispute over swing rights occurred. Her four-year-old girlfriend stomped her foot in the grass and cried, "But that's not fair!" "Oh, Katherine," Maisie said patronizingly, "everyone knows that life isn't fair."

It was the classic response of a second child. Funny how kids understand fairness from the moment there is more than one glass of orange juice to be filled. Like hawks, they watch how many cookies are dished out; the bigger the family, the more intense the surveillance.

And fairness isn't confined to equal portions. If you don't play fair, it means you steal, cheat, hog, hoard, and break your word. These are universal no-no's. It's not fair to butt in line. Or to break a promise. Or to copy someone's homework. Or to change the rules of the game. It's also not fair to take advantage of someone's goodwill.

A parent must be clear about his own standards of fairness, and impart these standards purposefully to his child. To develop a sense of fair play, the young child will first internalize the concepts given to him by his parents. (I do it because Mommy says so.) Then, having internalized his parents' standards, the child will begin to develop empathetic reactions to other people's feelings. (When I don't share my trucks other children feel sad or angry.) The child's final stage of development occurs when he is able to define standards of fair play for himself, and apply them voluntarily.

Some people, it seems, never learn to play by the rules; their greed overcomes them. In fact, if some of the Wall Street players of the 1980s had taken to heart the stories that follow, they might not be facing indictments today. Greed is commonplace, even banal, in the classic folktale. It is also the mother of injustice, and why some people, no matter how good they have it, refuse to play fair—a throwback to the infant who wants and wants and wants.

But as Maisie points out, that's life. The good guy doesn't always come out on top. Yet the lesser individual takes the road of pretty predictable damnation. These stories show some dubious strategies and their outcomes.

"The Ten Commandments"

from the Holy Bible, King James version, Exodus 20:1–17

1 And God spake all these words, saying,

2 I am the Lord thy God, which have brought thee out of the land of Egypt, out of the house of bondage.

3 Thou shalt have no other gods before me.

4 Thou shalt not make unto thee any graven image, or any likeness of any thing that is in heaven above, or that is in the earth beneath, or that is in the water under the earth:

5 Thou shalt not bow down thyself to them, nor serve them: for I the Lord thy God am a jealous God, visiting the iniquity of the fathers upon the children unto the third and fourth generation of them that hate me;

6 And showing mercy unto thousands of them that love me, and keep my commandments.

7 Thou shalt not take the name of the Lord thy God in vain; for the Lord will not hold him guiltless that taketh his name in vain.

8 Remember the sabbath day, to keep it holy.

9 Six days shalt thou labour, and do all thy work:

10 But the seventh day is the sabbath of the Lord thy God: in it thou shalt not do any work, thou, nor thy son, nor thy daughter, thy manservant, nor thy maidservant, nor thy cattle, nor thy stranger that is within thy gates:

11 For in six days the Lord made heaven and earth, the sea, and all that in them is, and rested the seventh day: wherefore the Lord blessed the sabbath day, and hallowed it.

12 Honour thy father and thy mother: that thy days may be long upon the land which the Lord thy God giveth thee.

13 Thou shalt not kill.

14 Thou shalt not commit adultery.

15 Thou shalt not steal.

16 Thou shalt not bear false witness against thy neighbour.

17 Thou shalt not covet thy neighbour's house, thou shalt not covet thy neighbour's wife, nor his manservant, nor his maidservant, nor his ox, nor his ass, nor any thing that is thy neighbour's.

"The Griffin and the Minor Canon"
by Frank Stockton

This is one of my favorite tales. A griffin, who has come to torment the town, meets his nemesis in a minor canon and the two wrestle with each other. But when the town turns on the canon, it is the griffin who is outraged; how unjust to abandon your great defender! Please give this a good and expressive reading. Your children will love it.

Over the great door of an old, old church, which stood in a quiet town of a faraway land, there was carved in stone the figure of a large griffin. The old-time sculptor had done his work with great care, but the image he had made was not a pleasant one to look at. It had a large head, with enormous open mouth and savage teeth; from its back arose great wings, armed with sharp hooks and prongs; it had stout legs in front, with projecting claws; but there were no legs behind—the body running out into a long and powerful tail, finished off at the end with a barbed point. This tail was coiled up under it, the end sticking up just behind its wings.

The sculptor, or the people who had ordered his stone figure, had evidently been very much pleased with it, for little copies of it, also in stone, had been placed here and there along the sides of the church not very far from the ground, so that people could easily look at them and ponder on their curious forms. There were a great many other sculptures on the outside of this church—saints, martyrs, grotesque heads of men, beasts, and birds, as well as those of other creatures, which cannot be named, because nobody knows exactly what they were—but none were so curious and interesting as the great griffin over the door and the little griffins on the sides of the church.

A long, long distance from the town, in the midst of dreadful wilds scarcely known to man, there dwelt the Griffin whose image had been put up over the church door. In some way or other, the old-time sculptor had seen him, and afterward, to the best of his memory, had copied his

91

figure in stone. The Griffin had never known this until, hundreds of years afterward, he heard from a bird, from a wild animal, or in some manner which it is not now easy to find out, that there was a likeness of him on the old church in the distant town.

Now, this Griffin had no idea how he looked. He had never seen a mirror, and the streams where he lived were so turbulent and violent that a quiet piece of water, which would reflect the image of anything looking into it, could not be found. Being, as far as could be ascertained, the very last of his race, he had never seen another griffin. Therefore it was that when he heard of this stone image of himself, he became very anxious to know what he looked like, and at last determined to go to the old church and see for himself what manner of being he was. So he started off from the dreadful wilds, and flew on and on until he came to the countries inhabited by men, where his appearance in the air created great consternation; but he alighted nowhere, keeping up a steady flight until he reached the suburbs of the town which had his image on its church. Here, late in the afternoon, he alighted in a green meadow by the side of a brook and stretched himself on the grass to rest. His great wings were tired, for he had not made such a long flight in a century or more.

The news of his coming spread quickly over the town, and the people, frightened nearly out of their wits by the arrival of so extraordinary a visitor, fled into their houses and shut themselves up. The Griffin called loudly for someone to come to him, but the more he called, the more afraid the people were to show themselves. At length, he saw two laborers hurrying to their homes through the fields, and in a terrible voice he commanded them to stop. Not daring to disobey, the men stood, trembling.

"What is the matter with you all?" cried the Griffin. "Is there not a man in your town who is brave enough to speak to me?"

"I think," said one of the laborers, his voice shaking so that his words could hardly be understood, "that—perhaps—the Minor Canon—would come."

"Go, call him then!" said the Griffin. "I want to see him."

The Minor Canon, who filled a subordinate position in the old church, had just finished the afternoon services and was coming out of the church with three aged women who had formed the weekday congregation. He was a young man of a kind disposition, and very anxious to do good to the people of the town. Apart from his duties in the church, where he conducted services every weekday, he visited the sick and the poor, counseled and assisted persons who were in trouble, and taught a school composed entirely of the bad children in the town with whom nobody else would have anything to do. Whenever the people wanted something difficult done for them, they always went to the Minor Canon. Thus it was that the laborer thought of the young priest when he found that someone must come and speak to the Griffin.

The Minor Canon had not heard of the strange event, which was known to the whole town except himself and the three old women, and when he was informed of it and was told that the Griffin had asked to see him, he was greatly amazed and frightened.

"Me!" he exclaimed. "He has never heard of me! What should he want with me?"

"Oh, you must go instantly!" cried the two men. "He is very angry now because he has been kept waiting so long; and nobody knows what may happen if you don't hurry to him."

The poor Minor Canon would rather have had his hand cut off than go out to meet an angry griffin; but he felt that it was his duty to go, for it would be a woeful thing if injury should come to the people of the town because he was not brave enough to obey the summons of the Griffin. So, pale and frightened, he started off.

"Well," said the Griffin, as soon as the young man came nearer, "I am glad to see that there is someone who has the courage to come to me."

The Minor Canon did not feel very courageous, but he bowed his head.

"Is this the town," said the Griffin, "where there is a church with a likeness of myself over one of the doors?"

The Minor Canon looked at the frightful creature before him and saw that he was, without doubt, exactly like the stone image on the church. "Yes," he said, "you are right."

"Well, then," said the Griffin, "will you take me to it? I wish very much to see it."

The Minor Canon instantly thought that if the Griffin entered the town without the people knowing what he came for, some of them would probably be frightened to death, and so he sought to gain time to prepare their minds.

"It is growing dark now," he said, very much afraid, as he spoke, that his words might enrage the Griffin, "and objects on the front of the church cannot be seen clearly. It will be better to wait until morning, if you wish to get a good view of the stone image of yourself."

"That will suit me very well," said the Griffin. "I see you are a man of good sense. I am tired, and I will take a nap here on this soft grass while I cool my tail in the little stream that runs near me. The end of my tail gets red-hot when I am angry or excited, and it is quite warm now. So you may go; but be sure and come early tomorrow morning and show me the way to the church."

The Minor Canon was glad enough to take his leave, and hurried into the town. In front of the church he found a great many people assembled to hear his report of his interview with the Griffin. When they found that the creature had not come to spread ruin and devastation, but simply to see his stony likeness on the church, they showed neither relief nor gratification, but began to upbraid the Minor Canon for consenting to conduct the creature into the town.

"What could I do?" cried the young man. "If I should not bring him, he would come himself, and perhaps end by setting fire to the town with his red-hot tail."

Still the people were not satisfied, and a great many plans were proposed to prevent the Griffin from coming into the town. Some elderly persons urged that the young men should go out and kill him; but the young men scoffed at such a ridiculous idea. Then someone said that it would be a good thing to destroy the stone image so that the Griffin would have no excuse for entering the town; and this proposal was received with such favor that many people ran for hammers, chisels, and crowbars with which to tear down and break up the stone griffin. But the Minor Canon resisted this plan with all the strength of his mind and body. He assured the people that this action would enrage the Griffin beyond measure, for it would be impossible to conceal from him that his image had been destroyed during the night. But the people were so determined to break up the stone griffin that the Minor Canon saw there was nothing for him to do but to stay there and protect it. All night he walked up and down in front of the church door, keeping away the men who brought ladders by which they might mount to the great stone griffin and knock it to pieces with their hammers and crowbars. After many hours, the people were obliged to give up their attempts and went home to sleep; but the Minor Canon remained at his post till early morning, and then he hurried away to the field where he had left the Griffin.

The monster had just awakened, and rising to his forelegs and shaking himself, he said that he was ready to go into the town. The Minor Canon therefore walked back, the Griffin flying slowly through the air at a short distance above the head of his guide. Not a person was to be seen in the streets, and they proceeded directly to the front of the church, where the Minor Canon pointed out the stone griffin.

The real Griffin settled down in the little square before the church and gazed earnestly at his sculptured likeness. For a long time he looked at it. First he put his head on one side, and then he put it on the other; then he shut his right eye and gazed with his left, after which he shut his left eye and gazed with his right. Then he moved a little to one side and looked at the image, then he moved the other way. After a while he said to the Minor Canon, who had been standing by all this time, "It is, it must be, an excellent likeness! That breadth between the eyes, that expansive forehead, those massive jaws! I feel that it must resemble me. If there is any fault to find with it, it is that the neck seems a little stiff. But that is nothing. It is an admirable likeness— admirable!"

The Griffin sat looking at his image all the morning and all the afternoon. The Minor Canon had been afraid to go away and leave him, and had hoped all through the day that he would soon be satisfied with his inspection and fly away home. But by evening, the poor young man was utterly exhausted and felt that he must eat and sleep. He frankly admitted this fact to the Griffin, and asked him if he would not like something to eat. He said this because he felt obliged in politeness to do so, but as soon as he had spoken the words, he was seized with dread lest the monster should demand half a dozen babies or some tempting repast of that kind.

"Oh, no," said the Griffin. "I never eat between the equinoxes. At the vernal and the autumnal equinox I take a good meal, and that lasts me for half a year. I am extremely regular in my habits, and do not think it healthful to eat at odd times. But if you need food, go and get it, and I will return to the soft grass where I slept last night and take another nap."

The next day, the Griffin came again to the little square before the church and remained there until evening, steadfastly regarding the stone griffin over the door. The Minor Canon came once or twice to look at him, and the Griffin seemed very glad to see him; but the young clergyman could not stay as he had done before, for he had many duties to perform. Nobody went to the church, but the people came to the Minor Canon's house and anxiously asked him how long the Griffin was going to stay.

"I do not know," he answered, "but I think he will soon be satisfied with regarding his stone likeness and then he will go away."

But the Griffin did not go away. Morning after morning he came to the church, but after a time he did not stay there all day. He seemed to have taken a great fancy to the Minor Canon, and followed him about as he pursued his various avocations. He would wait for him at the side door of the church, for the Minor Canon held services every day, morning and evening, though nobody came now.

"If anyone should come," he said to himself, "I must be found at my post."

When the young man came out, the Griffin would accompany him on his visits to the sick and the poor, and would often look in the windows of the schoolhouse where the Minor Canon was teaching his unruly scholars. All the other schools were closed, but the parents of the Minor Canon's scholars forced them to go to school, because they were so bad they could not endure them all day at home—Griffin or no

Griffin. But it must be said they generally behaved very well when that great monster sat up on his tail and looked in at the schoolroom window.

When it was perceived that the Griffin showed no signs of going away, all the people who were able to do so left the town. The canons and the higher officers of the church had fled away during the first day of the Griffin's visit, leaving behind only the Minor Canon and some of the men who opened the doors and swept the church. All the citizens who could afford it shut up their houses and traveled to distant parts, and only the working people and the poor were left behind. After some days, these ventured to go about and attend to their business, for if they did not work, they would starve. They were getting a little used to seeing the Griffin, and having been told that he did not eat between equinoxes, they did not feel so much afraid of him as before.

Day by day, the Griffin became more and more attached to the Minor Canon. He kept near him a great part of the time, and often spent the night in front of the little house where the young clergyman lived alone. This strange companionship was often burdensome to the Minor Canon; but on the other hand, he could not deny that he derived a great deal of benefit and instruction from it. The Griffin had lived for hundreds of years, and had seen much, and he told the Minor Canon many wonderful things.

"It is like reading an old book," said the young clergyman to himself; "but how many books I would have had to read before I would have found out what the Griffin told me about the earth, the air, the water, about minerals, and metals, and growing things, and all the wonders of the world!"

Thus the summer went on, and drew toward its close. And now the people of the town began to be very much troubled again.

"It will not be long," they said, "before the autumnal equinox is here, and then that monster will want to eat. He will be dreadfully hungry, for he has taken so much exercise since his last meal. He will devour our children. Without doubt, he will eat them all. What is to be done?"

To this question no one could give an answer, but all agreed that the Griffin must not be allowed to remain until the approaching equinox. After talking over the matter a great deal, a crowd of the people went to the Minor Canon at a time when the Griffin was not with him.

"It is all your fault," they said, "that that monster is among us. You brought him here, and you ought to see that he goes away. It is only on your account that he stays here at all, for, although he visits his image every day, he is with you the greater part of the time. If you were not here, he would not stay. It is your duty to go away and then he will follow you, and we shall be free from the dreadful danger which hangs over us."

"Go away!" cried the Minor Canon, greatly grieved at being spoken to in such a way. "Where shall I go? If I go to some other town, shall I not take this trouble there? Have I a right to do that?"

"No," said the people, "you must not go to any other town. There is no town far enough away. You must go to the dreadful wilds where the Griffin lives; and then he will follow you and stay there."

They did not say whether or not they expected the Minor Canon to stay there also, and he did not ask them anything about it. He bowed his head, and went into his house to think. The more he thought, the more clear it became in his mind that it was his duty to go away and thus free the town from the presence of the Griffin.

That evening, he packed a leather bag full of bread and meat, and early the next morning he set out on his journey to the dreadful wilds. It was a long, weary, and doleful journey, especially after he had gone beyond the habitations of men, but the Minor Canon kept on bravely and never faltered. The way was longer than he had expected, and his provisions soon grew so scanty that he was obliged to eat but a little every day, but he kept up his courage and pressed on, and after many days of toilsome travel, he reached the dreadful wilds.

When the Griffin found that the Minor Canon had left the town, he seemed sorry, but showed no disposition to go and look for him. After a few days had passed, he became much annoyed, and asked some of the people where the Minor Canon had gone. But, although the citizens had been so anxious that the young clergyman should go to the dreadful wilds, thinking that the Griffin would immediately follow him, they were now afraid to mention the Minor Canon's destination, for the monster seemed angry already, and if he should suspect their trick, he would doubtless become very much enraged. So everyone said he did not know, and the Griffin wandered about disconsolately. One morning he looked into the Minor Canon's schoolhouse, which was always empty now, and thought that it was a shame that everything should suffer on account of the young man's absence.

"It does not matter so much about the church," he said to himself, "for nobody went there; but it is a pity about the school. I think I will teach it myself until he returns."

It was the hour for opening the school, and the Griffin went inside and pulled the rope which rang the school bell. Some of the children who heard the bell ran in to see what was the matter, supposing it to be a joke of one of their companions; but when they saw the Griffin they stood astonished and scared.

"Go tell the other scholars," said the monster, "that school is about to open, and that if they are not all here in ten minutes I shall come after them."

In seven minutes, every scholar was in place.

Never was seen such an orderly school. Not a boy or girl moved or uttered a whisper. The Griffin climbed into the master's seat, his wide wings spread on each side of him, because he could not lean back in his chair while they stuck out behind, and his great tail coiled around in front of the desk, the barbed end sticking up ready to tap any boy or girl who might misbehave.

The Griffin now addressed the scholars, telling them that he intended to teach them while their master was away. In speaking, he tried to imitate, as far as possible, the mild and gentle tones of the Minor Canon; but it must be admitted that in this he was not very successful. He had paid a good deal of attention to the studies of the school, and he determined not to try to teach them anything new, but to review them in what they had been studying; so he called up the various classes and questioned them upon their previous lessons. The children racked their brains to remember what they had learned. They were so afraid of the Griffin's displeasure that they recited as they never recited before. One of the boys, far down in his class, answered so well that the Griffin was astonished.

"I should think you would be at the head," said he. "I am sure you have never been in the habit of reciting so well. Why is this?"

"Because I did not choose to take the trouble," said the boy, trembling in his boots. He felt obliged to speak the truth, for all the children thought that the great eyes of the Griffin could see right through them, and that he would know when they told a falsehood.

"You ought to be ashamed of yourself," said the Griffin. "Go down to the very tail of the class; and if you are not at the head in two days, I shall know the reason why."

The next afternoon this boy was Number One.

It was astonishing how much these children now learned of what they had been studying. It was as if they had been educated over again. The Griffin used no severity toward them, but there was a look about him which made them unwilling to go to bed until they were sure they knew their lessons for the next day.

The Griffin now thought that he ought to visit the sick and poor; and he began to go about the town for this purpose. The effect upon the sick was miraculous. All, except those who were very ill indeed, jumped from their beds when they heard he was coming, and declared themselves quite well. To those who could not get up, he gave herbs and roots, which none of them had ever before thought of as medicines, but which the Griffin had seen used in various parts of the world; and most of them recovered. But, for all that, they afterward said that no matter what happened to them, they hoped they should never again have such a doctor coming to their bedsides, feeling their pulses and looking at their tongues.

As for the poor, they seemed to have utterly disappeared. All those who had depended upon charity for their daily bread were at work in some way or other, many of them offering to do odd jobs for their neighbors just for the sake of their meals—a thing which before had been seldom heard of in the town. The Griffin could find no one who needed his assistance.

The summer had now passed, and the autumnal equinox was

rapidly approaching. The citizens were in a state of great alarm and anxiety. The Griffin showed no signs of going away, but seemed to have settled himself permanently among them. In a short time the day for his semiannual meal would arrive, and then what would happen? The monster would certainly be very hungry, and would devour all their children.

Now they greatly regretted and lamented that they had sent away the Minor Canon; he was the only one on whom they could have depended in this trouble, for he could talk freely with the Griffin and so find out what could be done. But it would not do to be inactive. Some step must be taken immediately. A meeting of the citizens was called, and two old men were appointed to go and talk to the Griffin. They were instructed to offer to prepare a splendid dinner for him on equinox day—one which would entirely satisfy his hunger. They would offer him the fattest mutton, the most tender beef, fish and game of various sorts, and anything of the kind that he might fancy. If none of these suited, they were to mention that there was an orphan asylum in the next town.

"Anything would be better," said the citizens, "than to have our dear children devoured."

The old men went to the Griffin; but their propositions were not received with favor.

"From what I have seen of the people of this town," said the monster, "I do not think I could relish anything which was prepared by them. They appear to be all cowards, and therefore mean and selfish. As for eating one of them, old or young, I could not think of it for a moment. In fact, there was only one creature in the whole place for whom I could have had any appetite, and that was the Minor Canon, who has gone away. He was brave and good and honest, and I think I should have relished him."

"Ah!" said one of the old men very politely, "in that case I wish we had not sent him to the dreadful wilds!"

"What!" cried the Griffin. "What do you mean? Explain instantly what you are talking about!"

The old man, terribly frightened at what he had said, was obliged to tell how the Minor Canon had been sent away by the people, in the hope that the Griffin might be induced to follow him.

When the monster heard this, he became furiously angry. He dashed away from the old men, and spreading his wings, flew backward and forward over the town. He was so much excited that his tail became red-hot and glowed like a meteor against the evening sky. When at last he settled down in the little field where he usually rested and thrust his tail into the brook, the steam arose like a cloud and the water of the stream ran hot through the town. The citizens were greatly frightened, and bitterly blamed the old man for telling the Griffin about the Minor Canon.

"It is plain," they said, "that the Griffin intended at last to go and look for him, and we should have been saved. Now, who can tell what misery you have brought upon us?"

The Griffin did not remain long in the little field. As soon as his tail was cool, he flew to the town hall and rang the bell. The citizens knew that they were expected to come there; and although they were afraid to go, they were still more afraid to stay away, and they crowded into the hall. The Griffin was on the platform at one end, flapping his wings and walking up and down, and the end of his tail was still so warm that it slightly scorched the boards as he dragged it after him.

When everybody who was able to come was there, the Griffin stood still and addressed the meeting.

"I have had a very low opinion of you," he said, "ever since I discovered what cowards you are, but I had no idea that you were so ungrateful, selfish, and cruel as I now find you to be. Here was your Minor Canon, who labored day and night for your good, and thought of nothing else but how he might benefit you and make you happy; and as soon as you imagine yourselves threatened with a danger—for well I know you are dreadfully afraid of me—you send him off, caring not whether he returns or perishes, hoping thereby to save yourselves. Now, I had conceived a great liking for that young man, and had intended, in a day or two, to go and look him up. But I have changed my mind about him. I shall go and find him, but I shall send him back here to live among you, and I intend that he shall enjoy the reward of his labor and his sacrifices.

"Go, some of you, to the officers of the church, who were so cowardly as to run away when I first came here, and tell them never to return to this town under penalty of death. And if, when your Minor Canon comes back to you, you do not bow yourselves before him, put him in the highest place among you, and serve and honor him all his life, beware of my terrible vengeance! There were only two good things in this town: the Minor Canon and the stone image of myself over your church door. One of these you have sent away, and the other I shall carry away myself."

With these words he dismissed the meeting; and it was time, for the end of his tail had become so hot that there was danger of it setting fire to the building.

The next morning the Griffin came to the church, and tearing the stone image of himself from its fastenings over the great door, he grasped it with his powerful forelegs and flew up into the air. Then, after hovering over the town for a moment, he gave his tail an angry shake and took up his flight to the dreadful wilds. When he reached this desolate region, he set the stone griffin upon a ledge of a rock which rose in front of the dismal cave he called his home. There the image occupied a position somewhat similar to that it had had over the church door; and the Griffin, panting with the exertion of carrying such an enormous load so great a distance, lay down upon the ground and regarded it with much satisfaction. When he felt somewhat rested, he went to look for the Minor Canon. He found the young man, weak and half starved, lying under the shadow of a rock. After picking him up and carrying him to his cave, the Griffin flew away to a distant marsh, where he procured some roots and herbs that he well knew were strengthening and beneficial to man, though he had never tasted them himself. After eating these, the Minor Canon was greatly revived, and sat up and listened while the Griffin told him what had happened in the town.

"Do you know," said the monster, when he had finished, "that I have had, and still have, a great liking for you?"

"I am very glad to hear it," said the Minor Canon, with his usual politeness.

"I am not at all sure that you would be," said the Griffin, "if you thoroughly understood the state of the case; but we will not consider that now. If some things were different, other things would be otherwise. I have been so enraged by discovering the manner in which you have been treated, that I have determined that you shall at last enjoy the rewards and honors to which you are entitled. Lie down and have a good sleep, and then I will take you back to the town."

As he heard these words, a look of trouble came over the young man's face.

"You need not give yourself any anxiety," said the Griffin, "about my return to the town. I shall not remain there. Now that I have that admirable likeness of myself in front of my cave, where I can sit at my leisure and gaze upon its noble features, I have no wish to see that abode of cowardly and selfish people."

The Minor Canon, relieved from his fears, lay back and dropped into a doze; and when he was sound asleep, the Griffin took him up and carried him back to the town. He arrived just before daybreak, and putting the young man gently on the grass in the little field where he himself used to rest, the monster, without having been seen by any of the people, flew back to his home.

When the Minor Canon made his appearance in the morning among the citizens, the enthusiasm and cordiality with which he was received was truly wonderful. He was taken to a house which had been occupied by one of the banished high officers of the place, and everyone was anxious to do all that could be done for his health and comfort. The people crowded into the church when he held services, so the three old women who used to be his weekday congregation could not get to the best seats, which they had always been in the habit of taking; and the parents of the bad children determined to reform them at home, in order that he might be spared the trouble of keeping up his former school. The Minor Canon was appointed to the highest office of the old church, and before he died, he became a bishop.

During the first years after his return from the dreadful wilds, the people of the town looked up to him as a man to whom they were bound to do honor and reverence; but they often, also, looked up to the sky to see if there were any signs of the Griffin coming back. However, in the course of time, they learned to honor and reverence their former Minor Canon without the fear of being punished if they did not do so.

But they need never have been afraid of the Griffin. The autumnal equinox came around, and the monster ate nothing. If he could not have the Minor Canon, he did not care for anything. So, lying down, with his eyes fixed upon the great stone griffin, he gradually declined and died. It was a good thing for some of the people of the town that they did not know this.

If you should ever visit the old town, you would still see the little griffins on the side of the church; but the great stone griffin that was over the door is gone.

"The Fire on the Mountain"

by Harold Courlander

This is an Ethiopian tale by a marvelous storyteller about an unjust chieftain who learns a powerful lesson about fair play. Injustice rankles all children, and they will respond mightily when Arha is robbed of his reward unfairly. The matter is resolved quite neatly.

People say that in the old days in the city of Addis Ababa there was a young man by the name of Arha. He had come as a boy from the country of Gurage, and in the city he became the servant of a rich merchant, Haptom Hasei.

Haptom Hasei was so rich that he owned everything money could buy, and often he was very bored because he had tired of everything he knew, and there was nothing new for him to do.

One cold night, when the damp wind was blowing across the plateau, Haptom called to Arha to bring wood for the fire. When Arha was finished, Haptom began to talk.

"How much cold can a man stand?" he said, speaking at first to himself. "I wonder if it would be possible for a man to stand on the highest peak, Mount Sululta, where the coldest winds blow, through an entire night without blankets or clothing and yet not die?"

"I don't know," Arha said. "But wouldn't it be a foolish thing?"

"Perhaps, if he had nothing to gain by it, it would be a foolish thing to spend the night that way," Haptom said. "But I would be willing to bet that a man couldn't do it."

"I am sure a courageous man could stand naked on Mount Sululta throughout an entire night and not die of it," Arha said. "But as for me, it isn't my affair, since I've nothing to bet."

"Well, I'll tell you what," Haptom said. "Since you are so sure it can be done, I'll make a bet with you anyway. If you can stand among the rocks on Mount Sululta for an entire night without food or water, or clothing or blankets or fire, and not die of it, then I will give you ten acres of good farmland for your own, with a house and cattle."

Arha could hardly believe what he had heard.

"Do you really mean this?" he asked.

"I am a man of my word," Haptom replied.

"Then tomorrow night I will do it," Arha said, "and afterward, for all the years to come, I shall till my own soil."

But he was very worried, because the wind swept bitterly across that peak. So in the morning Arha went to a wise old man from the Gurage tribe and told him of the bet he had made. The old man listened quietly and thoughtfully, and when Arha had finished he said, "I will help you. Across the valley from Sululta is a high rock, which can be seen in the daytime. Tomorrow night, as the sun goes down, I shall build a fire there, so that it can be seen from where you stand on the peak. All night long you must watch the light of my fire. Do not close your eyes or let the darkness creep upon you. As you watch my fire, think of its warmth, and think of me, your friend, sitting there tending it for you. If you do this you will survive, no matter how bitter the night wind."

Arha thanked the old man warmly and went back to Haptom's house with a light heart. He told Haptom he was ready, and in the afternoon Haptom sent him, under the watchful eyes of other servants, to the top of Mount Sululta. There, as night fell, Arha removed his clothes and stood in the damp, cold wind that swept across the plateau with the setting sun. Across the valley, several miles away, Arha saw the light of his friend's fire, which shone like a star in the blackness.

The wind turned colder and seemed to pass through his flesh and chill the marrow in his bones. The rock on which he stood felt like ice. Each hour the cold numbed him more, until he thought he would never be warm again, but he kept his eyes upon the twinkling light across the valley, and remembered that his old friend sat there tending a fire for him. Sometimes wisps of fog blotted out the light, and then he strained to see until the fog passed. He sneezed and coughed and shivered, and began to feel ill. Yet all night through he stood there, and only when the dawn came did he put on his clothes and go down the mountain back to Addis Ababa.

Haptom was very surprised to see Arha, and he questioned his servants thoroughly.

"Did he stay all night without food or drink or blankets or clothing?"

"Yes," his servants said. "He did all of these things."

"Well, you are a strong fellow," Haptom said to Arha. "How did you manage to do it?"

"I simply watched the light of a fire on a distant hill," Arha said.

"What! You watched a fire? Then you lose the bet, and you are still my servant, and you own no land!"

"But this fire was not close enough to warm me, it was far across the valley!"

"I won't give you the land," Haptom said. "You didn't fulfill the conditions. It was only the fire that saved you."

Arha was very sad. He went again to his old friend of the Gurage tribe and told him what had happened.

"Take the matter to the judge," the old man advised him.

Arha went to the judge and complained, and the judge sent for Haptom. When Haptom told his story, and the servants said once more that Arha had watched a distant fire across the valley, the judge said, "No, you have lost, for Haptom Hasei's condition was that you must be without fire."

Once more Arha went to his old friend with the sad news that he was doomed to the life of a servant, as though he had not gone through the ordeal on the mountaintop.

"Don't give up hope," the old man said. "More wisdom grows wild in the hills than in any city judge."

He got up from where he sat and went to find a man named Hailu, in whose house he had been a servant when he was young. He explained to the good man about the bet between Haptom and Arha, and asked if something couldn't be done.

"Don't worry about it," Hailu said after thinking for a while. "I will take care of it for you."

Some days later Hailu sent invitations to many people in the city to come to a feast at his house. Haptom was among them, and so was the judge who had ruled Arha had lost the bet.

When the day of the feast arrived, the guests came riding on mules with fine trappings, their servants strung out behind them on foot. Haptom came with twenty servants, one of whom held a silk umbrella over his head to shade him from the sun, and four drummers played music that signified the great Haptom was here.

The guests sat on soft rugs laid out for them and talked. From the kitchen came the odors of wonderful things to eat: roast goat, roast corn and durra, pancakes called injera, and many tantalizing sauces. The smell of the food only accentuated the hunger of the guests. Time passed. The food should have been served, but they didn't see it, only smelled vapors that drifted from the kitchen. The evening came, and still no food was served. The guests began to whisper among themselves. It was very curious that the honorable Hailu had not had the food brought out. Still the smells came from the kitchen. At last one of the guests spoke out for all the others: "Hailu, why do you do this to us? Why do you invite us to a feast and then serve us nothing?"

"Why, can't you smell the food?" Hailu asked with surprise.

"Indeed we can, but smelling is not eating; there is no nourishment in it!"

"And is there warmth in a fire so distant that it can hardly be seen?" Hailu asked. "If Arha was warmed by the fire he watched while standing on Mount Sululta, then you have been fed by the smells coming from my kitchen."

The people agreed with him; the judge now saw his mistake, and Haptom was shamed. He thanked Hailu for his advice, and announced that Arha was then and there the owner of the land, the house, and the cattle.

Then Hailu ordered the food brought in, and the feast began.

"The Fisherman and His Wife"

by the Brothers Grimm

> *I do not know of a greedier character in folk literature than the wife of the fisherman. If anyone has ever been out of line, it is she. When we intrude upon another's goodwill we are not playing fair. This story makes the point dramatically that greed, in the end, begets woe.*

There was once upon a time a Fisherman who lived with his wife in a miserable hovel close by the sea, and every day he went out fishing. Once as he was sitting with his rod, looking at the clear water, his line suddenly went down, far down below, and when he drew it up again, he brought out a large Flounder. The Flounder said to him, "Hark you, Fisherman, I pray you, let me live. I am no Flounder really, but an enchanted prince. What good will it do you to kill me? I should not be good to eat. Put me in the water again, and let me go." "Come," said the Fisherman, "there is no need for so many words about it—a fish that can talk I should certainly let go, anyhow." With that he put him back again into the clear water, and the Flounder went to the bottom, leaving a long streak of blood behind him. The Fisherman then got up and went home to his wife in the hovel.

"Husband," said the woman, "have you caught nothing today?" "No," said the man, "I did catch a Flounder, who said he was an enchanted prince, so I let him go." "Did you not wish for anything first?" said the woman. "No," said the man, "what should I wish for?" "Ah," said the woman, "it is surely hard to have to live always in this dirty hovel; you might have wished for a small cottage for us. Go back and call him. Tell him we want to have a small cottage; he will certainly give us that." "Ah," said the man, "why should I go there again?" "Why?" said the woman. "You did catch him, and you let him go again. He is sure to do it. Go at once." The man still did not quite like to go, but did not like to oppose his wife either, and he went to the sea.

When he got there the sea was all green and yellow, and no longer so smooth, so he stood and said,

> "Flounder, Flounder in the sea,
> Pray thee harken unto me:
> My wife Ilsebil must have her will,
> And sends me to ask a gift of thee."

The Flounder came swimming to him and said, "Well, what does she want then?" "Ah," said the man, "I did catch you, and my wife says I really ought to have wished for something. She does not want to live in a wretched hovel any longer; she would like to have a cottage." "Go, then," said the Flounder, "she has it already."

When the man went home, his wife was no longer in the hovel, but instead there stood a small cottage, and she was sitting on a bench before the door. Then she took him by the hand and said to him, "Just come inside. Look, now isn't this a great deal better?" So they went in, and there was a small porch, and a pretty little parlor and bedroom, and a kitchen and pantry, with the best of furniture, and fitted up with the most beautiful things made of tin and brass, whatsoever was wanted. And behind the cottage there was a small yard, with hens and ducks and a little garden with flowers and fruit. "Look," said the wife, "is not that nice!" "Yes," said the husband, "and so we must always think it—now we will live quite contented." "We will think about that," said the wife. With that they ate something and went to bed.

Everything went well for a week or so, and then the woman said, "Hark you, husband, this cottage is far too small for us, and the garden and yard are little; the Flounder might just as well have given us a larger house. I should like to live in a great stone castle. Go to the Flounder, and tell him to give us a castle." "Ah, wife," said the man, "the cottage is quite good enough. Why should we live in a castle?" "What?" said the woman, "just go there, the Flounder can surely say yes to that." "No, wife," said the man, "the Flounder has just given us the cottage. I do not like to go back so soon. It might make him angry." "Go," said the woman, "he can do it quite easily, and will be glad to do it. Just you go to him."

The man's heart grew heavy, and he would not go. He said to himself, "It is not right," and yet he went. And when he came to the sea the water was quite purple and dark-blue, and gray and thick, and no longer so green and yellow, but was still quiet. And he stood there and said,

> "Flounder, Flounder in the sea,
> Pray thee harken unto me:
> My wife Ilsebil must have her will,
> And sends me to ask a gift of thee."

"Well, what does she want then?" said the Flounder. "Alas," said the man, half scared, "she wants to live in a great stone castle." "Go to it, then, she is standing before the door," said the Flounder.

The man went away, intending to go home, but when he got there, he found a great stone palace, and his wife was just standing on the steps going in, and she took him by the hand and said, "Come in." So he went in with her, and in the castle was a great hall paved with marble, and many servants, who flung wide the doors; and the walls were all bright with beautiful hangings, and in the rooms were chairs and tables of pure gold, and crystal chandeliers hung from the ceiling, and all the rooms and bedrooms had carpets, and food and wine of the very best were standing on all the tables, so that they nearly broke down beneath it. Behind the house, too, there was a great courtyard, with stables for horses and cows, and the very best of carriages; there was a magnificent large garden, too, with the most beautiful flowers and fruit trees, and a park quite half a mile long, in which were stags, deer, and hares, and everything that could be desired. "Come," said the woman, "isn't that beautiful?" "Yes, indeed," said the man, "now let it be; and we will live in this beautiful castle and be content." "We will consider about that," said the woman, "and sleep upon it." Thereupon they went to bed.

Next morning the wife awoke first, and it was just daybreak, and from her bed she saw the beautiful country lying before her. Her husband was still stretching himself, so she poked him in the side with her elbow and said, "Get up, husband, and just peep out of the window.

Look you, couldn't we be the King over all that land? Go to the Flounder. We will be the King." "Ah, wife," said the man, "why should we be King? I do not want to be King." "Well," said the wife, "if you won't be King, I will; go to the Flounder, for I will be King." "Ah, wife," said the man, "why do you want to be King? I do not like to say that to him." "Why not?" said the woman; "go to him this instant; I must be King!" So the man went, and was quite unhappy because his wife wished to be King. "It is not right; it is not right," thought he. He did not wish to go, but yet he went.

And when he came to the sea, it was quite dark-gray, and the water heaved up from below, and smelled putrid. Then he went and stood by it, and said,

> "Flounder, Flounder in the sea,
> Pray thee harken unto me:
> My wife Ilsebil must have her will,
> And sends me to ask a gift of thee."

"Well, what does she want then?" said the Flounder. "Alas," said the man, "she wants to be King." "Go to her; she is King already."

So the man went, and when he came to the palace, the castle had become much larger, and had a great tower and magnificent ornaments, and the sentinel was standing before the door, and there were numbers of soldiers with kettle drums and trumpets. And when he went inside the house, everything was of real marble and gold, with velvet covers and great golden tassels. Then the doors of the hall were opened, and there was the court in all its splendor, and his wife was sitting on a high throne of gold and diamonds, with a great crown of gold on her head, and a scepter of pure gold and jewels in her hand, and on both sides of her stood her maids-in-waiting in a row, each of them always one head shorter than the last.

Then he went and stood before her, and said, "Ah, wife, and now you are King." "Yes," said the woman, "now I am King." So he stood and looked at her, and when he had looked at her thus for some time, he said, "And now that you are King, let all else be. Now we will wish for nothing more." "No, husband," said the woman, quite anxiously, "I find time passes very heavily. I can bear it no longer. Go to the Flounder—I am King, but I must be Emperor too." "Oh, wife, why do you wish to be Emperor?" "Husband," said she, "go to the Flounder. I will be Emperor." "Alas, wife," said the man, "he cannot make you Emperor; I may not say that to the fish. There is only one Emperor in the land. An Emperor the Flounder cannot make you! I assure you he cannot."

"What!" said the woman, "I am the King, and you are nothing but my husband. Will you go this moment? Go at once! If he can make a king he can make an emperor. I will be Emperor; go instantly." So he was forced to go. As the man went, however, he was troubled in mind, and thought to himself: "It will not end well. It will not end well! Emperor is too shameless! The Flounder will at last be tired out."

With that he reached the sea, and the sea was quite black and thick, and began to boil up from below, so that it threw up bubbles, and such a sharp wind blew over it that it curdled, and the man was afraid. He went and stood by it, and said,

> "Flounder, Flounder in the sea,
> Pray thee harken unto me:
> My wife Ilsebil must have her will,
> And sends me to ask a gift of thee."

"Well, what does she want then?" said the Flounder. "Alas, Flounder," said he, "my wife wants to be Emperor." "Go to her," said the Flounder; "she is Emperor already."

So the man went, and when he got there the whole palace was made of polished marble with alabaster figures and golden ornaments, and soldiers were marching before the door blowing trumpets and beating cymbals and drums; and in the house, barons and counts and dukes were going about as servants. Then they opened the doors to him, which were of pure gold. And when he entered, there sat his wife on a throne, which was made of one piece of gold, and was quite two miles high; and she wore a great golden crown that was three yards high and set with diamonds and carbuncles, and in one hand she had the scepter and in the other the imperial orb; and on both sides of her stood the yeomen of the guard in two rows, each being smaller than the one before him, from the biggest giant, who was two miles high, to the very smallest dwarf, just as big as my thumb. And before the throne stood a number of princes and dukes.

Then the man went and stood among them, and said, "Wife, are you Emperor now?" "Yes," said she, "now I am Emperor." Then he stood and looked at her well, and when he had looked at her thus for some time, he said, "Ah, wife, be content, now that you are Emperor." "Husband," said she, "why are you standing there? Now I am Emperor, but I will be Pope too. Go to the Flounder." "Oh, wife," said the man, "what will you not wish for? You cannot be Pope. There is but one in Christendom; he cannot make you Pope." "Husband," said she, "I will be Pope. Go immediately; I must be Pope this very day." "No, wife," said the man, "I do not like to say that to him; that would not do. It is too much; the Flounder can't make you Pope." "Husband," said she, "what nonsense! If he can make an emperor, he can make a pope. Go to him directly. I am Emperor, and you are nothing but my husband. Will you go at once?"

Then he was afraid and went; but he was quite faint, and shivered and shook, and his knees and legs trembled. And a high wind blew over the land, and the clouds flew, and toward evening all grew dark, and the leaves fell from the trees, and the water rose and roared as if it were boiling, and splashed upon the shore; and in the distance he saw ships that were firing guns in their sore need, pitching and tossing on the waves. And yet in the midst of the sky there was still a small bit of blue, though on every side it was as red as in a heavy storm. So, full of despair, he went and stood in much fear and said,

> "Flounder, Flounder in the sea,
> Pray thee harken unto me:
> My wife Ilsebil must have her will,
> And sends me to ask a gift of thee."

"Well, what does she want now?" said the Flounder. "Alas," said the man, "she wants to be Pope." "Go to her then," said the Flounder, "she is Pope already."

So he went, and when he got there, he saw what seemed to be a large church surrounded by palaces. He pushed his way through the crowd. Inside, however, everything was lighted up with thousands and thousands of candles, and his wife was clad in gold, and she was sitting on a much higher throne, and had three great golden crowns on, and around and about her there was much ecclesiastical splendor; and on both sides of her was a row of candles the largest of which was as tall as the very tallest tower, down to the very smallest kitchen candle, and all the emperors and kings were on their knees before her, kissing her shoe. "Wife," said the man, and looked attentively at her, "are you now Pope?" "Yes," said she, "I am Pope." So he stood and looked at her, and it was just as if he were looking at the bright sun. When he had stood looking at her thus for a short time, he said, "Ah, wife, if you are Pope, do let well alone!" But she looked as stiff as a post, and did not move or show any signs of life. Then said he, "Wife, now that you are Pope, be satisfied. You cannot become anything greater now." "I will consider about that," said the woman. Thereupon they both went to bed, but she was not satisfied, and greediness let her have no sleep, for she was continually thinking what there was left for her to be.

The man slept well and soundly, for he had run about a great deal during the day; but the woman could not fall asleep at all, and flung herself from one side to the other the whole night through, thinking always what more was left of her to be, but unable to call to mind anything else. At length the sun began to rise, and when the woman saw the red of dawn, she sat up in bed and looked at it. And when, through the window, she saw the sun thus rising, she said, "Cannot I, too, order the sun and moon to rise? Husband," she said, poking him in the ribs with her elbow, "wake up! Go to the Flounder, for I wish to be even as God is." The man was still half asleep, but he was so horrified that he fell out of bed. He thought he must have heard amiss, and rubbed his eyes, and said, "Alas, wife, what are you saying?" "Husband," said she, "if I can't order the sun and moon to rise, and have to look on and see the sun and moon rising, I can't bear it. I shall not know what it is to have another happy hour unless I can make them rise myself." Then she looked at him so terribly that a shudder ran over him, and she said, "Go at once; I wish to be like unto God." "Alas, wife," said the man, falling on his knees before her, "the Flounder cannot do that; he can make an emperor and a pope; I beseech you, go on as you are, and be Pope." Then she fell into a rage, and her hair flew wildly about her head, and she cried, "I will not endure this, I'll not bear it any longer. Will you go this instant?" Then he put on his trousers and ran away like a madman. But outside a great storm was raging, and blowing so hard that he could scarcely keep his feet; houses and trees toppled over, the mountains trembled, rocks rolled into the sea, the sky was pitch-black, and it thundered and lightninged, and the sea came in with black waves as high as church towers and mountains, and all with crests of white foam at the top. Then he cried, but could not hear his own words,

> "Flounder, Flounder in the sea,
> Pray thee harken unto me:
> My wife Ilsebil must have her will,
> And sends me to ask a gift of thee."

"Well, what does she want then?" said the Flounder. "Alas," said he, "she wants to be like unto God." "Go to her and you will find her back again in the dirty hovel." And there they are still living to this day.

"Two of Everything"
by Alice Ritchie

A rather mad Chinese folktale about unbridled greed. It seems to amuse children greatly. They love the ending!

Mr. and Mrs. Hak-Tak were rather old and rather poor. They had a small house in a village among the mountains and a tiny patch of green land on the mountainside. Here they grew the vegetables that were all they had to live on, and when it was a good season and they did not need to eat up everything as soon as it was grown, Mr. Hak-Tak took what they could spare in a basket to the next village, which was a little larger than theirs, and sold it for as much as he could get and bought some oil for their lamp, and fresh seeds, and every now and then, but not often, a piece of cotton stuff to make new coats and trousers for himself and his wife. You can imagine they did not often get the chance to eat meat.

Now, one day it happened that when Mr. Hak-Tak was digging in his precious patch, he unearthed a big brass pot. He thought it strange that it should have been there for so long without his having come across it before, and he was disappointed to find that it was empty; still, he thought they would find some use for it, so when he was ready to go back to the house in the evening he decided to take it with him. It was very big and heavy, and in his struggles to get his arms around it and raise it to a good position for carrying, his purse, which he always took with him in his belt, fell to the ground, and to be quite sure he had it safe, he put it inside the pot and so staggered home with his load.

As soon as he got into the house Mrs. Hak-Tak hurried from the inner room to meet him.

"My dear husband," she said, "whatever have you got there?"

"For a cooking pot it is too big; for a bath a little too small," said Mr. Hak-Tak. "I found it buried in our vegetable patch and so far it has been useful in carrying my purse home for me."

"Alas," said Mrs. Hak-Tak, "something smaller would have done as well to hold any money we have or are likely to have," and she stooped over the pot and looked into its dark inside.

As she stooped, her hairpin—for poor Mrs. Hak-Tak had only one hairpin for all her hair and it was made of carved bone—fell into the pot. She put in her hand to get it out again, and then she gave a loud cry, which brought her husband running to her side.

"What is it?" he asked. "Is there a viper in the pot?"

"Oh, my dear husband," she cried. "What can be the meaning of this? I put my hand into the pot to fetch out my hairpin and your purse, and look, I have brought out two hairpins and two purses, both exactly alike."

"Open the purse. Open both purses," said Mr. Hak-Tak. "One of them will certainly be empty."

But not a bit of it. The new purse contained exactly the same number of coins as the old one—for that matter, no one could have said which was the new and which the old—and it meant, of course, that the Hak-Taks had exactly twice as much money in the evening as they had had in the morning.

"And two hairpins instead of one!" cried Mrs. Hak-Tak, forgetting in her excitement to do up her hair, which was streaming over her shoulders. "There is something quite unusual about this pot."

"Let us put in the sack of lentils and see what happens," said Mr. Hak-Tak, also becoming excited.

They heaved in the bag of lentils and when they pulled it out again—it was so big it almost filled the pot—they saw another bag of exactly the same size waiting to be pulled out in its turn. So now they had two bags of lentils instead of one.

"Put in the blanket," said Mr. Hak-Tak. "We need another blanket for the cold weather." And, sure enough, when the blanket came out, there lay another behind it.

"Put my wadded coat in," said Mr. Hak-Tak, "and then when the cold weather comes there will be one for you as well as for me. Let us put in everything we have in turn. What a pity we have no meat or tobacco, for it seems that the pot cannot make anything without a pattern."

Then Mrs. Hak-Tak, who was a woman of great intelligence, said, "My dear husband, let us put the purse in again and again and again. If we take two purses out each time we put one in, we shall have enough money by tomorrow evening to buy everything we lack."

"I am afraid we may lose it this time," said Mr. Hak-Tak, but in the end he agreed, and they dropped in the purse and pulled out two, then they added the new money to the old and dropped it in again and pulled out the larger amount twice over. After a while the floor was covered with old leather purses and they decided just to throw the money in by itself. It worked quite as well and saved trouble; every time, twice as much money came out as went in, and every time they added the new coins to the old and threw them all in together. It took them some hours to tire of this game, but at last Mrs. Hak-Tak said, "My dear husband, there is no need for us to work so hard. We shall see to it that the pot does not run away, and we can always make more money as we want it. Let us tie up what we have."

It made a huge bundle in the extra blanket and the Hak-Taks lay and looked at it for a long time before they slept, and talked of all the things they would buy and the improvements they would make in the cottage.

The next morning they rose early and Mr. Hak-Tak filled a wallet with money from the bundle and set off for the big village to buy more things in one morning than he had bought in a whole fifty years.

Mrs. Hak-Tak saw him off and then she tidied up the cottage and put the rice on to boil and had another look at the bundle of money, and made herself a whole set of new hairpins from the pot, and about twenty candles instead of the one which was all they had possessed up to now. After that she slept for a while, having been up so late the night before, but just before the time when her husband should be back, she awoke and went over to the pot. She dropped in a cabbage leaf to make sure it was still working properly, and when she took two leaves out she sat down on the floor and put her arms around it.

"I do not know how you came to us, my dear pot," she said, "but you are the best friend we ever had."

Then she knelt up to look inside it, and at that moment her husband came to the door, and turning quickly to see all the wonderful things he had bought, she overbalanced and fell into the pot.

Mr. Hak-Tak put down his bundles and ran across and caught her by the ankles and pulled her out, but, oh, mercy, no sooner had he set her carefully on the floor then he saw the kicking legs of another Mrs. Hak-Tak in the pot! What was he to do? Well, he could not leave her there, so he caught her ankles and pulled, and another Mrs. Hak-Tak, so exactly like the first that no one would have told one from the other, stood beside them.

"Here's an extraordinary thing," said Mr. Hak-Tak, looking help-lessly from one to the other.

"I will not have a second Mrs. Hak-Tak in the house!" screamed the old Mrs. Hak-Tak.

All was confusion. The old Mrs. Hak-Tak shouted and wrung her hands and wept, Mr. Hak-Tak was scarcely calmer, and the new Mrs. Hak-Tak sat down on the floor as if she knew no more than they did what was to happen next.

"One wife is all I want," said Mr. Hak-Tak, "but how could I have left her in the pot?"

"Put her back in it again!" cried Mrs. Hak-Tak.

"What? And draw out two more?" said her husband. "If two wives are too many for me, what should I do with three? No! No!" He stepped back quickly as if he were stepping away from the three wives and, missing his footing, lo and behold, he fell into the pot!

Both Mrs. Hak-Taks ran and each caught an ankle and pulled him out and set him on the floor, and there, oh, mercy, was another pair of kicking legs in the pot! Again each caught hold of an ankle and pulled, and soon another Mr. Hak-Tak, so exactly like the first that no one could have told one from the other, stood beside them.

Now, the old Mr. Hak-Tak liked the idea of his double no more than Mrs. Hak-Tak had liked the idea of hers. He stormed and raged and scolded his wife for pulling him out of the pot, while the new Mr. Hak-Tak sat down on the floor beside the new Mrs. Hak-Tak and looked as if, like her, he did not know what was going to happen next.

Then the old Mrs. Hak-Tak had a very good idea. "Listen, my dear husband," she said, "now, do stop scolding and listen, for it is really a good thing that there is a new one of you as well as a new one of me. It means that you and I can go on in our usual way, and these new people, who are ourselves and yet not ourselves, can set up house together next door to us."

And that is what they did. The old Hak-Taks built themselves a fine new house with money from the pot, and they built one just like it next door for the new couple, and they lived together in the greatest friendliness, because, as Mrs. Hak-Tak said, "The new Mrs. Hak-Tak is really more than a sister to me, and the new Mr. Hak-Tak is really more than a brother to you."

The neighbors were very much surprised, both at the sudden wealth of the Hak-Taks and at the new couple who resembled them so strongly that they must, they thought, be very close relations of whom they had never heard before. They said, "It looks as though the Hak-Taks, when they so unexpectedly became rich, decided to have two of everything, even of themselves, in order to enjoy their money more."

CHAPTER SIX

Never Give Up

"Sometimes when I look at my father, I am stirred to unholy anger. I think, God help me, Roy Luther, I don't want you dead, and that's the truth. But since it's going to happen anyhow, I wish it could hurry up and be over with, for it's pulling us to pieces and I need to get on with things and fix them around so that life will be easier for those of us who are left.

"And I get scared and I think, but how am I going to do this? Who will show me and who will help me?

"And then I get madder and I say to myself, Aw, quit your bellyaching. There's a way; all you have to do is find it."

From *Where the Lilies Bloom*
by Vera and Bill Cleaver

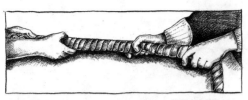 One would be hard pressed to find an American schoolchild—or adult—who has not read "The Little Engine That Could." When her little boy became partially trapped beneath an automobile, a woman suddenly recalled the story of the determined little engine. Instead of panicking, she summoned almost supernatural strength and, chanting to herself "I think I can, I think I can," lifted the car just high enough to release the young boy.

A mature human being does not give up when forces make life difficult. The virtue required is called perseverance, and individuals who are well trained in it make the world go around: they are the entrepreneurs, the artists, the athletes, and builders. They are also the people who create long and durable marriages, strong families, and great friendships.

Perseverance is learned in tiny increments, and teaching it means inspiring the will to conform to a random intellectual goal. It's not about *making* a child perform a task; it's about developing his courage, discipline, willpower, and endurance.

At age seven, your child is truly ready to practice the virtue of perseverance by taking on narrowly defined tasks with specific goals. Homework is the obvious arena, but chores around the home also provide opportunities. The idea is not to heap piles of work on your child, but to select one or two projects or duties that your child can start and successfully complete.

For some children, perseverance is a cakewalk; they are born with a sense of determination and conscientiousness. Others have the attention span of a small toad, and getting them to complete the smallest task is an ordeal. This child will develop the virtue in time, it will just take more time.

Unfortunately, by the time a child has reached his preteen years parents are not so influential, and direct lessons about this virtue become difficult. It is we who now must persevere! At this point, more than ever, it is crucial to sprinkle your child's life with words that build patience and endurance—like "no," "wait a while," "think it over," "have it later," or "save for it." It is brutal to shower your child with every want and whim he expresses, and especially unloving to gratify those wishes instantly.

In addition, your personal example is the most edifying tool. A parent who makes life look too easy does his child no favor. (There is a reason we all know our own parents walked five miles to school every day, usually during blizzards.) While you obviously do not want to come off as a martyr, you do want your child to know that Mom and Dad give 110 percent as a matter of routine.

For the lackadaisical child, stories can reveal so much. In every story, between "once upon a time" and "they lived happily ever after" lies a series of tests, such as loneliness, abandonment, poverty, murder, illness, abuse, boredom—every demon you could imagine. The hero or heroine of the story can take a lot of detours; the only thing he can't do is "give up."

If you give up, the story is over, in literature, just as it is in life.

"The Ugly Duckling"
by Hans Christian Andersen

Part of never giving up is accepting the hand that's dealt you.
The ugly duckling had no choice but to live out his destiny, but he
never seemed to despair. His reward, as we all know, was great.

It was lovely summer weather in the country. The wheat was golden and the oats still green. The hay was stacked in the rich low meadows, and around about field and meadow lay great woods, in the midst of which were deep lakes.

In the sunniest spot stood an old mansion surrounded by a deep moat, and great coarse weeds grew from the walls of the house right down to the water's edge. Some of them were so tall that a small child could stand upright under them. In among the weeds, it was as se-cluded as in the depths of a forest, and there a duck was sitting on her nest. Her little ducklings were just about to be hatched, but she was quite tired of sitting, for it had lasted such a long time. Moreover, she had very few visitors, as the other ducks liked swimming about in the moat better than waddling up to sit under the tall weeds and gossip with her.

At last one egg after another began to crack. "Cheep, cheep!" they said. All the chicks had come to life and were poking their heads out.

"Quack, quack!" said the duck, and then they all quacked their hardest and looked about them on all sides among the green weeds. Their mother allowed them to look as much as they liked, for green is good for the eyes.

"How big the world is, to be sure!" said all the young ones. They certainly now had ever so much more room to move about than when they were inside their eggshells.

"Do you imagine this is the whole world?" said the mother. "It stretches a long way on the other side of the garden, right into the parson's field, though I have never been as far as that. I suppose you are

126

all here now?" She got up and looked about. "No, I have not got you all yet! The biggest egg is still there. How long is this going to take?" she said, and settled herself on the nest again.

"Well, how are you getting on?" said an old duck who had come to pay her a visit.

"This last egg is taking such a long time!" answered the sitting duck. "The shell will not crack. But look at the others. They are the finest ducklings I have ever seen. They are all exactly like their father, the rascal! Yet he never comes to see me."

"Let me look at the egg which won't crack," said the old duck. "You must be sure that it is not a turkey's egg! I was cheated like that once and I had no end of trouble and worry with the creatures, for I may tell you that they are afraid of the water. I simply could not get them into it. I quacked and snapped at them, but it all did no good. Let me see the egg! Yes, it is a turkey's egg. You just leave it alone, and teach the other children to swim."

"I will sit on it a little longer. I have sat so long already that I may as well go on."

"Please yourself," said the old duck, and away she went.

At last the big egg cracked. "Cheep, cheep!" said the young one and tumbled out. How big and ugly he was! The duck looked at him.

"That is a monstrous big duckling," she said. "None of the others looked like that. I wonder if it really is a turkey. Well, we shall soon find that out. Into the water he shall go, if I have to kick him in myself."

Next day was glorious and the sun shone on all the green weeds. The mother duck with her whole family went down to the moat.

Splash! into the water she sprang. "Quack, quack," she said, and one duckling plumped in after the other. The water dashed over their heads, but they came up again and floated beautifully. Their legs went of themselves, and they were all there. Even the big ugly gray one swam about with them.

"No, that is no turkey," she said. "See how beautifully he uses his legs and how erect he holds himself. He is my own chick, after all, and not bad-looking when you come to look at him properly. Quack, quack!

Now come with me and I will take you out into the world and introduce you to the duckyard. But keep close to me all the time so that no one will tread upon you. And beware of the cat!"

Then they went into the duckyard. There was a great uproar going on, for two broods were fighting for the head of an eel, and in the end the cat captured it.

"That's how things go in this world," said the mother duck, and she licked her bill, because she had wanted the eel's head herself.

"Now use your legs," said she. "Mind you quack properly, and bend your necks to the old duck over there. She is the grandest of us all. And do you see? She has a red rag around her leg. This is a wonderfully fine thing, and the most extraordinary mark of distinction any duck can have. It shows clearly that she is not to be parted with, and that she is worthy of recognition both by beasts and men! Quack, now! Don't turn your toes in! A well brought-up duckling keeps his legs wide apart just like Father and Mother. That's it. Now bend your necks and say quack!"

They did as they were bid, but the other ducks around about looked at them and said, quite loudly, "Just look there! Now we are to have that tribe, just as if there were not enough of us already. And, oh dear, how ugly that duckling is! We won't stand him." And a duck flew at him at once and bit him in the neck.

"Let him be," said the mother. "He is doing no harm."

"Very likely not," said the biter. "But he is so ungainly and queer that he must be whacked."

"Those are handsome children that mother has," said the old duck with the rag around her leg. "They are all good-looking except this one, but he is not a good specimen. It's a pity you can't make him over again."

"That can't be done, your grace," said the mother duck. "He is not handsome, but he is a thoroughly good creature, and he swims as beautifully as any of the others. I think I might venture even to add that I think he will improve as he goes on, or perhaps in time he may grow smaller. He was too long in the egg, and so he has not come out with a very good figure." And then she patted his neck and stroked him down. "Besides, he is a drake," said she. "So it does not matter so much. I believe he will be very strong, and I don't doubt but he will make his way in the world."

"The other ducklings are very pretty," said the old duck. "Now make yourselves quite at home, and if you find the head of an eel you may bring it to me."

After that they felt quite at home. But the poor duckling who had been the last to come out of the shell, and who was so ugly, was bitten, pushed about, and made fun of both by the ducks and the hens. "He is too big," they all said. And the turkey cock, who was born with his spurs on and therefore thought himself quite an emperor, puffed himself up like a vessel in full sail, made for him, and gobbled and gobbled till he became quite red in the face. The poor duckling was at his wit's end, and did not know which way to turn. He was in despair because he was so ugly and the butt of the whole duckyard.

So the first day passed, and afterward matters grew worse and worse. The poor duckling was chased and hustled by all of them. Even his brothers and sisters ill-used him. They were always saying, "If only the cat would get ahold of you, you hideous object!" Even his mother said, "I wish to goodness you were miles away." The ducks bit him, the hens pecked him, and the girl who fed them kicked him aside.

Then he ran off and flew right over the hedge, where the little birds flew up into the air in a fright.

"That is because I am so ugly," thought the poor duckling, shutting his eyes, but he ran on all the same. Then he came to a great marsh where the wild ducks lived. He was so tired and miserable that he stayed there the whole night. In the morning the wild ducks flew up to inspect their new comrade.

"What sort of a creature are you?" they inquired, as the duckling turned from side to side and greeted them as well as he could. "You are frightfully ugly," said the wild ducks, "but that does not matter to us, so long as you do not marry into our family." Poor fellow! He had not thought of marriage. All he wanted was permission to lie among the rushes and to drink a little of the marsh water.

He stayed there two whole days. Then two wild geese came, or rather two wild ganders. They were not long out of the shell and therefore rather pert.

"I say, comrade," they said, "you are so ugly that we have taken quite a fancy to you! Will you join us and be a bird of passage? There is another marsh close by, and there are some charming wild geese there. All are sweet young ladies who can say quack! You are ugly enough to make your fortune among them." Just at that moment, bang! bang! was heard up above, and both the wild geese fell dead among the reeds, and the water turned bloodred. Bang! bang! went the guns, and flocks of wild geese flew from the rushes and the shot peppered among them again.

There was a grand shooting party, and the sportsmen lay hidden around the marsh. Some even sat on the branches of the trees which overhung the water. The blue smoke rose like clouds among the dark trees and swept over the pool.

The retrieving dogs wandered about in the swamp—splash! splash! The rushes and reeds bent beneath their tread on all sides. It was terribly alarming to the poor duckling. He twisted his head around to get it under his wing, and just at that moment a frightful big dog appeared close beside him. His tongue hung right out of his mouth and his eyes glared wickedly. He opened his great chasm of a mouth close to the duckling. Showed his teeth, and—splash!—went on without touching him.

"Oh, thank Heaven!" sighed the duckling. "I am so ugly that even the dog won't bite me!"

Then he lay quite still while the shots whistled among the bushes, and bang after bang rent the air. It only became quiet late in the day, but even then the poor duckling did not dare to get up. He waited several hours more before he looked about, and then he hurried away from the marsh as fast as he could. He ran across fields and meadows, and there was such a wind that he had hard work to make his way.

Toward night he reached a poor little cottage. It was such a miserable hovel that it could not make up its mind which way even to fall, and so it remained standing. The wind whistled so fiercely around the duckling that he had to sit on his tail to resist it, and it blew harder and ever harder. Then he saw that the door had fallen off one hinge and hung so crookedly that he could creep into the house through the crack, and so he made his way into the room.

An old woman lived here with her cat and her hen. The cat would arch his back, purr, and give off electric sparks if you stroked his fur the wrong way. The hen had quite tiny short legs, but laid good eggs, and the old woman was as fond of her as if she had been her own child.

In the morning the strange duckling was discovered immediately, and the cat began to purr and the hen to cluck.

"What on earth is that?" said the old woman, looking around, but her sight was not good and she thought the duckling was a fat duck which had escaped. "This is a wonderful find!" said she. "Now I shall have duck eggs—if only it is not a drake. We must wait and see about that."

So she took the duckling on trial for three weeks, but no eggs made their appearance. The cat was master of this house and the hen its mistress. They always said, "We and the world," for they thought that they represented half of the world, and that quite the better half.

The duckling thought there might be two opinions on the subject, but the hen would not hear of it.

"Can you lay eggs?" she asked.

"No."

"Have the goodness to hold your tongue then!"

And the cat said, "Can you arch your back, purr, or give off sparks?"

"No."

"Then you had better keep your opinions to yourself when people of sense are speaking!"

The duckling sat in the corner nursing his ill humor. Then he began to think of the fresh air and the sunshine and an uncontrollable longing seized him to float on the water. At last he could not help telling the hen about it.

"What on earth possesses you?" she asked. "You have nothing to do. That is why you get these crazy thoughts into your head. Lay some eggs or take to purring, and you will get over it."

"But it is so delicious to float on the water," said the duckling. "It is so delicious to feel it rushing over your head when you dive to the bottom."

"That would be a fine amusement!" said the hen. "I think you have gone mad. Ask the cat about it. He is the wisest creature I know. Ask him if he is fond of floating on the water or diving under it. I say nothing about myself. Ask our mistress herself, the old woman. There is no one in the world cleverer than she is. Do you suppose she has any desire to float on the water or to duck underneath it?"

"You do not understand me," said the duckling.

"Well, if we don't understand you, who should? I suppose you don't consider yourself cleverer than the cat or the old woman, not to mention me! Don't make a fool of yourself, child, and thank your stars for all the good we have done you. Have you not lived in this warm room, and in such society that you might have learned something? But you are an idiot, and there is no pleasure in associating with you. You may believe me: I mean you well. I tell you home truths, and there is no surer way than that of knowing who are one's friends. You just set about laying some eggs, or learn to purr, or to emit sparks."

"I think I will go into the wide world," said the duckling.

"Oh, do so by all means," said the hen.

So away went the duckling. He floated on the water and ducked underneath it, but he was looked at askance and was slighted by every living creature for his ugliness. Now autumn came. The leaves in the woods turned yellow and brown. The wind took hold of them, and they danced about. The sky looked very cold and the clouds hung heavy with snow and hail. A raven stood on the fence and croaked, "Caw, caw!" from sheer cold. It made one shiver only to think of it. The poor duckling certainly was in a bad case!

One evening, the sun was just setting in wintry splendor when a flock of beautiful large birds appeared out of the bushes. The duckling had never seen anything so beautiful. They were dazzlingly white with long, waving necks. They were swans, and uttering a peculiar cry they spread out their magnificent broad wings and flew away from the cold regions to warmer lands and open seas. They mounted so high, so very high, and the ugly little duckling became strangely uneasy. He circled around and around in the water like a wheel, craning his neck up into the air after them. Then he uttered a shriek so piercing and so strange that he was quite frightened by it himself. Oh, he could not forget those beautiful birds, those happy birds. And as soon as they were out of sight, he ducked right down to the bottom, and when he came up again he was quite beside himself. He did not know what the birds were, or whither they flew, but all the same he was more drawn toward them than he had ever been by any creatures before. He did not envy them in the least. How could it occur to him even to wish to be such a marvel of beauty? He would have been thankful if only the ducks would have tolerated him among them—the poor ugly creature.

The winter was so bitterly cold that the duckling was obliged to swim about in the water to keep it from freezing over, but every night the hole in which he swam got smaller and smaller. Then it froze so hard that the surface ice cracked, and the duckling had to use his legs all the time so that the ice should not freeze around him. At last he was so weary that he could move no more, and he was frozen fast into the ice.

Early in the morning a peasant came along and saw him. He went out onto the ice and hammered a hole in it with his heavy wooden shoe, and carried the duckling home to his wife. There he soon revived. The children wanted to play with him, but the duckling thought they were going to ill-use him, and rushed in his fright into the milk pan, and the milk spurted out all over the room. The woman shrieked and threw up her hands. Then he flew into the butter cask, and down into the meal tub and out again. Just imagine what he looked like by this time! The woman screamed and tried to hit him with her tongs. The children tumbled over one another in trying to catch him, and they screamed with laughter. By good luck the door stood open, and the duckling flew out among the bushes and the newly fallen snow. And he lay there thoroughly exhausted.

But it would be too sad to mention all the privation and misery he had to go through during the hard winter. When the sun began to shine warmly again, the duckling was in the marsh, lying among the rushes. The larks were singing and the beautiful spring had come.

Then all at once he raised his wings and they flapped with much greater strength than before and bore him off vigorously. Before he knew where he was, he found himself in a large garden where the apple trees were in full blossom and the air was scented with lilacs, the long branches of which overhung the indented shores of the lake. Oh, the spring freshness was delicious!

Just in front of him he saw three beautiful white swans advancing toward him from a thicket. With rustling feathers they swam lightly over the water. The duckling recognized the majestic birds, and he was overcome by a strange melancholy.

"I will fly to them, the royal birds, and they will hack me to pieces because I, who am so ugly, venture to approach them. But it won't matter! Better be killed by them than be snapped at by the ducks, pecked by the hens, spurned by the henwife, or suffer so much misery in the winter."

So he flew into the water and swam toward the stately swans. They saw him and darted toward him with ruffled feathers.

"Kill me!" said the poor creature, and he bowed his head toward the water and awaited his death. But what did he see reflected in the transparent water?

He saw below him his own image, but he was no longer a clumsy dark-gray bird, ugly and ungainly. He was himself a swan! It does not matter in the least having been born in a duckyard, if only you come out of a swan's egg!

He felt quite glad of all the misery and tribulation he had gone through, for he was the better able to appreciate his good fortune now and all the beauty that greeted him. The big swans swam around and around him and stroked him with their bills.

Some little children came into the garden with corn and pieces of bread, which they threw into the water, and the smallest one cried out, "There is a new one!" The other children shouted with joy, "Yes, a new one has come." And they clapped their hands and danced about, running after their father and mother. They threw the bread into the water, and one and all said, "The new one is the prettiest of them all. He is so young and handsome." And the old swans bent their heads and did homage before him.

He felt quite shy, and hid his head under his wing. He did not know what to think. He was very happy, but not at all proud, for a good heart never becomes proud. He thought of how he had been pursued and scorned, and now he heard them all say that he was the most beautiful of all beautiful birds. The lilacs and elders bent their boughs right down into the water before him, and the bright sun was warm and cheering. He rustled his feathers and raised his slender neck aloft, saying with a grateful heart, "I never dreamt of so much happiness when I was the Ugly Duckling!"

"Onawandah"

by Louisa May Alcott

*This is the story of a courageous American Indian child who
was misunderstood and maligned by a handful of white settlers,
and who went on to prove their prejudices sorely misguided. This
is a marvelous story about valor and persistence.*

Long ago, when hostile Indians haunted the great forests, and every
settlement had its fort for the protection of the inhabitants, in one of the
towns on the Connecticut River lived Parson Bain and his little son and
daughter. The wife and mother was dead; but an old servant took care
of them, and did her best to make Reuben and Eunice good children.
Her direct threat, when they were naughty, was, "The Indians will come
and fetch you, if you don't behave." So they grew up in great fear of the
red men. Even the friendly Indians, who sometimes came for food or
powder, were regarded with suspicion by the people. No man went to
work without his gun nearby. On Sundays, when they trudged to the
rude meetinghouse, all carried the trusty rifle on the shoulder, and
while the pastor preached, a sentinel mounted guard at the door, to give
warning if canoes came down the river or a dark face peered from the
wood.

One autumn night, when the first heavy rains were falling and a
cold wind whistled through the valley, a knock came at the minister's
door and, opening it, he found an Indian boy, ragged, hungry, and
foot-sore, who begged for food and shelter. In his broken way, he told
how he had fallen ill and been left to die by enemies who had taken him
from his own people months before; how he had wandered for days till
almost sinking; and that he had come now to ask for help, led by the
hospitable light in the parsonage window.

"Send him away, Master, or harm will come of it. He is a spy, and
we shall be scalped by the murdering Injuns who are waiting in the
wood," said old Becky harshly; while little Eunice hid in the old

servant's ample skirts, and twelve-year-old Reuben laid his hand on his crossbow, ready to defend his sister if need be.

But the good man drew the poor lad in, saying, with his friendly smile, "Shall not a Christian be as hospitable as a godless savage? Come in, child, and be fed; you sorely need rest and shelter."

Leaving his face to express the gratitude he had no words to tell, the boy sat by the comfortable fire and ate like a famished wolf, while Becky muttered her forebodings and the children eyed the dark youth at a safe distance. Something in his pinched face, wounded foot, and eyes full of dumb pain and patience touched the little girl's tender heart, and yielding to a pitiful impulse, she brought her own basin of new milk and, setting it beside the stranger, ran to hide behind her father, suddenly remembering that this was one of the dreaded Indians.

"That was well done, little daughter. Thou shalt love thine enemies, and share thy bread with the needy. See, he is smiling; that pleased him, and he wishes us to be his friends."

But Eunice ventured no more that night, and quaked in her little bed at the thought of the strange boy sleeping on a blanket before the fire below. Reuben hid his fears better, and resolved to watch while the others slept; but was off as soon as his curly head touched the pillow, and dreamed of tomahawks and war whoops till morning.

Next day, neighbors came to see the waif, and one and all advised sending him away as soon as possible, since he was doubtless a spy, as Becky said, and would bring trouble of some sort.

"When he is well, he may go whithersoever he will; but while he is too lame to walk, weak with hunger, and worn out with weariness, I will harbor him. He cannot feign suffering and starvation like this. I shall do my duty, and leave the consequences to the Lord," answered the parson, with such pious firmness that the neighbors said no more.

But they kept a close watch upon Onawandah when he went among them, silent and submissive, but with the proud air of a captive prince, and sometimes a fierce flash in his black eyes when the other lads taunted him about his red skin. He was very lame for weeks, and could only sit in the sun, weaving pretty baskets for Eunice, and shaping bows and arrows for Reuben. The children were soon his friends, for with them he was always gentle, trying in his soft language and expressive gestures to show his goodwill and gratitude; for they defended him against their ruder playmates and, following their father's example, trusted and cherished the homeless youth.

When he was able to walk he taught the boy to shoot and trap the wild creatures of the wood, to find fish where others failed, and to guide himself in the wilderness by star and sun, wind and water. To Eunice he brought little offerings of bark and feathers; taught her to make moccasins of skin, belts of shells, or pouches gay with porcupine quills and colored grass. He would not work for old Becky—who plainly showed her distrust—saying, "A brave does not grind corn and bring wood; that is squaw's work. Onawandah will hunt and fish and fight for you, but no more." And even the request of the parson could not win obedience in this, though the boy would have died for the good man.

Winter came, and the settlers fared hardly through the long months, when the drifts rose to the eaves of their low cabins, and the stores, carefully harvested, failed to supply even their simple wants. But the minister's family never lacked for wild meat, for Onawandah proved himself a better hunter than any man in the town, and the boy of sixteen led the way on his snowshoes when they went to track a bear to its den, chase the deer for miles, or shoot the wolves that howled about their homes in the winter nights.

"Be of good cheer, little daughter; I shall be gone but three days, and our brave Onawandah will guard you well," said the parson one April morning as he mounted his horse to visit a distant settlement, where the bitter winter had brought sickness and death to more than one household.

The boy showed his white teeth in a bright smile as he stood beside the children, while Becky croaked, with a shake of the head, "I hope you mayn't find you've warmed a viper in your bosom, Master."

Two days later, it seemed as if Becky was a true prophet, and that the confiding minister had been terribly deceived; for Onawandah went out to hunt, and that night the awful war whoop woke the sleeping villagers to find their houses burning, while the hidden

Indians shot at them by the light of the fires kindled by dusky scouts. In terror and confusion the whites fled to the fort; and while the men fought bravely, the women held blankets to catch arrows and bullets, or bound up the hurts of their defenders.

It was all over by daylight, and the red men sped away up the river with several prisoners and such booty as they could plunder from the deserted houses. Not till all fear of a return of their enemies was over did the poor people venture to leave the fort and seek their ruined homes. Then it was discovered that Becky and the parson's children were gone, and great was the bewailing, for the good man was much beloved by his flock.

Suddenly the smothered voice of Becky was heard by a party of visitors, calling dolefully, "I am here, betwixt the beds. Pull me out, neighbors, for I am half dead with fright and smothering."

The old woman was quickly extricated from her hiding place, and with much energy declared that she had seen Onawandah, disguised with war paint, among the Indians, and that he had torn away the children from her arms before she could fly from the house.

"He chose his time well, when they were defenseless, dear lambs! Spite of all my warnings, Master trusted him, and this is the thanks we get. Oh, my poor master! How can I tell him this heavy news?"

There was no need to tell it; for, as Becky sat moaning and beating her breast on the fireless hearth, and the sympathizing neighbors stood about her, the sound of horse's hooves was heard, and the parson came down the hilly road like one riding for his life. He had seen the smoke afar off, guessed the sad truth, and hurried on, to find his home in ruins and to learn by his first glance at the faces around him that his children were gone.

When he had heard all there was to tell, he sat down upon his door stone with his head in his hands, praying for strength to bear a grief too deep for words. The wounded and weary men tried to comfort him with hope, and the women wept with him as they hugged their own babies closer to the hearts that ached for the lost children. Suddenly a stir went through the mournful group, as Onawandah came from the wood with a young deer upon his shoulders, and amazement in his face as he saw the desolation before him. Dropping his burden, he stood an instant looking with eyes that kindled fiercely; then he came bounding toward them, undaunted by the hatred, suspicion, and surprise plainly written on the countenances before him. He missed his playmates, and asked but one question: "The boy? the little squaw?—where gone?"

His answer was a rough one, for the men seized him and poured forth the tale, heaping reproaches upon him for such treachery and ingratitude. He bore it all in proud silence till they pointed to the poor father whose dumb sorrow was more eloquent than all their wrath. Onawandah looked at him, and the fire died out of his eyes as if quenched by the tears he would not shed. Shaking off the hands that held him, he went to his good friend, saying with passionate earnestness "Onawandah is not traitor! Onawandah remembers. Onawandah grateful! You believe?"

The poor parson looked up at him, and could not doubt his truth; for genuine love and sorrow ennobled the dark face, and he had never known the boy to lie.

"I believe and trust you still, but others will not. Go, you are no longer safe here, and I have no home to offer you," said the parson sadly, feeling that he cared for none, unless his children were restored to him.

"Onawandah has no fear. He goes; but he comes again to bring the boy, the little squaw."

Few words, but they were so solemnly spoken that the most unbelieving were impressed; for the youth laid one hand on the gray head bowed before him, and lifted the other toward heaven, as if calling the Great Spirit to hear his vow.

A relenting murmur went through the crowd, but the boy paid no heed as he turned away, and with no arms but his hunting knife and bow, no food but such as he could find, no guide but the sun by day, the stars by night, he plunged into the pathless forest and was gone.

Then the people drew a long breath, and muttered to one another, "He will never do it, yet he is a brave lad for his years."

"Only a shift to get off with a whole skin, I warrant you. These varlets are as cunning as foxes," added Becky, sourly.

The parson alone believed and hoped, though weeks and months went by, and his children did not come.

Meantime, Reuben and Eunice were far away in an Indian camp, resting as best they could after the long journey that followed that dreadful night. Their captors were not cruel to them, for Reuben was a stout fellow and, thanks to Onawandah, could hold his own with the boys who would have tormented him if he had been feeble or cowardly. Eunice also was a hardy creature for her years, and when her first fright and fatigue were over, made herself useful in many ways among the squaws, who did not let the pretty child suffer greatly; though she was neglected, because they knew no better.

Life in a wigwam was not a life of ease, and fortunately the children were accustomed to simple habits and the hardships that all endured in those early times. But they mourned for home till their young faces were pathetic with longing, and their pillows of dry leaves were often wet with tears in the night. Their clothes grew ragged, their hair unkempt, their faces tanned by sun and wind. Scanty food and exposure to all weathers tried the strength of their bodies, and uncertainty as to their fate saddened their spirits; yet they bore up bravely, and said their prayers faithfully, feeling sure that God would bring them home to Father in His own good time.

One day, when Reuben was snaring birds in the wood—for the Indians had no fear of such young children venturing to escape—he heard the cry of a quail, and followed it deeper and deeper into the forest, till it ceased, and with a sudden rustle Onawandah rose up from the brakes, his finger on his lips to prevent any exclamation that might betray him to other ears and eyes.

"I come for you and little Laraka," which was the name he gave Eunice, meaning *wild rose*. "I take you home. Not know me yet. Go and wait."

He spoke low and fast; but the joy in his face told how glad he was to find the boy after his long search, and Reuben clung to him, trying not to disgrace himself by crying like a girl in his surprise and delight.

Lying hidden in the tall brakes they talked in whispers, while one told of the capture, and the other of a plan for escape; for, though a friendly tribe, these Indians were not Onawandah's people, and they must not suspect that he knew the children, else they might be separated at once.

"Little squaw betray me. You watch her. Tell her not to cry out, and not to speak to me any time. When I say come, we go—fast—in the night. Not ready yet."

These were the orders Reuben received, and when he could compose himself he went back to the wigwams, leaving his friend in the wood, while he told the good news to Eunice and prepared her for the part she must play.

Fear had taught her self-control, and the poor child stood the test well, working off her relief and rapture by pounding corn in the stone mortar till her little hands were blistered, and her arms ached for hours afterward.

Not till the next day did Onawandah make his appearance, and then he came limping into the village, weary, lame, and half starved after his long wandering in the wilderness. He was kindly welcomed, and his story believed, for he told only the first part, and said nothing of his life among the white men. He hardly glanced at the children when they were pointed out to him by their captors, and scowled at poor Eunice, who forgot her part in her joy, and smiled as she met the dark eyes that till now had always looked kindly at her. A touch from Reuben warned her, and she was glad to hide her confusion by shaking her long hair over her face, as if afraid of the stranger.

Onawandah took no further notice of them, but seemed to be very lame with the old wound in his foot, which prevented his being obliged to hunt with the men. He was resting and slowly gathering strength for the hard task he had set himself, while he waited for a safe time to save the children.

At last, in the early autumn, all the men went off on the warpath, leaving only boys and women behind. Then Onawandah's eyes began to kindle, and Reuben's heart beat fast, for both felt that their time for escape had come.

All was ready, and one moonless night the signal was given. A cricket chirped shrilly outside the tent where the children slept with one old squaw. A strong hand cut the skin beside their bed of fir boughs, and two trembling creatures crept out to follow the tall shadow that flitted noiselessly before them into the darkness of the wood. Not a broken twig, a careless step, or a whispered word betrayed them, and they vanished as swiftly and silently as hunted deer flying for their lives.

Till dawn they hurried on, Onawandah carrying Eunice, whose strength soon failed, and Reuben manfully shouldering the hatchet and the pouch of food. At sunrise they hid in a thicket by a spring and rested, while waiting for the friendly night to come again. Then they pushed on, and fear gave wings to their feet, so that by another morning they were far enough away to venture to travel more slowly and sleep at night.

If the children had learned to love and trust the Indian boy in happier times, they adored him now, and came to regard him as an earthly Providence, so faithful, brave, and tender was he; so forgetful of himself, so bent on saving them. He never seemed to sleep, ate the poorest morsels or went without any food when provision failed; let no danger daunt him, no hardship wring complaint from him; but went on through the wild forest, led by guides invisible to them, till they began to hope that home was near.

Twice he saved their lives. Once, when he went in search of food, leaving Reuben to guard his sister, the children, being very hungry, ignorantly ate some poisonous berries that looked like wild cherries, and were deliciously sweet. The boy generously gave most of them to Eunice, and soon was terror-stricken to see her grow pale and cold and deathly ill. Not knowing what to do, he could only rub her hands and call wildly for Onawandah.

The name echoed through the silent wood, and though far away, the keen ear of the Indian heard it. His fleet feet brought him back in time, and his knowledge of wild roots and herbs made it possible to save the child when no other help was at hand.

"Make fire. Keep warm. I soon come," he said, after hearing the story and examining Eunice, who could only lift her eyes to him, full of childish confidence and patience.

Then he was off again, scouring the woods like a hound on the scent, searching everywhere for the precious little herb that would counteract the poison. Anyone watching him would have thought him crazy as he rushed hither and thither, tearing up the leaves, creeping on his hands and knees that it might not escape him, and when he found it, springing up with a cry that startled the birds, and carried hope to poor Reuben, who was trying to forget his own pain in his anxiety for Eunice, whom he thought dying.

"Eat, eat, while I make drink. All safe now," cried Onawandah, as he came leaping toward them with his hands full of green leaves, and his dark face shining with joy.

The boy was soon relieved, but for hours they hung over the girl, who suffered sadly, till she grew unconscious and lay as if dead. Reuben's courage failed then, and he cried bitterly, thinking how hard it would be to leave the dear little creature under the pines and go home alone to Father. Even Onawandah lost hope for a while, and sat like a bronze statue of despair, with his eyes fixed on his Wild Rose, who seemed fading away too soon.

Suddenly he rose, stretched his arms to the west, where the sun was setting splendidly, and in his own musical language prayed to the Great Spirit. The Christian boy fell upon his knees, feeling that the only help was in the Father who saw and heard them even in the wilderness. Both were comforted, and when they turned to Eunice there was a faint tinge of color on the pale cheeks, as if the evening red kissed her. The look of pain was gone, and she slept quietly without the moans that had made their hearts ache before.

"He hears! He hears!" cried Onawandah, and for the first time Reuben saw tears in his keen eyes, as the Indian boy turned his face to the sky full of gratitude that no words were sweet enough to tell.

In the morning she was safe, and great was the rejoicing; but for two days the little invalid was not allowed to continue the journey, much as they longed to hurry on. It was a pretty sight, the bed of hemlock boughs spread under a green tent of woven branches, and on the pillow of moss the pale child watching the flicker of sunshine through the leaves, listening to the babble of a brook close by, or sleeping tranquilly, lulled by the murmur of the pines. Patient, loving, and grateful, it was a pleasure to serve her, and both the lads were faithful nurses. Onawandah cooked birds for her to eat, and made a pleasant drink of the wild raspberry leaves to quench her thirst. Reuben snared rabbits, that she might have nourishing food, and longed to shoot a deer for provision, that she might not suffer hunger again on their journey. The boyish desire led him deeper into the wood than it was wise for him to go alone, for it was nightfall, and wild creatures haunted the forest in those days. The fire, which Onawandah kept constantly burning, guarded their little camp where Eunice lay; but Reuben, with no weapon but his bow and hunting knife, was beyond this protection when he at last gave up his vain hunt and turned homeward. Suddenly, the sound of stealthy steps startled him, but he could see nothing through the dusk at first, and hurried on, fearing that some treacherous Indian was following him. Then he remembered his sister, and resolved not to betray her resting place if he could help it, for he had learned courage from Onawandah, and longed to be as brave and generous as his dusky hero.

So he paused to watch and wait, and soon saw the gleam of two fiery eyes, not behind, but above him, in a tree. Then he knew it was an "Indian devil," as they called a species of fierce wildcat that lurked in the thickets and sprang on its prey like a small tiger.

"If I could only kill it alone, how proud Onawandah would be of me," thought Reuben, burning for the good opinion of his friend.

It would have been wiser to hurry on and give the beast no time to spring; but the boy was overbold, and fitting an arrow to the string, aimed at the bright eyeball and let fly. A sharp snarl showed that some harm was done and, rather daunted by the savage sound, Reuben raced away, meaning to come back next day for the prize he hoped he had secured.

But soon he heard the creature bounding after him, and he uttered one ringing shout for help, feeling too late that he had been foolhardy. Fortunately he was nearer camp than he thought. Onawandah heard him and was there in time to receive the wildcat as, mad with the pain of the wound, it sprung at Reuben. There was no time for words, and the boy could only watch in breathless interest and anxiety the fight which went on between the brute and the Indian.

It was sharp but short, for Onawandah had his knife, and as soon as he could get the snarling, struggling beast down, he killed it with a skillful stroke. But not before it had torn and bitten him more dangerously than he knew, for the dusk hid the wounds, and excitement kept him from feeling them at first. Reuben thanked him heartily, and accepted his first words of warning with grateful docility; then both hurried back to Eunice, who till next day knew nothing of her brother's danger.

Onawandah made light of his scratches, as he called them, got their supper, and sent Reuben early to bed, for tomorrow they were to start again.

Excited by his adventure, the boy slept lightly, and waking in the night saw by the flicker of the fire Onawandah binding up a deep wound in his breast with wet moss and his own belt. A stifled groan betrayed how much he suffered; but when Reuben went to him, he would accept no help, said it was nothing, and sent him back to bed, preferring to endure the pain in stern silence, with true Indian pride and courage.

Next morning, they set out and pushed on as fast as Eunice's strength allowed. But it was evident that Onawandah suffered much, though he would not rest, forbade the children to speak of his wounds, and pressed on with feverish haste, as if he feared that his strength would not hold out. Reuben watched him anxiously, for there was a look in his face that troubled the boy and filled him with alarm, as well as with remorse and love.

In three days they reached the river and, as if Heaven helped them in their greatest need, found a canoe, left by some hunter, near the shore. In they sprang, and let the swift current bear them along, Eunice kneeling in the bow like a little figurehead of hope, Reuben steering with his paddle, and Onawandah sitting with arms tightly folded over his breast, as if to control the sharp anguish of the neglected wound.

Hour after hour they floated down the great river, looking eagerly for signs of home, and then at last they entered the familiar valley. While the little girl cried for joy, and the boy paddled as he had never done before, Onawandah sat erect with his haggard eyes fixed on the dim distance, and sang his death song in a clear, strong voice—though every breath was pain—bent on dying like a brave, without complaint or fear.

At last they saw the smoke from the cabins on the hillside, and hastily mooring the canoe, all sprung out, eager to be at home after their long and perilous wandering. But as his foot touched the land, Onawandah felt that he could do no more, and stretching his arms toward the parsonage, the windows of which glimmered as hospitably as they had done when he first saw them, he said with a pathetic sort of triumph in his broken voice, "Go. I cannot. Tell the good father, Onawandah not lie, not forget. He keep his promise."

"Rescue!"
from Dolphin Island
by Arthur C. Clarke

This adventure tale is told in the twenty-first century, where advanced research about dolphins is taking place. Johnny, shipwrecked, is saved by the dolphins himself. He never loses hope, and against great odds makes his way to his new home on Dolphin Island.

As those fins sliced toward the raft, cutting through the water with incredible speed, Johnny thought of all the gruesome tales he had read about sharks and shipwrecked sailors. He drew himself up into as little space as possible, at the center of the packing case. It wobbled alarmingly, and he realized how small a push would be needed to turn it over. To his surprise, he felt little fear, only a kind of numbed regret and a hope that, if the worst came to the worst, it would all be over quickly. And it seemed a pity, too, that no one would ever know what had happened to him. . . .

Then the water around the raft was full of sleek gray bodies, switchbacking along the surface in a graceful roller-coaster motion. Johnny knew almost nothing about the creatures of the sea, but surely, sharks did not swim in this fashion. And these animals were breathing air, just as he was; he could hear them wheezing as they went by, and he caught glimpses of blowholes opening and closing. Why, of course— they were dolphins!

Johnny relaxed and no longer tried to hide himself in the middle of his raft. He had often seen dolphins in movies or on television, and he knew that they were friendly, intelligent creatures. They were playing like children among the wreckage of the *Santa Anna*, butting at the floating debris with their streamlined snouts, making the strangest whistling and creaking noises as they did so. A few yards away, one had reared its head completely out of the water and was balancing a plank on its nose, like a trained animal in a circus act; it seemed to be saying to its companions, "Look at me—see how clever I am!"

The strange, nonhuman but intelligent head turned toward Johnny, and the dolphin dropped its plaything with an unmistakable gesture of surprise. It sank back into the water, squeaking with excitement, and a few seconds later Johnny was surrounded by glistening, inquisitive faces. They were smiling faces, too, for the mouths of the dolphins seemed to be frozen in a kind of fixed grin—one so infectious that Johnny found himself smiling back at them.

He no longer felt alone; now he had companionship, even though it was not human and could do nothing to help him. It was fascinating to watch the leathery dove-gray bodies moving around him with such effortless ease as they hunted among the debris of the *Santa Anna.* They were doing this, Johnny soon realized, purely out of playfulness and fun; they were more like lambs gamboling in a spring meadow than anything he had ever expected to find in the sea.

The dolphins continued to bob up and look at him from time to time, as if making sure that he had not run away. They watched with great curiosity as he pulled off his sodden clothing and spread it to dry in the sun, and they seemed to be giving the matter careful thought when Johnny asked them solemnly, "Well, what shall I do now?"

One answer to that question was obvious: he had to arrange some shelter from the tropical sun before it roasted him alive. Luckily, this problem was quickly solved; he was able to build a little wigwam from some pieces of driftwood which he lashed together with his handkerchief and then covered with his shirt. When he had finished, he felt quite proud of himself, and hoped that his audience appreciated his cleverness.

Now he could do nothing but lie down in the shade and conserve his strength while the wind and the currents carried him to an unknown fate. He did not feel hungry, and though his lips were already dry, it would be several hours before thirst became a serious problem.

The sea was much calmer now, and low, oily waves were rolling past with a gentle, undulating motion. Somewhere Johnny had come across the phrase, "Rocked in the cradle of the deep." Now he knew exactly what it meant. It was so soothing, so peaceful here that he could almost forget his desperate position; he was content to stare at the blue sea and the blue sky, and to watch the strange yet beautiful animals that glided and swooped around him, sometimes hurling their bodies clear out of the water in the sheer joy of life. . . .

Something jolted the raft, and he awoke with a start. For a moment he could hardly believe that he had been sleeping and that the sun was now almost overhead. Then the raft jerked again—and he saw why.

Four dolphins, swimming side by side, were pushing the raft through the water. Already it was moving faster than a man could swim, and it was still gaining speed. Johnny stared in amazement at the animals splashing and snorting only inches away from him; was this another of their games?

Even as he asked himself that question, he knew that the answer was No. The whole pattern of their behavior had changed completely; this was deliberate and purposeful. Playtime was over. He was the center of a great pack of the animals, all now moving steadily in the same direction. There were scores, if not hundreds, ahead and behind, to right and left, as far as he could see. He felt that he was moving across the ocean in the midst of a military formation—a brigade of cavalry.

He wondered how long they would keep it up, but they showed no signs of slackening. From time to time, one of the dolphins would drop away from the raft, and another would immediately take its place so that there was no loss of speed. Though it was very hard to judge how fast he was moving, Johnny guessed that the raft was being pushed along at over five miles an hour. There was no way of telling, however, whether he was moving north, south, east, or west; he could get no compass bearings from the almost vertical sun.

Not until much later in the day did he discover that he was heading toward the west, for the sun was going down in front of him. He was glad to see the approach of night, and looked forward to its coolness after the scorching day. By this time he was extremely thirsty; his lips were parched and cracked, and though he was tantalized by the water all around him, he knew it would be dangerous to drink it. His thirst was so overpowering that he did not feel any hunger; even if he had some food, he would be unable to swallow it.

It was a wonderful relief when the sun went down, sinking in a blaze of gold and red. Still the dolphins drove on into the west, beneath the stars and the rising moon. If they kept this up all through the night, Johnny calculated, they would have carried him the best part of a hundred miles. They must have a definite goal, but what could it be? He began to hope that there was land not far away, and that for some unknown reason these friendly and intelligent creatures were taking him to it. But why they were going to all this trouble he could not imagine.

The night was the longest that Johnny had ever known, for his growing thirst would not allow him to sleep. To add to his distress, he had been badly sunburned during the day, and he kept twisting and turning on the raft in a vain attempt to find a comfortable position. Most of the time he lay flat on his back, using his clothes to protect the sore spots, while the moon and stars crept across the sky with agonizing slowness. Sometimes the brilliant beacon of a satellite would drift from west to east, traveling much more swiftly than any of the stars, and in the opposite direction. It was maddening to know that up on the space stations were men and instruments that could easily locate him—if they bothered to search. But, of course, there was no reason why they should.

At last the moon went down, and in the brief darkness before dawn the sea once more came alight with phosphorescence. The graceful, superbly streamlined bodies all around the raft were outlined with fire; every time one of them shot into the air, the trajectory of its leap was a glowing rainbow in the night.

This time Johnny did not welcome the dawn; now he knew how pitiful his defenses were against the tropical sun. He reerected his little tent, crept beneath it, and tried to turn his thoughts away from drink.

It was impossible. Every few minutes he found himself picturing cold milk shakes, glasses of iced fruit juice, water flowing from faucets in sparkling streams. Yet he had been adrift for not more than thirty hours; men had survived without water for much longer than that.

The only thing that kept up his spirits was the determination and energy of his escort. The school still drove on into the west, carrying the raft before it with undiminished speed. Johnny no longer puzzled himself about the mystery of the dolphins' behavior; that was a problem that would solve itself in good time—or not at all.

And then, about midmorning, he caught his first glimpse of land. For many minutes he was afraid that it was merely a cloud on the horizon—but if so it was strange that it was the only cloud in the sky and that it lay dead ahead. Before long he could not doubt that it was an island, though it seemed to float clear of the water, and the heat haze made its outlines dance and shimmer against the skyline.

An hour later, he could see its details clearly. It was long and low and completely covered with trees. A narrow beach of dazzling white sand surrounded it, and beyond the beach there seemed to be a very wide, shallow reef, for there was a line of white breakers at least a mile out at sea.

At first Johnny could see no signs of life, but at last, with great relief, he spotted a thin stream of smoke rising from the wooded interior. Where there was smoke there were human beings—and the water which his whole body was now craving.

He was still several miles from the island when the dolphins gave him a bad shock; they were turning aside as if to bypass the land that was now so close. Then Johnny understood what they were doing. The reef was too great an obstacle; they were going to outflank it and approach the island from the other side.

The detour took at least an hour, but Johnny's mind was at rest, now that he felt sure that he was nearing safety. As the raft and its untiring escort swung around to the western side of the island, he saw first a small group of boats at anchor, then some low white buildings, then a collection of huts with dark-skinned people moving among them. There was a fairly large community here, on this lonely speck in the Pacific.

Now at last the dolphins seemed a little hesitant, and Johnny got the impression that they were reluctant to go into the shallow water.

They pushed the raft slowly past the anchored boats, then backed off as if to say, "It's up to you now."

Johnny felt an overwhelming impulse to say some words of thanks, but his mouth was too dry for speech. So he stepped quietly off the raft, found himself in water only waist deep, and waded ashore.

There were people running along the beach toward him, but they could wait. He turned toward the lovely, powerful creatures who had brought him on this incredible journey, and waved them a grateful farewell. Already they were turning back toward their home, in the deep water of the open sea.

Then something seemed to happen to his legs, and as the sand came up to hit him, dolphins, island, and everything else vanished from his consciousness.

"Pandora's Box"

by Nathaniel Hawthorne

This story is not so much about persistence but hope, which is one of life's great gifts. Hope drives persistence. "Pandora's Box" tells of our foibles, how our follies push us to the edge, and how through the kindness of the gods, there is always hope.

Long, long ago, when this old world was still very young, there was a boy named Epimetheus. He had neither father nor mother; and to keep him company, a little girl, who, like himself, had no father or mother, was sent from a far country to live with him and be his playmate. Her name was Pandora.

The first thing Pandora saw when she came to the cottage where Epimetheus lived was a great wooden box. "What have you in the box, Epimetheus?" she asked.

"That is a secret," answered Epimetheus, "and you must not ask any questions about it. The box was left here to be kept safely and I myself do not know what is in it."

"But who gave it to you?" asked Pandora. "And where did it come from?"

"That's a secret too," answered Epimetheus.

"How tiresome." Pandora pouted. "I wish that ugly box were out of the way!" And she looked very cross.

"Oh, come, don't think of it anymore," cried Epimetheus. "Let's play games outdoors with the other children."

It is thousands of years since Epimetheus and Pandora were alive. Then, everybody was a child. The children needed no fathers and mothers to take care of them because there was no danger or trouble of any kind. There was always plenty to eat and drink. Whenever a child wanted his dinner he found it growing on a tree, and he could see next morning's breakfast just getting ready to be plucked.

Most wonderful of all, the children never quarreled among themselves, nor did they ever cry. Those ugly little winged monsters called Troubles had never yet been seen on earth. Probably the worst annoyance that a child had ever experienced was Pandora's at not being able to find out the secret of the mysterious box.

At first this was only the shadow of a Trouble, but it grew bigger every day.

"Where could the box have come from?" Pandora kept saying. "And what in the world can be inside it?"

"Always talking about that box!" said Epimetheus. "I do wish you'd talk of something else. Come, let's go and gather some ripe figs and eat them under the trees for our supper. And I know a vine that has the juiciest, sweetest grapes you ever tasted."

"Always talking about grapes and figs!" cried Pandora peevishly.

"Well, then," said Epimetheus, "let us run out and have a merry time with our playmates."

"I am tired of merry games! This ugly box! I think about it all the time. You must tell me what is in it!"

"As I have said fifty times over, I do not know," replied Epimetheus, now a little provoked.

"You might open it," said Pandora, looking sideways at Epimetheus.

Epimetheus looked so shocked at the idea of opening a box that had been given to him in trust, that Pandora thought it best not to suggest it anymore. "At least," she said, "you could tell me how it came here."

"It was left at the door," replied Epimetheus, "just before you came, by a person who looked very smiling and intelligent. He could hardly keep from laughing as he put it down. He wore an odd kind of cloak and a cap that seemed to be made partly of feathers so that it looked as if it had wings."

"What sort of staff had he?" asked Pandora.

"Oh, the most curious staff you ever saw!" cried Epimetheus. "It seemed like two serpents twisting around a stick, and was carved so naturally that, at first, I thought the serpents were alive."

"I know him," said Pandora thoughtfully. "It was Mercury. No one else has such a staff. He brought me here as well as that box. I am sure he meant the box for me, and perhaps there are pretty clothes in it for us to wear and toys for us to play with."

"It may be so," said Epimetheus, turning away, "but until Mercury comes back and tells us so, we have neither of us the right to lift the lid of the box."

For the first time since Pandora had come there, Epimetheus went out without asking her to go with him. Pandora stood gazing at the box. Although she had called it ugly a hundred times, it actually was very handsome and would have been an ornament in any room.

It was made of beautiful dark wood so highly polished that Pandora could see her face in it. The edges and corners were wonderfully carved. Around the margin there were figures and faces of graceful men and women and pretty children playing among the leaves and flowers. All were combined in a design of exquisite harmony. But here and there, peering out from among the carved leaves, Pandora once or twice imagined she saw a face not quite so lovely. When she looked more closely, however, and touched the spot with her fingers, she could discover nothing of the kind.

But the most beautiful face of all was the one in the center of the lid. It had a wreath of flowers around its brow. Pandora had looked at this face a great many times. Some days she thought it had a very grave look, which made her rather afraid, while at other times its expression was lively and mischievous.

The box was not fastened with a lock and key like most boxes, but with a strange knot of gold cord. There never was a knot so queerly tied. It seemed to have no beginning and no end, but was twisted so cunningly, with so many ins and outs, that not even the cleverest fingers could undo it.

Pandora began to examine the knot to find out how it had been made. "I believe I am beginning to see how it is done," she said to herself. "I am sure I could tie it up again after undoing it. There would be no harm in that, surely. I needn't open the box even if I undo the knot."

First, however, Pandora tried to lift the box. It was heavy—too heavy for her. She could only raise one end of the box a few inches from the floor and let it fall again with a loud thump. A moment afterward, she thought she heard something stir inside the box. She put her ear as close to the box as possible and listened. There did seem to be a kind of low murmuring within! Or was it only the ringing in Pandora's ears? Her curiosity was greater than ever.

She took the golden knot in her fingers and without quite intending it, she was soon busily trying to undo it.

Meanwhile the bright sunshine came through the open window. She could hear the happy voices of the children playing in the distance. What a beautiful day it was! Perhaps she could leave the troublesome knot alone and run out to join her playmates.

All this time, however, her fingers were busy with the knot. Then she happened to glance at the flower-wreathed face on the lid. The face seemed to be grinning at her!

"That face looks very mischievous," thought Pandora. "I wonder if it is smiling because I am doing wrong! I have a good mind to leave the box alone and run away."

But just at that moment she gave the knot a little shake. As if by magic the gold cord untwined itself, and there was the box without any fastening.

"This is the strangest thing I have ever known," said Pandora, a little frightened. "What will Epimetheus say? And how can I tie it up again?"

She tried once or twice, but the knot would not come right. It had untied itself so suddenly that she could not remember how the strings had been twisted together. So there was nothing to be done but to let the box remain unfastened until Epimetheus should come home.

"But," thought Pandora, "when Epimetheus finds the knot untied, he will know I did it. How shall I ever make him believe I haven't looked into the box?"

And then the thought came to her naughty head that since Epimetheus would believe she had looked into the box, she might as well do so.

She looked at the face with the wreath, and it seemed to smile at

157

her invitingly, as if to say, "Do not be afraid. What harm can there possibly be in raising the lid for a moment?" And she thought she heard within more distinctly than before, the murmur of small voices that seemed to whisper, "Let us out, dear Pandora, let us out."

"What can it be?" said Pandora. "Is there something alive in the box? Yes, I must see. Only one little peep and the lid will be shut down as safely as ever. There cannot be any harm in just one little peep!"

All this time Epimetheus had been playing with the other children in the fields, but he did not feel happy. This was the first time he had played without Pandora, and he was so cross and discontented that the other children could not think what was the matter with him. Up to this time, you see, everyone in all the world had always been happy. No one had been very ill or naughty or unhappy, for the world was still new and beautiful.

Epimetheus could not understand what was the matter with him and he decided to go back to Pandora. On the way, he gathered roses, lilies, and orange blossoms to make a bouquet for her. He noticed in the sky a great black cloud, which was creeping nearer and nearer the sun. Just as Epimetheus reached the cottage door, the cloud went right over the sun and made everything look dark and sad.

Epimetheus entered quietly, for he wanted to surprise Pandora with the bouquet. Pandora had put her hand on the lid of the box and was just going to open it. Epimetheus saw this quite well, and if he had cried out at once it would have given Pandora such a fright she would have let go of the lid.

But now Epimetheus was just as curious as Pandora to see what was inside. If there was anything pretty or valuable in the box he meant to take half for himself.

As Pandora raised the lid, the cottage grew very dark, for the black cloud now covered the sun entirely and a heavy peal of thunder was heard. But Pandora was too busy and excited to notice this. She lifted the lid right up, and at once a swarm of creatures with wings brushed past her as they flew out of the box.

At the same instant she heard Epimetheus cry out in pain, "Oh, I am stung! I am stung!"

Pandora let the lid fall with a crash and looked up to see what had happened to Epimetheus. The thundercloud had so darkened the room that she could scarcely see. But she heard a disagreeable buzz-buzzing, as if a great many huge flies had flown in, and soon she saw a crowd of ugly little winged shapes darting about like bats, and armed with terribly long stings in their tails. One of these had stung Epimetheus, and it was not long before Pandora herself began to scream in pain and fear. An ugly little monster had settled on her forehead and would have stung her if Epimetheus had not run forward and brushed it off.

Now these ugly creatures were the whole family of Earthly Troubles. There were bad tempers; there were a great many kinds of cares; there were more than a hundred and fifty sorrows; there were more kinds of naughtiness than it would be of any use to talk about. In fact all the sorrows and worries that have since troubled the world had been shut up in that mysterious box. It had been given to Epimetheus and Pandora to be kept safely. If only these two had obeyed Mercury and left the box alone, all would have gone well. No grown person would ever have been sad, and no child would have had cause to shed a single tear from that hour until this moment.

It was impossible for the two children to keep the ugly swarm in their own little cottage. The first thing they did was to fling open the windows and doors in hopes of getting rid of them. And, sure enough, away flew the winged Troubles and so pestered and tormented the small people everywhere that none of them so much as smiled for many days afterward.

Meanwhile Pandora and Epimetheus remained in their cottage. Both of them had been grievously stung. Epimetheus sat down sullenly with his back to Pandora while Pandora flung herself sobbing on the floor and rested her head on the lid of the fatal box.

Suddenly there was a gentle tap-tap inside.

"Who are you?" asked Pandora. "Who are you inside this horrid box?"

A sweet voice spoke from within: "Only lift the lid and you shall see."

"No, no," answered Pandora, again beginning to sob. "I have had enough of lifting the lid! There are plenty of your ugly brothers and sisters already flying about the world. You need not think I would be so foolish as to let you out!"

"Ah, but I am not one of those," the sweet voice said. "They are no brothers or sisters of mine, as you will see, if only you will let me out!"

The voice sounded so kind and cheery that it was almost impossible to refuse it anything. Pandora's heart had grown lighter at every word. Epimetheus, too, had heard the voice.

"Dear Epimetheus," cried Pandora, "shall I lift the lid again?"

"Just as you please," said Epimetheus. "You have done so much mischief already that perhaps you may as well do a little more. One other Trouble can make no great difference."

"You might speak a little more kindly!" murmured Pandora.

"Ah, naughty boy," laughed the little voice from within the box. "He knows he is longing to see me. Come, dear Pandora, lift the lid. I am in a great hurry to comfort you."

"Epimetheus," exclaimed Pandora, "come what may, I am resolved to open the box!"

"As the lid seems very heavy," cried Epimetheus, running across the room, "I will help you."

This time both children opened the box. Out flew a bright, sunny, fairylike creature that hovered about the room throwing a light wherever she went. She flew to Epimetheus and with her finger touched his brow where the Trouble had stung him, and immediately the pain was gone. Then she kissed Pandora and her hurt was better at once.

"Pray, who are you, beautiful creature?" asked Pandora.

"I am called Hope," answered the sunshiny figure. "I was packed into the box so that I might comfort people when that swarm of ugly Troubles was let loose among them."

"What lovely wings you have!" exclaimed Pandora. "They are colored like the rainbow!"

"Yes, they are like the rainbow," said Hope, "because, happy as my nature is, I am made of tears as well as smiles."

"And will you stay with us?" asked Epimetheus, "forever and ever?"

"Yes, I shall stay with you as long as you live," said Hope. "There may come times when you will think I have vanished. But again and again, perhaps when you least dream of it, you shall see the glimmer of my wings on the ceiling of your cottage. But you must trust my promise that I will never leave you."

"Yes, we do trust you," cried both children.

And all the rest of their lives when Troubles would come back and buzz about their heads, they would wait patiently till Hope, the fairy with the rainbow wings, came back to heal and comfort them.

"Finn and the Snakes"
from The Green Hero: The Early Adventures of Finn McCool
by Bernard Evslin

One of the greatest folk heroes of all time, Finn McCool is a little bit clown and a lot prince. Mr. Evslin's writing is sheer poetry. Here is an excerpt from a book that deserves a full reading.

Finn McCool was a giant, but much too small for the work; the runt of the litter, he was, yards shorter than his brothers and sisters, which was embarrassing. In fact, it is a better thing altogether to be a large dwarf than a small giant. Such a thing has been known to spoil a man's disposition entirely. But it didn't spoil Finn's. He quickly learned how things were in the world, and said to himself, "Can't afford to be bad-tempered, not till I get a reputation."

To go back a bit, though. When Finn was an infant he shared his crib with a girl-baby named Murtha, whose own mother, a giantess, had been killed by an avalanche she started herself by throwing her husband headfirst off a mountain because he'd said something rude. So Finn shared his crib with young Murtha, and his porridge bowl, and his rattle, and such.

Now, it is well-known that infants are nasty, squalling, damp objects, except to their mothers, perhaps, but this Murtha was something else. Even as an infant she was beautiful. Her skin was ivory and pink, and she was never bald for an instant, but was born with a marvelous black fleece of hair, and had eyes that were neither green nor blue, but violet—rare for eyes. And teeth—a full set of them—so she was able to bite Finn quite early. On the other hand, her smile flashed like a stream when the sun hits it. She was a lovely creature, and young Finn fell in love with her immediately, just like that, and had resolved to marry her before he was three days old, but decided to keep it secret awhile because he knew she wasn't ready to listen to proposals. Nevertheless, his love for her was so great that he couldn't rest for trying to win her admiration, which was difficult to do; she didn't seem to notice him particularly with her violet eyes, except when she decided to bite him or snatch his bottle. She would lie on her back dreamily watching the clouds go by—their cradle was a leather sling set in an oak tree; this is the way with giant babies—and he did not know what to do to attract her attention.

He noticed that she did not like slithery things. Worms made her unhappy. She would grab a wolfhound by his whiskers and kiss him on the nose, but spiders were a different matter entirely; she hated them and was afraid. This set Finn to thinking.

"My short time in the world has taught me that the way to a young lady's heart is by being very brave. Yes, even if you're not, you must make her believe you are; that's just as good. Now, to be brave is dangerous sometimes, but if you're a lad of ideas you can get around that part maybe."

He thought and thought and put together a bit of a plan. "Now, it's a fact she's afraid of worms," he said to himself. "This is quite plain. Oh yes, terrified of the tiny things, bless her heart. But why? They can't hurt her. They cannot bite or sting. Why then does she fear them? It is their shape, perhaps, for what else is there about them? And that they crawl on their bellies, squiggling along, for what else is it they do? Now, when a worm falls off the branch into the cradle I might boldly brush it away from her, but that is not very impressive, after all. She might appreciate it, to be sure, but she would not go mad with admiration. No, no. I must do something more splendid, more bold, bigger altogether. What then is a big worm? Big worm . . . why, yes—a snake. That's anyone's idea of a big worm, I should think. Now, if she's afraid of worms, she would go absolutely stark blue with terror, the beautiful child, if she saw a snake, a sight she has been spared so far. If only I could rescue her from a snake, ah, that would be a thing to admire. This would count as a great deed. This would win Murtha's heart. She would know her cousin Finn is a hero, and fit to be wed. Yes, yes, I see it plain;

163

I must save her from a snake. There's a drawback though. I myself am by no means partial to serpents. Why, as I lie here and think about them, I can feel myself beginning to shiver and shake. I am still but a babe, I haven't come into my strength, and I couldn't handle the loopy beast if I did meet one. Nevertheless, for all the fear and doubt, there is an idea here and I must make it grow."

So he thought and thought until his eyes grew blurred with sleep, and the far stars trembled and went out. When he awoke, the first tatters of morning mist were beginning to flush with light. He swung himself out of his bullhide cradle, crept down the tree like a squirrel, and went into the wood. As he went he kept his eyes open, and kept thinking very hard. In the deep of the wood he rested himself under a tree. A strange bird screamed. Finn shivered. It was dark in the wood, not the safe darkness of night, but a green scary dusk of day half hidden. The bird screamed again. In the brush something snarled and pounced; something else spoke in pain, chipmunk perhaps, or rabbit.

"All the things here eat each other," he said to himself. "The big ones eat the small ones. An uncomfortable kind of arrangement, especially if you're small."

He felt fuller of sadness than he could hold, and he wept a tear. The tear fell, but did not vanish as tears usually do. It glittered upon the leaf mold, grew brighter, rose again toward his face. It was a tiny manikin, rising out of the earth. No bigger than a twig was he, with a squinched-up little nut of a face. Upon his head glistened Finn's tear, a crystal now, milky white as the moon, lighting up a space about the little man.

"Who are you?" said Finn.

"I am the Thrig of Tone."

"Are you now?"

"Have you heard of me?"

"No, sir."

"An ignorant lad you are then, for I am famous."

"What for?"

"Magic mostly. Mischief some. I'm much abused in certain quarters. But I'm a good one to know, I'll tell you that. Unless I happen to take a dislike to you, in which case you will regret our acquaintance."

"I see," said Finn.

"I doubt it. The thing about me is I'm not around very often, as it happens. A powerful curse is working upon me, you see. I'm the prisoner of a spell, woven by the wickedest old witch who was ever wooed by the evil and wore a black hat to her wedding—her name is Drabne of Dole. What can I do for you now?"

"You wish to do something for me?"

"I must."

"Why must you?"

"A condition of the curse. I'm a prisoner of the dust, you see, until the purest tear happens to fall on me. Then I come to life and wear it as a jewel and must serve the weeper, whoever it is."

"Did I weep a pure tear?"

"I'm here, am I not?"

"What makes a tear pure?"

"An extraordinary grief. Something outside the scheme of things, so odd it makes the gods laugh. And that laughter of the gods, which you know as the wind, means that someone somewhere has a grief he cannot handle. But it must be something special; plain things won't do, you know, not for the gods. They see enough of ordinary misery; they're no longer amused, they like something special. A crocodile moved to pity, perhaps; that roused me some time ago, and I had an adventure then. Or a king brought low. Yes, they like that. Or something wondrously beautiful made ugly, watching itself become so, and not able to stop. All this will set the night a-howling. What they found special in you, I don't know. But here I am. And there's the wind, hear it? What is your problem, lad?"

"Myself mostly. I come of a family of giants, and am small. I love someone who does not know what love is. And I have a bold deed in mind, but am afraid. Also, something pounced and something screamed, reminding me of the world's arrangements about big things eating small ones. Well, all this made me weep. Master Thrig of

Tone, sir, if you help me I shall be grateful, but I don't know how you can."

"What is this deed you have in mind?"

"Well, you see, this young lady I admire is much upset by the sight of a worm. Making me think that the sight of a snake would absolutely terrify her and make her feel affectionate toward her rescuer."

"Think you'd be much good at fighting off serpents? They're very strong, you know, just one long muscle. Makes it awkward when you start to wrestle them. Not only that, but a mouthful of secret weapons. Hollow teeth that squirt poison, making even the smallest serpent deadlier than wolf or bear. You absolutely sure it's a snake you want for your first bout, young Finn?"

"I am sure."

"Well, this requires a bit of thinking. Let's see. How can we do this with the most honor to you and the most effect on your little friend, and the least damage to both of you? And the most pleasure to the serpents, too, for they're the kind of creature that go along with nothing unless they're pleased. Pleased, yes, that's a thought. You play any musical instrument? Flute, for instance."

"Don't even know what it is. Sometimes, though, I shake my rattle a certain way that makes my blood dance. And Murtha sits there dancing without moving her legs."

"Rhythm section's all very well, but what snakes like is melody."

He broke a reed from a nearby clump, took out a knife no longer than a thorn and notched the reed, then gave it to Finn.

"What's this?"

"A reed, doctored according to me lights."

"What's it for?"

"Well, reeds have a hard life. You must understand that in the vegetable kingdom they're nowhere. Very bottom of the list. No leaves, no scent, not even any nuisance value like weeds. They are frail stalks, bowing before every wind. And yet, this is their magic. Their courtesy to the wind is a very special quality. For they are the first to recognize this cruel laughter of the gods, and so are attuned to human misery. Their weakness gives strength its meaning; their lowliness makes fame shine; their pity is the best description in all the world of cruelty. The owl hitting the mouse, a wasp stinging a beetle to death, the young boy drowned in the pride of swimming, the bride realizing that she has married wrong and that her mistake has become her life—all these things that make the gods laugh and the winds howl, the reeds know first. They bow to it. And as the wind seethes through them, they rustle in a kind of music. It all becomes music in them. Music, which is the essence of all man cannot say in words. And, if you take a reed and notch it in a certain way—like this—and give it to one who will whisper his own story to it, why, then a most exquisite music is made. And now happens the greatest joke of all, a joke on the gods themselves, those jesters. For hearing this music out of the reed, why, Evil itself, the simplified shape of evil, the snake, becomes enraptured and dances in slow loops of ecstasy. And a slight pause comes to evil arrangements. Strength is diverted from cruelty. The blackness of death is split for a moment, and a crystal light streams, making pictures in the head, and it seems to those listening that things might be different, might be better. But only for a split second. Then the music stops and all goes back to the way it was before. But in that moment the snakes have danced and the victim forgotten fear. D'you follow me, boy?"

"Will you teach me to play this thing?"

"Let me hear you whistle a tune. I can do nothing if you have no ear."

Finn whistled. He could do that. He had amused himself in his cradle, imitating birds. The Thrig nodded.

"Not entirely tone-deaf, I'm glad to hear. Perhaps I can . . . maybe so. Very well, let us begin."

"Now?"

"Always now when it comes to learning, especially something difficult."

"But I'm hungry, I'm cold, I'm sleepy."

"Tell it to the reed."

Now it is said that the Thrig of Tone and young Finn stayed under that oak tree a week of days and a week of nights piping duets. It rained sometimes, and the nights were cold. Nor did they stop for food. Pixies don't eat the stuff, and the Thrig had forgotten that humans do. All Finn had during this time was three mushrooms that happened to grow near where he was sitting. For his thirst he drank the rain. Oh, it was a difficult time he had, but it wasn't allowed to matter. The Thrig was a strict teacher, and kept Finn at it. What happened then was that the lad's hunger and thirst and sleepiness and loneliness wove themselves into the music, and the reeds added their own notes of pity and joy. And at the end of their time together under the oak tree you could not tell who was teacher and who was pupil; they played equally well.

They played so beautifully that the birds stopped their own singing to listen. Even the owl left off hunting, forgot her bloody hunger for a bit, and stood on a limb listening, hooting the tune softly to herself. The deer came, and wolves. Weasels, foxes, stoats, rabbits, bears, badgers, chipmunks, wild pigs. They came and stood in silent ranks at night, forgetting their enmity and fear as the moonlight sifted through the leaves and touched different fur with silver. Finally, two huge snakes came slithering out of their fearful nest and set among their coils, weaving a slow dance.

"Enough!" cried the Thrig of Tone. "Lesson's over, young Finn. You've learned what I can teach. You can pipe and the devil can dance."

"Thank you, sir," said Finn.

"I have done my good deed without interruption, and am free at last, I hope, from the wicked enchantment that binds me to the dust and allows me to see the sun only once every thousand years."

"I hope so indeed," said Finn. "My thanks to you, O Thrig of Tone. Perhaps I can return the favor one day. Farewell."

And he went piping off through the woods, followed by various beasts.

But it's not so easy to get away with a good deed on this spinning egg of a world. Evil has lidless eyes and does not sleep. At the very moment that Finn was ending his lesson, Drabne of Dole, deep in her hole, a thousand miles down, was gazing at a hand mirror, combing her snaky hair with the backbone of a fish. Then the mirror darkened; she could not see herself. And she knew that somewhere on earth a good deed was being born. For good, the mere breath of it, always darkened her mirror. She gnashed her teeth and stamped her foot, crying:

Oh, grief; oh, woe
I'll not have it,
No, no, no.
Not a shred of kindness
Not a ray of joy.
I'll bend him, rend him,
Tame him, maim him,
Whatever he be,
Larger or wee,
Man or boy.

So saying, she flapped her bat-wing sleeves and flew a thousand miles in a wink of an eye to the old oak tree where the Thrig of Tone stood gazing after Finn. She snatched him up and stuffed him into her purse, and flew back a thousand miles to her den. She took him to the stool where she sat to do her sewing, and bound him with thread, and stabbed him with a needle.

Stab and jab
Jab and stab.
Better talk,
Better gab.

"No," groaned the Thrig.

"Been doing good deeds again, haven't you? Let you out of my sight for a minute every thousand years, and up you pop into the light trying to help some poor fool do the right thing instead of taking life as it is. Well, you'll tell me now what you did, and I'll undo it."

"Never," said the Thrig.

"Never's a long time, little one, especially when there's pain attached. You'll tell me, for I'll torment you till you do.

I come and I go,
I fly and I spy.
I am Drabne of Dole
I live in a hole,
And I need to know.

"That's what witch means, small fool. Woman Who Knows. Now hear what I intend, Thrig of Tone, if you don't tell me straight. I'll round off your edges a bit and use you as a pincushion for the next thousand years. And it'll be pain, pain, pain all the time. I have plenty of tatters that need mending. My master's socks need doing too. His hooves, you know, they wear right through."

Thereupon she poked and prodded and jabbed and stabbed the poor little fellow until he could bear it no longer, and told her what he had done.

"Aha," she said. "It's a very good deed, indeed, but not too late to stop."

She threw him into her workbasket and stomped off to her big iron pot where it boiled over on its fire of brambles. She cast in the scale of a fishy thing that lives at the bottom of the sea and has neither sight nor touch nor any sense at all but is one blind suck. Henbane she added, and nightshade, wormwood, drearweed, and various poison fats that clog the sense, whispering all the while:

In this cauldron
Stew and roast.
Hearing ail,
Music fail.
Make him then
Deaf as post.

A smoke arose from the witch's brew, curling in the spirals of a most evil spell, and wafted itself out of her den and up the long way into the world. Flew into the wood and fumed around the flat head of one of the serpents who were following Finn, drawn by his music. This serpent straightaway fell deaf, heard nothing anymore, but followed along anyway, no longer dancing, only crawling, filling with stupefied wrath.

Finn knew nothing. He went skipping and piping through the wood until he came to his own village, silent now, for it was the hot golden after lunch hour when giants nap. He climbed into his bullhide cradle and gazed upon young Murtha, sleeping sweetly as a folded flower.

"Sleep, little beauty," he said. "Sleep, my flower. Dream whatever dreams you do, and I shall sit here and my music shall steal through your ears and into your dreams, and when you awake you will hear the same music and not know whether you are awake or asleep, seeing me or dreaming still. And when the snakes come and frighten you, it will be with the slowness of nightmare, and in the darkened enchantment of that half dream you will hear me play and see me do, and watch the writhing evil dance to my tune. So you will know me for what I am, and love me forever. Sleep then, sleep until you awake."

He sat cross-legged and began to pipe again. The wolves came, and the deer. Bear, fox, badger, rabbit, weasel. They stood at the foot of the tree, listening. Then, sure enough, he saw the serpents unreeling themselves through the branches of the tree, winding down toward his cradle.

"Strange," he thought to himself, "they were mottled green, both of them, but now one has changed color. It's a dull gray, like lead. Oh, well, I suppose he has changed his skin. Snakes do, I hear. What's the difference? I'll play and they shall dance."

The green snake was already dancing, slowly winding fold upon mottled fold on the limb from which the cradle swung. But the gray snake had crawled into the cradle itself, filling it with great coils of dully glimmering metal hide.

Murtha was awake now, staring with stark-wild violet eyes at what had come into her sleep. And Finn thought that he was locked in nightmare. For this snake was not dancing. Its tiny eyes were poison-red and seemed to be spinning, making Finn's head whirl with fear. Not dancing, this serpent, but oozing toward Finn. He curled the tip of his tail around the lad's ribs and began to squeeze. Finn felt his bones cracking. He could do nothing else, so he kept playing. He sat there piping although the breath was being choked out of him. As his sight darkened he saw the snake above still dancing. And Finn, knowing that he was being killed, put all his pain and all his fear and all his loneliness into the pipe, and the pipe answered.

Now the green snake above danced on, filled with the wild sleepy magic of this music. The last exquisite strains of Finn's fluting plaited the snake's loops with slow joy, so that the coils he wove were made of living cable, stronger than steel. And when he heard the music growing dim and saw the gray serpent throttling Finn, he simply cast a loop about the strangler and pressed the life out of its body, all without ceasing his dance.

Finn felt the coils lose their deathly grip; his breath came free. In the huge joy of breathing he blew so loud a blast upon his reed that the giants awoke and came running to see.

What they saw was young Finn sitting in his bullhide cradle piping a tune, and a huge green serpent dancing, and another metal-colored snake hanging limp and dead, while violet-eyed little Murtha shook her shoulders and snapped her fingers and smiled like the sun upon water.

"Finn!" cried his mother, snatching him up and hugging him to her. "Are you all right? Has the murdering beast harmed you, child?"

"I'm fine, Mother. Put me back and let me play."

Finn's mother was not much for weeping, but she wept then.

"Don't cry, Mother. Take the silver one, and skin off his hide and make yourself a belt."

"I'll do that, son. And know it for the finest girdle in all the world."

The giants were whispering to each other. " 'Tis a wonder now. A proud mother she is this day. Young Finn's a hero for all his small bones."

"Save a bit of the hide to make a drum for Murtha here," said Finn. "Do that, Mother, and she will drum to my fluting, and all will be well."

"Do it I will," said his mother. "As soon as the beast can be peeled."

"Answer me, darlin'," said Finn to Murtha. "Will you have a silver drum and beat the measure as I play?"

The giants shouted their pride. The animals bayed and bellowed and trumpeted. A muffled shriek of pain came from Drabne of Dole, for witches suffer when wickedness fails. And the birds in the trees made a racket of glee.

Young Murtha, though, said nothing at all; she wasn't one for answering questions. Besides, she was doing something new. She stood among the snake's coils and danced along with him. He swayed, casting his green loops about her like a garland come to life. The giants then began to dance, too, stomping the earth mightily, shaking the trees.

And Drabne of Dole, deep underground, whimpered and moaned and screamed, but no one heard her, for the day was full of joyful noise.

As for the Thrig of Tone, the witch's grief was his chance. He undid his bonds and escaped from her workbasket and made his way back to the wood. There he lives to this day, they say, doing sometimes good and sometimes mischief according to his mood, but mostly good nowadays, for the balance is so much the other way. Children still get lost in that wood, and when they are found, say that a manikin with a face like a nut taught them to take music out of a reed. He wears a crown, they say, which is a single crystal, tear-shaped, full of moonfire. Their parents laugh and tell them they were never lost at all but only asleep, dreaming. The children do not argue, but they know what they know. And it's a fact that children so lost and so found grow up fond of strange places and adventure. They go about the world confusing wind and laughter, tears and moon-crystals, teasing music out of reeds, heroes out of shadows, stories out of grief.

"Hope Is the Thing with Feathers"
by Emily Dickinson

Hope is the thing with feathers
That perches in the soul,
And sings the tune without the words,
And never stops at all,

And sweetest in the gale is heard;
And sore must be the storm
That could abash the little bird
That kept so many warm.

I've heard it in the chillest land,
And on the strangest sea;
Yet, never, in the extremity,
It asked a crumb of me.

"Try, Try Again"

Anonymous

'Tis a lesson you should heed,
    Try, try again;
If at first you don't succeed,
    Try, try again;
Then your courage should appear,
For, if you will persevere,
You will conquer, never fear;
    Try, try again.

Once or twice though you should fail,
    Try, try again;
If you would at last prevail,
    Try, try again;
If we strive, 'tis no disgrace
Though we do not win the race;
What should you do in the case?
    Try, try again.

Time will bring you your reward,
    Try, try again.
All that other folks can do,
Why, with patience, should not you?
Only keep this rule in view;
    Try, try again.

CHAPTER SEVEN

Love Your Neighbor

"There had never been such a Christmas. Now of course, right away, Laura and Mary should have thanked Mr. Edwards for bringing those lovely presents all the way from Independence. But they had forgotten all about Mr. Edwards. They had even forgotten Santa Claus. In a minute they would have remembered but before they did, Ma said gently, 'Aren't you going to thank Mr. Edwards?'

" 'Oh, thank you, Mr. Edwards! Thank you!' they said, and they meant it with all their hearts. Pa shook Mr. Edwards's hand, too, and shook it again. Pa and Ma and Mr. Edwards acted as if they were almost crying, Laura didn't know why. So she gazed again at her beautiful presents."

From *The Little House on the Prairie*
by LAURA INGALLS WILDER

Have you ever noticed that nobody in fairy tales ever makes it to the happy ending without help? (*Boing!* "Fairy" tale?) In stories, as in life, unexpected beneficiaries pop out of nowhere with solutions, inspirations, and gifts. I don't think there is a person alive who has not, in some way, been helped by a fairy godmother.

Teaching your child to love his neighbor is teaching him to be a friend to those in need, to be courteous to all he meets, and respectful of the individual. In many ways, this is the role of the fairy godmother. And though we are genetically "hard-wired" to feel empathy, our ability to give of ourselves to others is very much shaped by parents and culture. Americans are by nature generous; we are the world's unexpected helpers; our culture created the volunteer and perfected the charitable impulse. But it is not enough simply to be a do-gooder.

So many parents have quite beautiful intentions when it comes to teaching their children to "love their neighbor" through overt acts of kindness and charity. Doing good is important, but there is something deeper and more worthy—goodness itself—that needs to be inculcated.

This means that charity comes from the heart, not from sense of stylish obligation. I know many parents who support causes for the less privileged and yet treat with disdain a taxi driver or a waitress or a gas station attendant. I have seen children coming out of a charity event speak to a doorman as if he were not at all a human being. Truly loving one's neighbor means understanding at the core the dignity of all human beings. It means seeing and embracing the goodness of our fellows, not just doing good deeds.

Loving your neighbor isn't easy, and doesn't involve "feeling" love. It is a practice that arises out of an intellectual understanding of people's dignity and a decision to act lovingly toward people who may be essentially unlovable. And it does begin at home. We all have difficult relatives who are nearly impossible to tolerate for any length of time. There is no need to mask the difficulty of this kind of person to your child, but there is a need to practice a loving acceptance of this person, warts and all. Children do not see the unlovable the way we do, anyway. They almost naturally practice charity, until the world teaches them to be judges rather than lovers of their neighbors.

There is a moment in *To Kill a Mockingbird* when Dill, Jem, and Scout have decided to surprise Atticus, who is at the jailhouse facing down a mob full of whiskey-breath and anger. It's a lynching mob, and it aims to hang Atticus's client, Tom. The tension is thick, until Scout spots a familiar face:

> "Hey, Mr. Cunningham."
>
> The man did not hear me, it seemed.
>
> "Hey, Mr. Cunningham. How's your entailment gettin' along?"
>
> Mr. Walter Cunningham's legal affairs were well known to me; Atticus had once described them at length. The big man blinked and hooked his thumbs in his overall straps. He seemed uncomfortable; he cleared his throat and looked away. My friendly overture had fallen flat. . . .
>
> "Don't you remember me, Mr. Cunningham? I'm Jean Louise Finch. You brought us some hickory nuts one time, remember?" I began to sense the futility one feels when unacknowledged by a chance acquaintance.
>
> "I go to school with Walter," I began again. "He's your boy, ain't he? Ain't he, sir?"
>
> Mr. Cunningham was moved to a faint nod. He did know me, after all.
>
> "He's in my grade," I said, "and he does right well. He's a good boy," I added, "a real nice boy. We brought him home for dinner one time. Maybe he told you about me—I beat him up one time, but he was real nice about it. Tell him hey for me, won't you?"
>
> I began to feel sweat gathering at the edges of my hair; I could stand anything but a bunch of people looking at me. They were all quite still.
>
> "What's the matter?" I asked.

Atticus said nothing. I looked around and up at Mr. Cunningham, whose face was equally impassive. Then he did a peculiar thing. He squatted down and took me by both shoulders.

"I'll tell him you said hey, little lady," he said.

Then he straightened up and waved a big paw. "Let's clear out," he called. "Let's get going, boys."

Scout reached through the prejudice, the whiskey, and the mob mentality and saw a human being. Her own goodness dispelled, for just a moment, the hate in Cunningham's heart. If there is a big idea that we as a generation have lost, it is in the power of simple goodness. Scout's was the gesture of a fairy godmother who came along at the right moment, and for that moment provided a happy ending. Scout embodies the lesson of great religions and homespun philosophies: that it is *goodness*, in the end, that does the most good.

"The Good Samaritan"

from the Holy Bible, King James version, Luke 10:25–37

Ａnd, behold, a certain lawyer stood up, and tempted him, saying, Master, what shall I do to inherit eternal life?

He said unto him, What is written in the law? How readest thou?

And he answering said, Thou shalt love the Lord thy God with all thy heart, and with all thy soul, and with all thy strength, and with all thy mind; and thy neighbor as thyself.

And he said unto him, Thou hast answered right: this do, and thou shalt live.

But he, willing to justify himself, said unto Jesus, And who is my neighbor?

And Jesus answering said, A certain man went down from Jerusalem to Jericho, and fell among thieves, which stripped him of his raiment, and wounded *him,* leaving *him* half dead.

And by chance there came down a certain priest that way: and when he saw him, he passed by on the other side.

And likewise a Levite, when he was at the place, came and looked *on him,* and passed by on the other side.

But a certain Samaritan, as he journeyed, came where he was: and when he saw him, he had compassion on *him.*

And went to *him,* and bound up his wounds, pouring oil and wine, and set him on his own beast, and brought him to an inn, and took care of him.

And on the morrow when he departed, he took out two pence, and gave them to the host, and said unto him, Take care of him; and whatsoever thou spendest more, when I come again, I will repay thee.

Which now of these three, thinkest thou, was neighbor unto him that fell among the thieves?

And he said, He that showed mercy on him. Then said Jesus unto him, Go, and do thou likewise.

"Aunt Beast"
from A Wrinkle in Time
by Madeleine L'Engle

*One reason we should never despair is because there is good-
ness in the world, and as Madeleine L'Engle shows, even in other
worlds. (Another reason we should not despair is because Madeleine L'Engle is in the world!)*

*Hope and momentary salvation come in many forms, and in
this story, Meg is rescued by strange beasts on an unknown
planet. The enemy in this extraordinary book is IT, an all-
controlling mind, and Meg has been injured while trying to
escape its horrible clutches. Meg first ventured to this unknown
territory trying to save Mr. Murry, her own father; now she has
found her father, but her baby brother is lost in the dark mind of IT.
Here the family from Earth is faced with these strange beasts, and
they are trying to communicate.*

"N o!" Mr. Murry said sharply. "Please put her down."

A sense of amusement seemed to emanate from the beasts. The
tallest, who seemed to be the spokesman, said, "We frighten you?"

"What are you going to do with us?" Mr. Murry asked.

The beast said, "I'm sorry, we communicate better with the other
one." He turned toward Calvin. "Who are you?"

"I'm Calvin O'Keefe."

"What's that?"

"I'm a boy. A—a young man."

"You, too, are afraid?"

"I'm—not sure."

"Tell me," the beast said. "What do you suppose you'd do if three of
us suddenly arrived on your home planet."

"Shoot you, I guess," Calvin admitted.

"Then isn't that what we should do with you?"

Calvin's freckles seemed to deepen, but he answered quietly, "I'd really rather you didn't. I mean, the Earth's my home, and I'd rather be there than anywhere in the world—I mean, the universe—and I can't wait to get back, but we make some awful bloopers there."

The smallest beast, the one holding Meg, said, "And perhaps they aren't used to visitors from other planets."

"Used to it!" Calvin exclaimed. "We've never had any, as far as I know."

"Why?"

"I don't know."

The middle beast, a tremor of trepidation in his words, said, "You aren't from a dark planet, are you?"

"No." Calvin shook his head firmly, though the beast couldn't see him. "We're—we're shadowed. But we're fighting the shadow."

The beast holding Meg questioned, "You three are fighting?"

"Yes," Calvin answered. "Now that we know about it."

The tall one turned back to Mr. Murry, speaking sternly. "You. The oldest. Man. From where have you come? Now."

Mr. Murry answered steadily. "From a planet called Camazotz." There was a mutter from the three beasts. "We do not belong there," Mr. Murry said, slowly and distinctly. "We were strangers there as we are here. I was a prisoner there, and these children rescued me. My youngest son, my baby, is still there, trapped in the dark mind of IT."

Meg tried to twist around in the beast's arms to glare at her father and Calvin. Why were they being so frank? Weren't they aware of the danger? But again her anger dissolved as the gentle warmth from the tentacles flowed through her. She realized that she could move her fingers and toes with comparative freedom, and the pain was no longer so acute.

"We must take this child back with us," the beast holding her said.

Meg shouted at her father. "Don't leave me the way you left Charles!" With this burst of terror a spasm of pain racked her body and she gasped.

"Stop fighting," the beast told her. "You make it worse. Relax."

"That's what IT said," Meg cried. "Father! Calvin! Help!"

183

The beast turned toward Calvin and Mr. Murry. "This child is in danger. You must trust us."

"We have no alternative," Mr. Murry said. "Can you save her?"

"I think so."

"May I stay with her?"

"No. But you will not be far away. We feel that you are hungry, tired, that you would like to bathe and rest. And this little—what is the word?" the beast cocked its tentacles at Calvin.

"Girl," Calvin said.

"This little girl needs prompt and special care. The coldness of the—what is it you call it?"

"The Black Thing?"

"The Black Thing. Yes. The Black Thing burns unless it is counteracted properly." The three beasts stood around Meg, and it seemed that they were feeling into her with their softly waving tentacles. The movement of the tentacles was as rhythmic and flowing as the dance of an undersea plant, and lying there, cradled in the four strange arms, Meg, despite herself, felt a sense of security that was deeper than anything she had known since the days when she lay in her mother's arms in the old rocking chair and was sung to sleep. With her father's help she had been able to resist IT. Now she could hold out no longer. She leaned her head against the beast's chest, and realized that the gray body was covered with the softest, most delicate fur imaginable, and the fur had the same beautiful odor as the air.

I hope I don't smell awful to it, she thought. But then she knew with a deep sense of comfort that even if she did smell awful the beasts would forgive her. As the tall figure cradled her she could feel the frigid stiffness of her body relaxing against it. This bliss could not come to her from a thing like IT. IT could only give pain, never relieve it. The beasts must be good. They had to be good. She sighed deeply, like a very small child, and suddenly she was asleep.

When she came to herself again there was in the back of her mind a memory of pain, of agonizing pain. But the pain was over now and her body was lapped in comfort. She was lying on something wonderfully soft in an enclosed chamber. It was dark. All she could see were occasional tall moving shadows, which she realized were beasts walking about. She had been stripped of her clothes, and something warm and pungent was gently being rubbed into her body. She sighed and stretched and discovered that she could stretch. She could move again, she was no longer paralyzed, and her body was bathed in waves of warmth. Her father had not saved her; the beasts had.

"So you are awake, little one?" The words came gently to her ears. "What a funny little tadpole you are! Is the pain gone now?"

"All gone."

"Are you warm and alive again?"

"Yes, I'm fine." She struggled to sit up.

"No, lie still, small one. You must not exert yourself as yet. We will have a fur garment for you in a moment, and then we will feed you. You must not even try to feed yourself. You must be as an infant again. The Black Thing does not relinquish its victims willingly."

"Where are Father and Calvin? Have they gone back for Charles Wallace?"

"They are eating and resting," the beast said, "and we are trying to learn about each other and see what is best to help you. We feel now that you are not dangerous, and that we will be allowed to help you."

"Why is it so dark in here?" Meg asked. She tried to look around, but all she could see was shadows. Nevertheless there was a sense of openness, a feel of a gentle breeze moving lightly about, that kept the darkness from being oppressive.

Perplexity came to her from the beast. "What is this dark? What is this light? We do not understand. Your father and the boy, Calvin, have asked this, too. They say that it is night now on our planet, and that they cannot see. They have told us that our atmosphere is what they call opaque, so that the stars are not visible, and then they were surprised that we know stars, that we know their music and the movements of their dance far better than beings like you who spend hours studying them through what you call telescopes. We do not understand what this means, *to see*."

"Well, it's what things *look* like," Meg said helplessly.

"We do not know what things *look* like, as you say," the beast said.

"We know what things *are* like. It must be a very limiting thing, this seeing."

"Oh, no!" Meg cried. "It's—it's the most wonderful thing in the world!"

"What a very strange world yours must be!" the beast said, "that such a peculiar-seeming thing should be of such importance. Try to tell me, what is this thing called *light* that you are able to do so little without?"

"Well, we can't see without it," Meg said, realizing that she was completely unable to explain vision and light and dark. How can you explain sight on a world where no one has ever seen and where there is no need of eyes? "Well, on this planet," she fumbled, "you have a sun, don't you?"

"A most wonderful sun, from which comes our warmth, and the rays which give us our flowers, our food, our music, and all the things which make life and growth."

"Well," Meg said, "when we are turned toward the sun—our Earth, our planet, I mean, toward our sun—we receive its light. And when we're turned away from it, it is night. And if we want to see we have to use artificial lights."

"Artificial lights," the beast sighed. "How very complicated life on your planet must be. Later on you must try to explain some more to me."

"All right," Meg promised, and yet she knew that to try to explain anything that could be seen with the eyes would be impossible, because the beasts in some way saw, knew, understood, far more completely than she, or her parents, or Calvin, or even Charles Wallace.

"Charles Wallace!" she cried. "What are they doing about Charles Wallace? We don't know what IT's doing to him or making him do. Please, oh, please, help us!"

"Yes, yes, little one, of course we will help you. A meeting is in session right now to study what is best to do. We have never before been able to talk to anyone who has managed to escape from a dark planet, so although your father is blaming himself for everything that has happened, we feel that he must be quite an extraordinary person to get out of Camazotz with you at all. But the little boy, and I understand that he is a very special, a very important little boy—ah, my child, you must accept that this will not be easy. To go *back* through the Black Thing, *back* to Camazotz—I don't know. I don't know."

"But Father left him!" Meg said. "He's got to bring him back! He can't just abandon Charles Wallace!"

The beast's communication suddenly became crisp. "Nobody said anything about abandoning anybody. That is not our way. But we know that just because we want something does not mean that we will get what we want, and we still do not know *what* to do. And we cannot allow you, in your present state, to do anything that would jeopardize us all. I can see that you wish your father to go rushing back to Camazotz, and you could probably make him do this, and then where would we be? No. No. You must wait until you are more calm. Now, my darling, here is a robe for you to keep you warm and comfortable." Meg felt herself being lifted again, and a soft, light garment was slipped about her. "Don't worry about your little brother." The tentacles' musical words were soft against her. "We would *never* leave him behind the shadow. But for now you must relax, you must be happy, you must get well."

The gentle words, the feeling that this beast would be able to love her no matter what she said or did, lapped Meg in warmth and peace. She felt a delicate touch of tentacle to her cheek, as tender as her mother's kiss.

"It is so long since my own small ones were grown and gone," the beast said. "You are so tiny and vulnerable. Now I will feed you. You must eat slowly and quietly. I know that you are half starved, that you have been without food far too long, but you must not rush things or you will not get well."

Something completely and indescribably and incredibly delicious was put to Meg's lips, and she swallowed gratefully. With each swallow she felt strength returning to her body and she realized that she had had nothing to eat since the horrible fake turkey dinner on Camazotz which she had barely tasted. How long ago was her mother's stew? Time no longer had any meaning.

"How long does night last here?" she murmured sleepily. "It will be day again, won't it?"

"Hush," the beast said. "Eat, small one. During the coolness, which is now, we sleep. And, when you waken, there will be warmth again and many things to do. You must eat now, and sleep, and I will stay with you."

"What should I call you, please?" Meg asked.

"Well, now. First try not to say any words for just a moment. Think within your own mind. Think of all the things you call people, different kinds of people."

While Meg thought, the beast murmured to her gently. "No, *mother* is a special, a one-name; and a father you have here. Not just friend, nor teacher, nor brother, nor sister. What is *acquaintance*? What a funny, hard word. Aunt. Maybe. Yes, perhaps that will do. And you think of such odd words about me. *Thing,* and *monster*! *Monster,* what a horrid sort of word. I really do not think I am a monster. *Beast.* That will do. *Aunt Beast.*"

"Aunt Beast," Meg murmured sleepily, and laughed.

"Have I said something funny?" Aunt Beast asked in surprise. "Isn't Aunt Beast all right?"

"Aunt Beast is lovely," Meg said. "Please sing to me, Aunt Beast."

If it was impossible to describe sight to Aunt Beast, it would be even more impossible to describe the singing of Aunt Beast to a human being. It was a music even more glorious than the music of the singing creatures on Uriel. It was a music more tangible than form or sight. It had essence and structure. It supported Meg more firmly than the arms of Aunt Beast. It seemed to travel with her, to sweep her aloft in the power of song, so that she was moving in glory among the stars, and for a moment she, too, felt that the words Darkness and Light had no meaning, and only this melody was real.

Meg did not know when she fell asleep within the body of music. When she wakened Aunt Beast was asleep, too, the softness of her furry, faceless head drooping. Night had gone and a dull gray light filled the room. But she realized now that here on this planet there was no need for color, that the grays and browns merging into each other

188

were not what the beasts knew, and that what she, herself, saw was only the smallest fraction of what the planet was really like. It was she who was limited by her senses, not the blind beasts, for they must have senses of which she could not even dream.

She stirred slightly, and Aunt Beast bent over her immediately. "What a lovely sleep, my darling. Do you feel all right?"

"I feel wonderful," Meg said. "Aunt Beast, what is this planet called?"

"Oh, dear." Aunt Beast sighed. "I find it not easy at all to put things the way your mind shapes them. You call where you came from Camazotz?"

"Well, it's where we came from, but it's not our planet."

"You can call us Ixchel, I guess," Aunt Beast told her. "We share the same sun as lost Camazotz, but that, give thanks, is all we share."

"Are you fighting the Black Thing?" Meg asked.

"Oh, yes," Aunt Beast replied. "In doing that we can never relax. We are the called according to His purpose, and whom He calls, them He also justifies. Of course we have help, and without help it would be much more difficult."

"Who helps you?" Meg asked.

"Oh, dear, it is so difficult to explain things to you, small one. And I know now that it is not just because you are a child. The other two are as hard to reach into as you are. What can I tell you that will mean anything to you? Good helps us, the stars help us, perhaps what you would call *light* helps us, love helps us. Oh, my child, I cannot explain! This is something you just have to know or not know."

"But—"

"We look not at the things which are what you would call seen, but at the things which are not seen. For the things which are seen are temporal. But the things which are not seen are eternal."

"Aunt Beast, do you know Mrs. Whatsit?" Meg asked with a sudden flooding of hope.

"Mrs. Whatsit?" Aunt Beast was puzzled. "Oh, child, your language is so utterly simple and limited that it has the effect of extreme complication." Her four arms, tentacles waving, were outflung in a gesture of helplessness. "Would you like me to take you to your father and your Calvin?"

"Oh, yes, please!"

"Let us go, then. They are waiting for you to make plans. And we thought you would enjoy eating—what is it you call it? oh, yes, breakfast—together. You will be too warm in that heavy fur, now. I will dress you in something lighter, and then we will go."

As though Meg were a baby, Aunt Beast bathed and dressed her, and this new garment, though it was made of a pale fur, was lighter than the lightest summer clothes on earth. Aunt Beast put one tentacled arm about Meg's waist and led her through long, dim corridors in which she could see only shadows, and shadows of shadows, until they reached a large, columned chamber. Shafts of light came in from an open skylight and converged about a huge, round, stone table. Here were seated several of the great beasts, and Calvin and Mr. Murry, on a stone bench that circled the table. Because the beasts were so tall, even Mr. Murry's feet did not touch the ground, and lanky Calvin's long legs dangled as though he were Charles Wallace. The hall was partially enclosed by vaulted arches leading to long, paved walks. There were no empty walls, no covering roofs, so that although the light was dull in comparison to earth's sunlight, Meg had no feeling of dark or of chill. As Aunt Beast led Meg in, Mr. Murry slid down from the bench and hurried to her, putting his arms about her tenderly.

"They promised us you were all right," he said.

While she had been in Aunt Beast's arms Meg had felt safe and secure. Now her worries about Charles Wallace and her disappointment in her father's human fallibility rose like gorge in her throat.

"I'm fine," she muttered, looking not at Calvin or her father, but at the beasts, for it was to them she turned now for help. It seemed to her that neither her father nor Calvin were properly concerned about Charles Wallace.

"Meg!" Calvin said gaily. "You've never tasted such food in your life! Come and eat!"

Aunt Beast lifted Meg up onto the bench and sat down beside her, then heaped a plate with food, strange fruits and breads that tasted unlike anything Meg had ever eaten. Everything was dull and colorless and unappetizing to look at, and at first, even remembering the meal Aunt Beast had fed her the night before, Meg hesitated to taste, but once she had managed the first bite she ate eagerly; it seemed that she would never have her fill again.

The others waited until she slowed down. Then Mr. Murry said gravely, "We were trying to work out a plan to rescue Charles Wallace. Since I made such a mistake in tessering away from IT, we feel that it would not be wise for me to try to get back to Camazotz, even alone. If I missed the mark again I could easily get lost and wander forever from galaxy to galaxy, and that would be small help to anyone, least of all to Charles Wallace."

Such a wave of despondency came over Meg that she was no longer able to eat.

"Our friends here," he continued, "feel that it was only the fact that I still wore the glasses your Mrs. Who gave you that kept me within this solar system. Here are the glasses, Meg. But I am afraid that the virtue has gone from them and now they are only glass. Perhaps they were meant to help only once and only on Camazotz. Perhaps it was going through the Black Thing that did it." He pushed the glasses across the table at her.

"These people know about tessering," Calvin gestured at the circle of great beasts, "but they can't do it onto a dark planet."

"Have you tried to call Mrs. Whatsit?" Meg asked.

"Not yet," her father answered.

"But if you haven't thought of anything else, it's the *only* thing to do! Father, don't you care about Charles at all!"

At that Aunt Beast stood up, saying, "Child," in a reproving way. Mr. Murry said nothing and Meg could see that she had wounded him deeply. She reacted as she would have reacted to Mr. Jenkins. She scowled down at the table, saying, "We've *got* to ask them for help now. You're just stupid if you think we don't."

Aunt Beast spoke to the others. "The child is distraught. Don't judge her harshly. She was almost taken by the Black Thing. Sometimes we can't know what spiritual damage it leaves even when physical recovery is complete."

Meg looked angrily around the table. The beasts sat there, silent, motionless. She felt that she was being measured and found wanting.

Calvin swung away from her and hunched himself up. "Hasn't it occurred to you that we've been trying to tell them about our ladies? What do you think we've been up to all this time? Just stuffing our faces? Okay, you have a shot at it."

"Yes. Try, child." Aunt Beast seated herself again, and pulled Meg up beside her. "But I do not understand this feeling of anger I sense in you. What is it about? There is blame going on, and guilt. Why?"

"Aunt Beast, don't you know?"

"No," Aunt Beast said. "But this is not telling me about—whoever they are you want us to know. Try."

Meg tried. Blunderingly. Fumblingly. At first she described Mrs. Whatsit and her man's coat and multicolored shawls and scarves, Mrs. Who and her white robes and shimmering spectacles, Mrs. Which in her peaked cap and black gown quivering in and out of body. Then she realized that this was absurd. She was describing them only to herself. This wasn't Mrs. Whatsit or Mrs. Who or Mrs. Which. She might as well have described Mrs. Whatsit as she was when she took on the form of a flying creature of Uriel.

"Don't try to use words," Aunt Beast said soothingly. "You're just fighting yourself and me. Think about what they *are*. This *look* doesn't help us at all."

Meg tried again, but she could not get a visual concept out of her mind. She tried to think of Mrs. Whatsit explaining tessering. She tried to think of them in terms of mathematics. Every once in a while she thought she felt a flicker of understanding from Aunt Beast or one of the others, but most of the time all that emanated from them was gentle puzzlement.

"Angels!" Calvin shouted suddenly from across the table. "Guardian angels!" There was a moment's silence, and he shouted again, his face tense with concentration, "Messengers! Messengers of God!"

"I thought for a moment—" Aunt Beast started, then subsided, sighing. "No. It's not clear enough."

"How strange it is that they can't tell us what they themselves seem to know," a tall, thin beast murmured.

One of Aunt Beast's tentacled arms went around Meg's waist again. "They are very young. And on their Earth, as they call it, they never communicate with other planets. They revolve about all alone in space."

"Oh," the thin beast said. "Aren't they *lonely*?"

Suddenly a thundering voice reverberated throughout the great hall:

"WWEEE ARRE HHERRE!"

"Linda-Gold and the Old King"
by Anna Wahlenberg

*This is a simple tale about a child's kindness and goodness,
and how it melted the fears of an estranged king.*

Long, long ago there lived an old king who was rather eccentric.
People said he was odd because he had had many sorrows, poor old
king. His queen and children had died, and he himself said his heart
had been torn apart. Who had done that and how it had happened, he
never told; but it was someone with claws, he said, and since then he
imagined that everyone had claws on his hands.

No one was allowed to come nearer than two arms' lengths to the
king. His valets were not allowed to touch him, and his dining room
steward had to place his food at the very edge of the table. The king had
not shaken anyone's hand for many, many years. If people were careless
enough not to remember about the two arms' lengths, and came an inch
closer, the king had them put in irons for a week to refresh their
memory.

In all other ways, the old king was a good king. He governed his
subjects well and justly. Everyone was devoted to him, and the only
thing his people regretted was that he had not found a new queen, or
appointed anyone prince or princess to inherit the realm. When they
asked him about this, however, he always said, "Show me someone who
does not have claws, and I will let that person be my heir."

But no one ever appeared who, in the king's mind, did not have
claws. The claws might be under the fingernails, or curled in the palm,
but they were always there, he believed.

Now, one day it happened that the old king was walking alone in
the forest. He grew tired and sat down to rest on the moss and listen to
the birds singing in the trees. Suddenly a small girl rushed up the path,
her hair streaming behind. And when the king looked up, he saw in the
trees a shaggy gray beast with flashing eyes and a grinning red mouth.

It was a wolf, who wanted the little girl for breakfast. The old king rose and drew his sword, and straightaway the wolf turned in fear and ran back into the forest.

When the wolf had gone, the little girl began to weep and tremble. "Now you must walk home with me, too," she said, "or else the wolf will chase me again."

"Must I?" asked the king, who was not accustomed to taking orders.

"Yes. And my mother will give you a loaf of white bread for your trouble. My name is Linda-Gold, and my father is the miller on the other side of the forest."

What she said was right, the king decided. He couldn't very well let her be killed by the wolf, and so he was obliged to accompany her.

"You go first," he said. "I will follow behind you."

But the little girl did not dare walk first. "May I hold your hand?" she asked, and moved closer to him.

The king started, and looked closely at the little hand raised to his. "No, I am sure you have claws, too, though you are so small," he said.

Linda-Gold's eyes filled with tears, and she hid her hands behind her back. "My father says that, when all I have done is forgotten to cut my nails." She felt ashamed and looked at the ground. But then she asked if she might at least take hold of his mantle, and the king agreed to that. He simply could not make himself tell her to keep two arms' lengths away, for she was only a small child who would not understand.

So she skipped along beside him and told him of her cottage and all her toys. She had so many beautiful things she wanted to show him. There was a cow made of pine cones, with match sticks for legs; a boat made from an old wooden shoe, with burdock leaves for a sail; and then best of all was a doll her mother had sewn for her from an old brown apron and stuffed with yarn. It had a skirt made from the sleeve of a red sweater, and a blue ribbon at the neck, and her big brother had drawn a face on it with coal and put on a patch of leather for a nose.

It was odd, but the king listened patiently to all her chattering, and smiled. He was sure the little hand had claws, yet he let it pull and jerk at his mantle as much as it wished. But when Linda-Gold and the king came to the highway, and the mill was not far away, the king said good-bye. Now Linda-Gold could go home by herself.

But Linda-Gold was disappointed. She did not want to say good-bye so soon. She clung to his arm and tugged it, and begged him. How could he not want white bread, which was so good? It couldn't be true that he did not want to look at her fine toys! She would let him play with her doll all the evening, if only he would come home with her. She would give him a present—the boat with the burdock-leaf sails—because he had saved her from the wolf.

When none of this helped, she at last asked the king where he lived.

"In the castle," he said.

"And what is your name?"

"Old Man Graybeard."

"Good. Then I will come to visit you, Old Man Graybeard." And she took off her little blue checked scarf, and stood waving it as long as the king could see her—and he turned to look back quite often because he thought her the sweetest little girl he had met in a long time.

Even after he had returned to the castle, he still thought of Linda-Gold, wondering if she really would come to visit him. He was worried because she did not want to keep her little hands at a respectful distance, but he could not deny that he longed to see her.

The king was still thinking of Linda-Gold the next morning, and feeling sure that she would not dare venture out so far for fear of the wolf, when he heard a clear child's voice calling from the palace yard. He went to the balcony and saw Linda-Gold with a rag doll under her arm. She was arguing with the gatekeeper. She said she must speak to Old Man Graybeard about something very important.

But the gatekeeper just laughed at her and replied that no Old Man Graybeard lived there. Then Linda-Gold got angry. He mustn't say that, she insisted, for she herself knew very well Old Man Graybeard did live there. He had told her so himself.

Next she went up to the lady-in-waiting who had just come outside, and asked her advice. No, the lady-in-waiting had never heard of Old Man Graybeard, either, and she too laughed heartily.

But Linda-Gold did not give up. She asked the cook, she asked the steward of the household, and she asked all the courtiers, who had begun to gather in the courtyard to stare at her. She turned red in the face as they all laughed, and her lower lip began to tremble. Her eyes were full of tears, but she still maintained firmly in a clear voice, "He must be here, because he told me so himself."

The king called from his balcony, "Yes, here I am, Linda-Gold."

Linda-Gold looked up, gave a shout of joy, and jumped up and down in excitement. "Do you see, do you see!" she called in triumph. "I told you he was here."

The courtiers could do nothing but stare in surprise. The king had to command twice that Linda-Gold be brought to him before anyone obeyed. Then it was no less a person than the royal court's Master of Ceremonies who led her to the king's chamber. When the door opened, Linda-Gold ran straight to the king and set her rag doll on his knee.

"I will give you this instead of the boat," she said, "because I thought that since you saved me from the wolf you should have the best thing of all."

The rag doll was the ugliest, most clumsy little bundle imaginable, but the old king smiled as if he were quite delighted with it.

"Isn't she sweet?" asked Linda-Gold.

"Yes, very."

"Kiss her, then."

And so the king had to kiss the doll on its black, horrible mouth.

"Since you like her, you should thank me, don't you think?"

"Thank you," said the king, nodding in a friendly way.

"That wasn't right," said Linda-Gold.

"Not right? How should it be then?"

"When you say thank you, you must also pat my cheek," said Linda-Gold.

And so the king had to pat her on the cheek; but it was a warm, soft little cheek, and not at all unpleasant to pat.

"And now—" said Linda-Gold.

"Is there something more?" asked the king.

"Yes, I would like to pat your cheek, too."

Here the king hesitated. This was really too much for him.

"Because, you see," Linda-Gold went on, "I cut my fingernails," and she held up both her small chubby hands for the king to see. He had to look at them whether he liked it or not.

And truly, he could not see anything unusual on the pink fingertips. The nails were cut as close as a pair of scissors could do it, and there wasn't the trace of a claw.

"You can't say I have claws now, Graybeard," said Linda-Gold.

"No . . . hmm . . . well, pat me, then."

Linda-Gold flew up on his lap and stroked the old sunken cheeks and kissed them, and soon a couple of tears came rolling down. It was so long since the old king had known love.

Now he took Linda-Gold in his arms and carried her to the balcony. "Here you see the one you have always longed for," he called to those in the courtyard.

A loud cry of joy broke out among them. "Hurrah for our little princess. Hurrah! Hurrah!" they shouted.

Surprised and bewildered, Linda-Gold turned to the king and asked him what this meant.

"It means they like you because you have fine small hands which never scratch and have no claws," he said. Then he kissed the two little hands so that everyone could see, and from below the people shouted again, "Hurrah for our little princess!"

And that is how Linda-Gold became a princess and in the course of time inherited the realm of the old king.

From Little Women

by Louisa May Alcott

A peek at the four famous March girls at Christmas. Their father is off fighting the war and they are attempting with good humor to make do, and even act with kindness and charity to neighbors in need.

Playing Pilgrims

"Christmas won't be Christmas without any presents," grumbled Jo, lying on the rug.

"It's so dreadful to be poor!" sighed Meg, looking down at her old dress.

"I don't think it's fair for some girls to have plenty of pretty things, and other girls nothing at all," added little Amy, with an injured sniff.

"We've got Father and Mother and each other," said Beth contentedly, from her corner.

The four young faces on which the firelight shone brightened at the cheerful words, but darkened again as Jo said sadly, "We haven't got Father, and shall not have him for a long time." She didn't say "perhaps never," but each silently added it, thinking of Father far away, where the fighting was.

Nobody spoke for a minute; then Meg said in an altered tone, "You know the reason Mother proposed not having any presents this Christmas was because it is going to be a hard winter for everyone; and she thinks we ought not to spend money for pleasure, when our men are suffering so in the army. We can't do much, but we can make our little sacrifices, and ought to do it gladly. But I'm afraid I don't." Meg shook her head as she thought regretfully of all the pretty things she wanted.

199

"But I don't think the little we should spend would do any good. We've each got a dollar, and the army wouldn't be much helped by our giving that. I agree not to expect anything from Mother or you, but I do want to buy *Undine and Sintram* for myself; I've wanted it so long," said Jo, who was a bookworm.

"I have planned to spend mine on new music," said Beth, with a little sigh, which no one heard but the hearth brush and kettle holder.

"I shall get a nice box of Faber's drawing pencils; I really need them," said Amy decidedly.

"Mother didn't say anything about our money, and she won't wish us to give up everything. Let's each buy what we want, and have a little fun; I'm sure we work hard enough to earn it," cried Jo, examining the heels of her shoes in a gentlemanly manner.

"I know I do—teaching those tiresome children nearly all day, when I'm longing to enjoy myself at home," began Meg, in the complaining tone again.

"You don't have half such a hard time as I do," said Jo. "How would you like to be shut up for hours with a nervous, fussy old lady, who keeps you trotting, is never satisfied, and worries you till you're ready to fly out of the window or cry?"

"It's naughty to fret; but I do think washing dishes and keeping things tidy is the worst work in the world. It makes me cross; and my hands get so stiff, I can't practice well at all." Beth looked at her rough hands with a sigh that anyone could hear that time.

"I don't believe any of you suffer as I do," cried Amy, "for you don't have to go to school with impertinent girls who plague you if you don't know your lessons, and laugh at your dresses, and label your father if he isn't rich, and insult you when your nose isn't nice."

"If you mean *libel*, I'd say so, and not talk about *labels*, as if Papa was a pickle bottle," advised Jo, laughing.

"I know what I mean, and you needn't be *statirical* about it. It's proper to use good words, and improve your *vocabilary*," returned Amy with dignity.

"Don't peck at one another, children. Don't you wish we had the money Papa lost when we were little, Jo? Dear me, how happy and good we'd be, if we had no worries!" said Meg, who could remember better times.

"You said, the other day, you thought we were a deal happier than the King children, for they were fighting and fretting all the time, in spite of their money."

"So I did, Beth. Well, I think we are; for, although we do have to work, we make fun for ourselves, and are a pretty jolly set, as Jo would say."

"Jo does use such slang words!" observed Amy, with a reproving look at the long figure stretched on the rug. Jo immediately sat up, put her hands in her pockets, and began to whistle.

"Don't, Jo; it's so boyish!"

"That's why I do it."

"I detest rude, unladylike girls!"

"I hate affected, niminy-piminy chits!"

" 'Birds in their little nests agree,' " sang Beth, the peacemaker, with such a funny face that both sharp voices softened to a laugh, and the "pecking" ended for the time.

"Really, girls, you are both to be blamed," said Meg, beginning to lecture in her elder-sisterly fashion. "You are old enough to leave off boyish tricks, and to behave better, Josephine. It didn't matter so much when you were a little girl; but now you are so tall, and turn up your hair, you should remember that you are a young lady."

"I'm not! And if turning up my hair makes me one, I'll wear it in two tails till I'm twenty," cried Jo, pulling off her net, and shaking down a chestnut mane. "I hate to think I've got to grow up, and be Miss March, and wear long gowns, and look as prim as a China aster! It's bad enough to be a girl, anyway, when I like boys' games and work and manners! I can't get over my disappointment in not being a boy; and it's worse than ever now, for I'm dying to go and fight with Papa, and I can only stay at home and knit, like a poky old woman!" And Jo shook the blue army sock till the needles rattled like castanets, and her ball bounded across the room.

"Poor Jo! It's too bad, but it can't be helped; so you must try to be contented with making your name boyish, and playing brother to us girls," said Beth, stroking the rough head at her knee with a hand that all the dish washing and dusting in the world could not make ungentle to its touch.

"As for you, Amy," continued Meg, "you are altogether too particular and prim. Your airs are funny now; but you'll grow up an affected little goose if you don't take care. I like your nice manners and refined ways of speaking, when you don't try to be elegant. But your absurd words are as bad as Jo's slang."

"If Jo is a tomboy and Amy is a goose, what am I, please?" asked Beth, ready to share the lecture.

"You're a dear, and nothing else," answered Meg warmly. And no one contradicted her, for the "Mouse" was the pet of the family.

The four sisters sat knitting away in the twilight, while the December snow fell quietly without, and the fire crackled cheerfully within. It was a comfortable old room, though the carpet was faded and the furniture very plain. A good picture or two hung on the walls, books filled the recesses, chrysanthemums and Christmas roses bloomed in the windows, and a pleasant atmosphere of home peace pervaded it.

Margaret, the eldest of the four, was sixteen, and very pretty, being plump and fair, with large eyes, plenty of soft brown hair, a sweet mouth, and white hands, of which she was rather vain.

Fifteen-year-old Jo was very tall, thin, and brown, and reminded one of a colt; for she never seemed to know what to do with her long legs, which were very much in her way. She had a decided mouth, a comical nose, and sharp, gray eyes, which appeared to see everything, and were by turns fierce, funny, or thoughtful. Her long, thick hair was her one beauty; but it was usually bundled into a net, to be out of her way. Round shoulders had Jo, big hands and feet, a flyaway look to her clothes, and the uncomfortable appearance of a girl who was rapidly shooting up into a woman, and didn't like it.

Elizabeth—or Beth, as everyone called her—was a rosy, smooth-haired, bright-eyed girl of thirteen, with a shy manner, a timid voice, and a peaceful expression, which was seldom disturbed. Her father called her "Little Tranquillity," and the name suited her excellently, for she seemed to live in a happy world of her own, only venturing out to meet the few whom she trusted and loved. Amy, though the youngest, was a most important person—in her own opinion at least. A regular snow-maiden, with blue eyes, and yellow hair curling on her shoulders, pale and slender, and always carrying herself like a young lady mindful of her manners.

The clock struck six; and, having swept up the hearth, Beth put a pair of slippers down to warm. Somehow the sight of the old shoes had a good effect upon the girls. Mother was coming, and everyone brightened to welcome her. Meg stopped lecturing, and lighted the lamp; Amy got out of the easy chair without being asked; and Jo forgot how tired she was as she sat up to hold the slippers nearer to the blaze.

"They are quite worn out. Marmee must have a new pair."

"I thought I'd get her some with my dollar," said Beth.

"No, I shall!" cried Amy.

"I'm the oldest," began Meg, but Jo cut in with a decided, "I'm the man of the family now Papa is away, and I shall provide the slippers, for he told me to take special care of Mother while he was gone."

"I'll tell you what we'll do," said Beth. "Let's each get her something for Christmas, and not get anything for ourselves."

"That's like you, dear! What will we get?" exclaimed Jo.

Everyone thought soberly for a minute. Then Meg announced, as if the idea was suggested by the sight of her own pretty hands, "I shall give her a nice pair of gloves."

"Army shoes, best to be had," cried Jo.

"Some handkerchiefs, all hemmed," said Beth.

"I'll get a little bottle of cologne. She likes it, and it won't cost much, so I'll have some left to buy my pencils," added Amy.

"How will we give the things?"

"Put them on the table, and bring her in and see her open the bundles. Don't you remember how we used to do on our birthdays?" answered Jo.

"I used to be so frightened when it was my turn to sit in the big chair with the crown on, and see you all come marching around to give the presents, with a kiss. I liked the things and the kisses, but it was dreadful to have you sit looking at me while I opened the bundles," said Beth, who was toasting her face and the bread for tea at the same time.

"Let Marmee think we are getting things for ourselves, and then surprise her. We must go shopping tomorrow afternoon, Meg. There is so much to do about the play for Christmas night," said Jo, marching up and down with her hands behind her back and her nose in the air.

"I don't mean to act any more after this time. I'm getting too old for such things," observed Meg, who was as much a child as ever about "dressing-up" frolics.

"You won't stop, I know, as long as you can trail around in a white gown with your hair down, and wear gold-paper jewelry. You are the best actress we've got, and there'll be an end of everything if you quit the boards," said Jo. "We ought to rehearse tonight. Come here, Amy, and do the fainting scene, for you are as stiff as a poker in that."

"I can't help it. I never saw anyone faint, and I don't choose to make myself all black and blue, tumbling flat as you do. If I can go down easily, I'll drop. If I can't, I shall fall into a chair and be graceful. I don't care if Hugo does come at me with a pistol," returned Amy, who was not gifted with dramatic power, but was chosen because she was small enough to be borne out shrieking by the villain of the piece.

"Do it this way: Clasp your hands so, and stagger across the room, crying frantically, 'Roderigo! save me! save me!' " And away went Jo with a melodramatic scream which was truly thrilling.

Amy followed, but she poked her hands out stiffly before her, and jerked herself along as if she went by machinery. Her "Ow!" was more suggestive of pins being run into her than of fear and anguish.

Jo gave a despairing groan, and Meg laughed outright, while Beth let her bread burn as she watched the fun.

"It's no use! Do the best you can when the time comes, and if the audience laughs, don't blame me. Come on, Meg."

Then things went smoothly, for Don Pedro defied the world in a speech of two pages without a single break. Hagar, the witch, chanted an awful incantation over her kettleful of simmering toads, with weird effect. Roderigo rent his chains asunder manfully, and Hugo died in agonies of remorse and arsenic, with a wild "Ha! ha!"

"It's the best we've had yet," said Meg, as the dead villain sat up and rubbed his elbows.

"I don't see how you can write and act such splendid things, Jo. You're a regular Shakespeare!" exclaimed Beth, who firmly believed that her sisters were gifted with wonderful genius in all things.

"Not quite," replied Jo modestly. "I do think 'The Witch's Curse, an Operatic Tragedy,' is rather a nice thing; but I'd like to try *Macbeth*, if we only had a trap door for Banquo. I always wanted to do the killing part. 'Is that a dagger that I see before me?' " muttered Jo, rolling her eyes and clutching at the air, as she had seen a famous tragedian do.

"No, it's the toasting fork, with mother's shoe on it instead of the bread. Beth's stage-struck!" cried Meg, and the rehearsal ended in a general burst of laughter.

"Glad to find you so merry, my girls," said a cheery voice at the door, and actors and audience turned to welcome a tall, motherly lady, with a "can-I-help-you" look about her which was truly delightful. She was not elegantly dressed, but a noble-looking woman, and the girls thought the gray cloak and unfashionable bonnet covered the most splendid mother in the world.

"Well, dearies, how have you got on today? There was so much to do, getting the boxes ready to go tomorrow, that I didn't come home to dinner. Has anyone called, Beth? How is your cold, Meg? Jo, you look tired to death. Come and kiss me, baby."

While making the inquiries Mrs. March got her wet things off, her warm slippers on, and sitting down in the easy chair, drew Amy to her lap, preparing to enjoy the happiest hour of her busy day.

The girls flew about trying to make things comfortable, each in her own way. Meg arranged the tea table. Jo brought wood and set chairs, dropping, overturning, and clattering everything she touched. Beth trotted to and fro between parlor and kitchen, quiet and busy; while Amy gave directions to everyone, as she sat with her hands folded.

As they gathered about the table, Mrs. March said, with a particularly happy face, "I've got a treat for you after supper."

A quick, bright smile went around like a streak of sunshine. Beth clapped her hands, regardless of the biscuit she held, and Jo tossed up her napkin, crying, "A letter! a letter! Three cheers for Father!"

"Yes, a nice long letter. He is well, and thinks he shall get through the cold season better than we feared. He sends all sort of loving wishes for Christmas, and an especial message to you girls," said Mrs. March, patting her pockets as if she had a treasure there.

"Hurry and get done! Don't stop to quirk your little finger, and simper over your plate, Amy," cried Jo, choking in her tea, and dropping her bread, butter side down, on the carpet, in her haste to get at the treat.

Beth ate no more, but crept away, to sit in her shadowy corner and brood over the delight to come, till the others were ready.

"I think it was so splendid of Father to go as a chaplain when he was too old to be drafted, and not strong enough for a soldier," said Meg warmly.

"Don't I wish I could go as a drummer, or a nurse, so I could be near him and help him," exclaimed Jo, with a groan.

"It must be very disagreeable to be in a war and sleep in a tent, and eat all sorts of bad-tasting things, and drink out of a tin mug," sighed Amy.

"When will he come home, Marmee?" asked Beth, with a little quiver in her voice.

"Not for many months, dear, unless he is sick. He will stay and do his work faithfully as long as he can, and we won't ask for him back a minute sooner than he can be spared from this terrible war between the North and the South. Now come and hear the letter."

They all drew to the fire, Mother in the big chair with Beth at her feet, Meg and Amy perched on either arm of the chair, and Jo leaning on the back, where no one would see any sign of emotion if the letter should happen to be touching. Very few letters were written in those hard times that were not touching, especially those which fathers sent home. In this one little was said of the hardships endured, the dangers faced, or the homesickness conquered. It was a cheerful, hopeful letter, full of lively descriptions of camp life, marches, and military news. Only at the end did the writer's heart overflow with fatherly love and longing for the little girls at home.

"Give them all my dear love and a kiss. Tell them I think of them by day, pray for them by night, and find my best comfort in their affection at all times. A year seems very long to wait before I see them, but remind them that while we wait we may all work, so that these hard days need not be wasted. I know they will remember all I said to them, that they will be loving children to you, will do their duty faithfully, fight their enemies bravely, and conquer themselves so beautifully that when I come back to them I may be fonder and prouder than ever of my little women."

Everybody sniffed when they came to that part. Jo wasn't ashamed of the great tear that dropped off the end of her nose, and Amy never minded the rumpling of her curls as she hid her face on her Mother's shoulder and sobbed out, "I am a selfish girl! But I'll truly try to be better, so he mayn't be disappointed in me by and by."

"We all will!" cried Meg. "I think too much of my looks, and hate to work, but I won't any more, if I can help it."

"I'll try to be what he loves to call me, a 'little woman,' and not be rough and wild, but do my duty here instead of wanting to be somewhere else," said Jo, thinking that keeping her temper at home was a much harder task than facing a rebel or two down South.

Beth said nothing, but wiped away her tears with the blue army sock, and began to knit with all her might, losing no time in doing the duty that lay nearest her, while she resolved in her quiet little soul to be all that Father hoped to find her when the year brought around the happy coming home.

Mrs. March broke the silence that followed Jo's words by saying in her cheery voice, "Do you remember how you used to play *Pilgrim's Progress* when you were little things? Nothing delighted you more than to have me tie my piece bags on your backs for burdens, give you hats and sticks and rolls of paper, and let you travel through the house from the cellar, which was the City of Destruction, up, up, to the housetop, where you had all the lovely things you could collect to make a Celestial City."

"What fun it was, especially going by the lions, fighting Apollyon, and passing through the Valley where the hobgoblins were!" said Jo.

"I liked the place where the bundles fell off and tumbled downstairs," said Meg.

"My favorite part was when we came out on the flat roof where our flowers and arbors and pretty things were, and all stood and sang for joy up there in the sunshine," said Beth, smiling, as if that pleasant moment had come back to her.

"I don't remember much about it, except that I was afraid of the cellar and the dark entry, and always liked the cake and milk we had up at the top. If I wasn't too old for such things, I'd rather like to play it over again," said Amy, who began to talk of renouncing childish things at the mature age of twelve.

"We never are too old for this, my dear, because it is a play we are all playing àll the time in one way or another. Our burdens are here, our road is before us, and the longing for goodness and happiness is the guide that leads us through many troubles and mistakes to the peace which is a true Celestial City. Now, my little pilgrims, suppose you begin again, not in play, but in earnest, and see how far on you can get before Father comes home."

"Really, Mother? Where are our bundles?" asked Amy, who was a very literal young lady.

"Each of you told what your burden was just now, except Beth. I rather think she hasn't got any," said Mother.

"Yes, I have. Mine is dishes and dusters, and envying girls with nice pianos, and being afraid of people."

Beth's bundle was such a funny one that everybody wanted to laugh; but nobody did, for it would have hurt her feelings very much.

"Let us do it," said Meg thoughtfully. "It is only another name for trying to be good, and the story may help us; for though we do want to be good, it's hard work, and we forget, and don't do our best."

"We were in the Slough of Despond tonight, and Mother came and pulled us out as Help did in the book. We ought to have our roll of directions, like Christian. What shall we do about that?" asked Jo, delighted with the fancy which lent a little romance to the very dull task of doing her duty.

"Look under your pillows Christmas morning, and you will find your guide book," replied Mrs. March.

They talked over the new plan while old Hannah cleared the table. Then out came the four little workbaskets, and the needles flew as the girls made sheets for Aunt March. It was uninteresting sewing, but tonight no one grumbled. They adopted Jo's plan for dividing the long seams into four parts, and calling the quarters Europe, Asia, Africa, and America, and in that way got on capitally, especially when they talked about the different countries as they stitched their way through them.

At nine they stopped work, and sang, as usually, before they went to bed. No one but Beth could get much music out of the old piano; but she had a way of softly touching the yellow keys, and making a pleasant accompaniment to the simple songs. Meg had a voice like a flute, and she and her mother led the little choir. Amy chirped like a cricket, and Jo wandered through the airs at her own sweet will, always coming out at the wrong place with a croak or a quaver.

They had always done this from the time they could lisp "Crinkle, crinkle, 'ittle 'tar," and it had become a household custom, for the mother was a born singer. The first sound in the morning was her voice, as she went about the house singing like a lark; and the last sound at night was the same cheery sound, for the girls never grew too old for the familiar lullaby.

A Merry Christmas

Jo was the first to wake in the gray dawn of Christmas morning. No stockings hung at the fireplace, and for a moment she felt as much disappointed as she did long ago when her little sock fell down because it was so crammed with goodies. Then she remembered her mother's promise, and slipping her hand under her pillow, drew out a little crimson-covered book. She knew it very well, for it was that beautiful old story of the best life ever lived, and Jo felt that it was a true guide book for any pilgrim going the long journey.

Jo woke Meg with a "Merry Christmas," and bade her see what was under her pillow. A green-covered book appeared, with the same picture inside, and a few words written by their mother, which made their one present very precious in their eyes.

Presently Beth and Amy woke, to rummage and find their little books also—one dove-colored, the other blue. They all sat looking and talking while the east grew rosy with the coming day.

In spite of her small vanities, Margaret had a sweet and pious nature which unconsciously influenced her sisters, especially Jo, who loved her very tenderly, and obeyed her because her advice was so gently given.

"Girls," said Meg seriously, looking from the tumbled head beside her to the two little night-capped ones in the room beyond, "Mother wants us to read and love these books, and we must begin at once. We used to be faithful about it; but since Father went away, and all this war trouble unsettled us, we have neglected many things. You can do as you please; but I shall keep my book on the table here, and read a little every morning as soon as I wake, for I know it will do me good, and help me through the day."

Then she opened her new book and began to read. Jo put her arm around her, and leaning cheek to cheek, read also, with the quiet expression so seldom seen on her restless face.

"How good Meg is! Come, Amy, let's do as they do. I'll help you with the hard words, and they'll explain things if we don't understand," whispered Beth, very much impressed by the pretty books and her sisters' example.

"I'm glad mine is blue," said Amy. And then the rooms were very still while the pages were softly turned, and the winter sunshine crept in to touch the bright heads and serious faces with a Christmas greeting.

"Where is Mother?" asked Meg as she and Jo ran down to thank her for their gifts, half an hour later.

"Goodness only knows. Some poor creeter come a-beggin', and your ma went straight off to see what was needed. There never was such a woman for givin' away vittles and drink, clothes and firin'," replied Hannah, who had lived with the family since Meg was born.

"She will be back soon, I think; so fry your cakes, and have everything ready," said Meg, looking over the presents which were collected in a basket and kept under the sofa, ready to be produced at the proper time. "Why, where is Amy's bottle of cologne?" she added, as the little flask did not appear.

"She took it out a minute ago, and went off with it to put a ribbon on it, or some such notion," replied Jo, dancing about the room to take the first stiffness off the new warm slippers.

"How nice my handkerchiefs look, don't they? I marked them all myself," said Beth, looking proudly at the somewhat uneven letters which had cost her such labor.

"Bless the child! She's gone and put 'Mother' on them instead of 'M. March.' How funny!" cried Jo, taking up one.

"Isn't it right? I thought it was better to do it so, because Meg's initials are 'M. M.,' and I don't want anyone to use these but Marmee," said Beth, looking troubled.

"It's all right, dear, and a very pretty idea—quite sensible, too, for no one can ever mistake now. It will please her very much, I know," said Meg, with a frown for Jo and a smile for Beth.

"There's Mother. Hide the basket, quick!" cried Jo, as a door slammed, and steps sounded in the hall.

Amy came in hastily, and looked rather abashed when she saw her sisters all waiting for her.

"Where have you been, and what are you hiding behind you?" asked Meg, surprised to see, by her hood and cloak, that lazy Amy had been out so early.

"Don't laugh at me, Jo! I didn't mean anyone should know till the time came. I only meant to change the little bottle for a big one, and I gave all my money to get it, and I'm truly trying not to be selfish anymore."

As she spoke, Amy showed the handsome flask which replaced the cheap one; and looked so earnest and humble in her little effort to forget herself that Meg hugged her on the spot, and Jo pronounced her "a trump," while Beth ran to the window, and picked her finest rose to ornament the stately bottle.

"You see I felt ashamed of my present, after reading and talking about being good this morning. So I ran around the corner and changed it the minute I was up. I'm so glad, for mine is the handsomest now."

Another bang of the street door sent the basket under the sofa, and the girls to the table, eager for breakfast.

"Merry Christmas, Marmee! Many of them! Thank you for your books. We read some, and mean to every day," they cried, in chorus.

"Merry Christmas, little daughters! I'm glad you began at once, and hope you will keep on. But I want to say one word before we sit down. Not far away from here lies a poor woman, Mrs. Hummel, with a little newborn baby. Six children are huddled into one bed to keep from freezing, for they have no fire. There is nothing to eat over there; and the oldest boy came to tell me they were suffering hunger and cold. My girls, will you give them your breakfast as a Christmas present?"

They were all unusually hungry, having waited nearly an hour, and for a minute no one spoke; but only for a minute, for Jo exclaimed impetuously, "I'm so glad you came before we began!"

"May I go and help carry the things to the poor little children?" asked Beth eagerly.

"I shall take the cream and the muffins," added Amy, heroically giving up the articles she most liked.

Meg was already covering the buckwheats, and piling the bread on a big plate.

"I thought you'd do it," said Mrs. March, smiling as if satisfied. "You all help me, and when we come back we will have bread and milk for breakfast, and make it up at dinnertime."

They were soon ready, and the procession set out. Fortunately it was early, and they went through back streets, so few people saw them, and no one laughed at the queer party.

A poor, bare, miserable room it was, with broken windows, no fire, ragged bedclothes, a sick Mother, wailing baby, and a group of pale, hungry children cuddled under one old quilt, trying to keep warm.

How the big eyes stared and the blue lips smiled as the girls went in!

"Ach, mein Gott! It is good angels come to us!" said the poor woman, crying for joy.

"Funny angels in hoods and mittens," said Jo, and set them laughing.

In a few minutes it really did seem as if kind spirits had been at work there. Hannah, who had carried wood, made a fire, and stopped up the broken panes with old hats and her own cloak. Mrs. March gave the mother tea and gruel, and comforted her with promises of help, while she dressed the little baby as tenderly as if it had been her own. The girls, meantime, spread the table, set the children around the fire, and fed them like so many hungry birds—laughing, talking, and trying to understand the funny broken English.

"Das ist gut!" "Die Engel-kinder!" cried the poor things as they ate and warmed their purple hands at the comfortable blaze.

The girls had never been called angel children before, and thought it very agreeable, especially Jo, who had been considered a "Sancho" ever since she was born. That was a very happy breakfast, though they didn't get any of it; and when they went away, leaving comfort behind, I think there were not in all the city four merrier people than the hungry little girls who gave away their breakfasts and contented themselves with bread and milk on Christmas morning.

"That's loving our neighbor better than ourselves, and I like it," said Meg, as they set out their presents, while their Mother was upstairs collecting clothes for the poor Hummels.

Not a very splendid show, but there was a great deal of love done up in the few little bundles; and the tall vase of red roses, white chrysanthemums, and trailing vines, which stood in the middle, gave quite an elegant air to the table.

"She's coming! Strike up, Beth! Open the door, Amy! Three cheers for Marmee!" cried Jo, prancing about, while Meg went to conduct Mother to the seat of honor.

Beth played her gayest march, Amy threw open the door, and Meg acted as escort with great dignity. Mrs. March was both surprised and touched; and smiled with her eyes full as she examined her presents, and read the little notes which accompanied them. The slippers went on at once, a new handkerchief was slipped into her pocket, well scented with Amy's cologne, the rose was fastened to her bosom, and the nice gloves were pronounced a "perfect fit."

There was a good deal of laughing and kissing and explaining, in the simple loving fashion which makes these home festivals so pleasant at the time, so sweet to remember long afterward.

"Of Courtesy"

by Arthur Guiterman

Good Manners May in Seven Words Be Found:
Forget Yourself and Think of Those Around.

"The Miraculous Pitcher"

by Nathaniel Hawthorne

Here is the mythological version of the first good Samaritans,
told in a rich way by a great author.

Long, long ago, a good man and his wife lived in a little cottage on a hilltop. Their names were Philemon and Baucis. They were old and very poor, and they worked hard to earn their living, but they were happy all day long and they loved one another dearly.

They lived on their hilltop looking after their small garden and their beehives and tending their cow. They seldom had anything more to eat than bread and milk and vegetables, with sometimes a little honey from their beehives, or a few ripe pears or apples from the garden.

They were two of the kindest old people in the world, and would gladly have gone without their dinner any day rather than refuse a slice of bread or a cupful of milk to any hungry traveler who might stop at their cottage.

A beautiful village lay in the valley below the hilltop where the cottage of Philemon and Baucis stood. The valley, shaped like a bowl, was fertile with green meadows, gardens and orchards. But, sad to say, the people living in this pleasant fertile valley were selfish and hard-hearted, with never a thought of pity or kindness for the friendless or needy.

These villagers taught their children to be just as unkind as they were. They kept large fierce dogs, and whenever unfortunate strangers appeared in the village, the dogs would rush out barking and snarling at them. The children, too, were encouraged to run after them pelting them with stones and jeering at their shabby clothes.

What made it even worse was that if the strangers were rich people attended by servants, the villagers would be extra polite and would bow and scrape before them. If the children happened to be rude to these wealthy visitors, they had their ears boxed. As for the dogs, if a single dog dared so much as to growl at anyone who was rich, that dog was beaten and tied up without any supper.

One evening, Philemon and Baucis were sitting on a bench outside their doorway, talking quietly about their garden and enjoying the sunset.

Suddenly they were interrupted by the shouts of children and the angry barking of dogs in the village. The noise grew louder and louder until Philemon and Baucis could hardly hear each other speak.

"I have never heard the dogs bark so savagely," said Baucis.

"Nor the children shout so rudely," answered old Philemon.

They sat shaking their heads sorrowfully as the noise came nearer and nearer until they saw two strangers coming along the road on foot. Both travelers were very plainly dressed and looked as if they had no money for food or a night's lodging. Close behind them came the fierce dogs snarling at their heels and a little farther off ran a crowd of children who screamed shrilly and flung stones at the strangers.

"Good wife," said Philemon to Baucis, "I will go to meet these poor people while you prepare something for them to eat. Perhaps they feel too heavyhearted to climb the hill."

And he hastened forward, saying heartily, "Welcome, strangers! Welcome!"

"Thank you," answered the younger of the two travelers. "Yours is a kind welcome, very different from the one we just got in the village."

Philemon took a good look at him and his companion. The younger of the two strangers was slim and dressed in an odd kind of way. Though the evening was mild, he wore his cloak wrapped tightly about him. He had a cap on with a brim that stuck out over his ears. There was something queer, too, about his shoes, but as it was growing dark, Philemon could not see exactly what they were like.

Another thing struck Philemon. The younger stranger was so wonderfully light and active that it seemed as if his feet sometimes rose from the ground of their own accord and could be kept on the ground only with difficulty. He carried, besides, a staff which was the oddest

Philemon had ever seen. It was made of wood and had a little pair of wings near the tip. Two snakes carved in wood were twisting around the staff and these were so finely made that the old man almost thought he could see them wriggling.

The elder of the two strangers was very tall and walked calmly along. He seemed not to have noticed the barking dogs or the screaming children.

When they reached the cottage, Philemon said, "We are poor folk and haven't much to offer, but all we have is yours."

The strangers sat down on the bench and the younger one dropped his staff on the grass. And then a strange thing happened. The staff seemed to get up by itself and, spreading its little pair of wings, half hopped and half flew to lean itself against the wall of the cottage.

Before Philemon could ask any questions, the elder stranger said, "Was there not a lake long ago that covered this place where the village now stands?"

"Not in my time," said Philemon, "nor in my father's or grand-father's. There have always been meadows and gardens just as there are now and I suppose there always will be."

"That I am not so sure of," answered the stranger. "Since the people of that place have forgotten how to be kind, it might be better perhaps if a lake should be rippling over that village again." He looked sad and stern.

Philemon was sure now that he was not an ordinary wanderer. His clothes were old and shabby. Perhaps he was a learned man who wandered about the world seeking wisdom and knowledge.

Philemon turned to the younger traveler. "What is your name, my friend?" he asked.

"I am called Mercury," he said.

"Does your companion have as strange a name?" asked Philemon.

"You must ask the thunder to tell you," replied Mercury. "No other voice is loud enough."

Philemon did not quite know what to make of this, but the strangers appeared to be so kind and friendly that he began telling them about his good wife, Baucis, and what fine butter and cheese she made. He told them how happy they were in their little cottage and how they hoped that when they died, they might die together. The elder of the travelers listened to all this with a gentle smile on his stern face.

Now Baucis had the supper ready and called her husband to invite their guests to come in. "Had we known you were coming," she said, "my husband and I would have been happy to have gone without our supper, to give you a better one."

"Do not trouble yourself about that," said the elder of the strangers. "A cordial welcome is better than the best food and we were so hungry that whatever you have to offer will be a feast."

Then they all went into the cottage. As they turned into the doorway, that staff of Mercury's that had been leaning against the cottage wall opened its small wings and hopped up the steps and tap-tapped across the floor. It stopped behind the chair where Mercury sat. But Baucis and Philemon did not notice this. They were too busy attending to their guests.

On the table was half a loaf of brown bread and a bit of cheese, a pitcher with some milk, a little honey, and a bunch of purple grapes. Baucis filled two bowls with milk from the pitcher. "What delicious milk, Mother Baucis!" exclaimed Mercury. "May I have more? This has been such a warm day I am very thirsty."

"I am so sorry," said Baucis, "but there are barely a few drops left in the pitcher. If only we hadn't used so much milk for our supper before!"

"Let me see," said Mercury, picking up the pitcher. "Why, there certainly is more milk here." And he poured out a bowlful for himself and another for his companion.

Baucis could hardly believe her eyes.

In a few moments Mercury said, "Your milk is really the most delicious I have ever tasted. I must have just a little more."

As Baucis lifted the pitcher to pour out what she thought would be the very last drop of milk into the stranger's bowl, a wonderful stream of rich, fresh milk fell bubbling into it and overflowed onto the table.

The more Baucis poured, the more milk remained. The pitcher was always filled to the brim.

And so it was with the bread. Though it had been rather dry when Philemon and Baucis had had it for their supper, it was now as fresh and tasty as if it had just come from the oven. Baucis could hardly believe this was the loaf she had baked with her own hands.

Baucis sat down beside Philemon. "Did you ever hear of anything so wonderful?" she whispered.

"No, I never did," answered Philemon. "Perhaps you are imagining all this, my dear."

"Just one more bowl of milk, please," Mercury asked. This time Philemon lifted the pitcher himself and peeped into it. There wasn't a drop in it. Then all at once a little white fountain of milk gushed up from the bottom and soon the pitcher was filled again to its very brim.

In his amazement Philemon nearly dropped the miraculous pitcher. "Who are you?" he cried, gazing wide-eyed at the wonder-working strangers.

"We are your guests and your friends, my good Philemon," replied the elder traveler in his deep voice. "May that pitcher never be empty for yourselves or for any needy wayfarer."

The old people did not like to ask any more questions. They gave their beds to the strangers and they themselves lay down to sleep on the hard kitchen floor. In the morning they rose with the sun to help their guests make ready to continue their journey.

"If the villagers only knew what a pleasure it is to be kind to strangers, they would tie up their dogs and never allow their children to fling another stone," said Philemon.

"It is a sin and a shame for them to behave that way, and I mean to tell them so this very day," declared Baucis firmly.

"I'm afraid," said Mercury, smiling, "that you will find none of them home." And he pointed to the foot of the hill.

The old people looked at the elder traveler. His face had grown very grave and stern. "When men do not feel toward the poorest stranger as if he were a brother," he said in his deep voice, "they do not deserve to remain on Earth."

Philemon and Baucis turned toward the valley where just the evening before they had seen meadows, houses, gardens, and streets. But now there was not a sign of the village—or even of the valley.

"Alas! What has become of our poor neighbors?" asked the kind-hearted old people.

"They are not men and women any longer," answered the elder traveler in a voice like thunder. "Those wicked people of the valley have had their punishment. As for you, good Philemon and Baucis, your reward shall be anything you may wish for."

Philemon and Baucis looked at one another and whispered together for a moment. Then Philemon spoke to the gods. "Our wish, O great gods from High Olympus," the old man said slowly, "is that we may live the rest of our lives together. Neither of us wishes to live without the other."

"So be it," said the elder stranger, who was the god Jupiter. As he spoke, he and his companion vanished from sight like mist in the morning sun.

When Baucis and Philemon turned to go back to their little cottage, it had disappeared. In its place stood a white marble palace with a beautiful park around it. The kind old people lived there for many years, and to every traveler who passed that way they offered a drink from the ever bubbling pitcher.

Baucis and Philemon grew very, very old. Then one summer morning when guests came to visit them, neither Baucis nor Philemon could be found. The guests looked everywhere but it was of no use. Suddenly one of them noticed two large beautiful trees in the garden just in front of the doorway of the palace. One was an oak tree and the other a linden, and their branches were entwined so that they seemed to be embracing one another.

No one could remember having seen them before. While the guests wondered how such fine trees could possibly have grown up in one night, a gentle wind blew up that set the branches stirring.

A mysterious voice whispered from the oak, "I am Philemon." And from the linden came, "I am Baucis." Then the voices seemed to speak together.

Now the people knew that the good couple would live on for many, many years in the lovely trees. They would cast a pleasant shade for the weary traveler who rested under their branches, and they seemed to be forever saying, "Welcome, dear travelers, welcome."

"The Selfish Giant"

by Oscar Wilde

This is simply one of the most exquisite tales ever told.

Every afternoon, as they were coming from school, the children used to go and play in the Giant's garden.

It was a large, lovely garden, with soft green grass. Here and there over the grass stood beautiful flowers like stars, and there were twelve peach trees that in the Springtime broke out into delicate blossoms of pink and pearl and in the Autumn bore rich fruit. The birds sat on the trees and sang so sweetly that the children used to stop their games in order to listen to them. "How happy we are!" they cried to each other.

One day the Giant came back. He had been to visit his friend the Cornish ogre, and had stayed with him for seven years. After the seven years were over he had said all that he had to say, for his conversation was limited, and he determined to return to his own castle. When he arrived he saw the children playing in the garden.

"What are you doing here?" he cried in a very gruff voice, and the children ran away.

"My own garden is my own garden," said the Giant; "anyone can understand that, and I will allow nobody to play in it but myself." So he built a high wall all around it, and put up a notice board.

TRESPASSERS

WILL BE

PROSECUTED

He was a very selfish Giant.

The poor children had now nowhere to play. They tried to play on the road, but the road was very dusty and full of hard stones, and they did not like it. They used to wander around the high wall when their lessons were over, and talk about the beautiful garden inside. "How happy we were there!" they said to each other.

Then the Spring came, and all over the country there were little blossoms and little birds. Only in the garden of the Selfish Giant it was still Winter. The birds did not care to sing in it, as there were no children, and the trees forgot to blossom. Once a beautiful flower put its head out from the grass, but when it saw the notice board it was so sorry for the children that it slipped back into the ground again, and went off to sleep. The only people who were pleased were the Snow and the Frost. "Spring has forgotten this garden," they cried, "so we will live here all the year around." The Snow covered up the grass with her great white cloak, and the Frost painted all the trees silver. Then they invited the North Wind to stay with them, and he came. He was wrapped in furs, and he roared all day about the garden, and blew the chimney pots down. "This is a delightful spot," he said. "We must ask the Hail on a visit." So the Hail came. Every day for three hours he rattled on the roof of the castle till he broke most of the slates, and then he ran around and around the garden as fast as he could go. He was dressed in gray, and his breath was like ice.

"I cannot understand why the Spring is so late in coming," said the Selfish Giant as he sat at the window and looked out at his cold white garden; "I hope there will be a change in the weather."

But the Spring never came, nor the Summer. The Autumn gave golden fruit to every garden, but to the Giant's garden she gave none. "He is too selfish," she said. So it was always Winter there, and the North Wind and the Hail and the Frost and the Snow danced about through the trees.

One morning the Giant was lying awake in the bed when he heard some lovely music. It sounded so sweet to his ears that he thought it must be the King's musicians passing by. It was really only a little linnet singing outside his window, but it was so long since he had heard a bird sing in his garden that it seemed to him to be the most beautiful music in the world. Then the Hail stopped dancing over his head, and the North Wind ceased roaring, and a delicious perfume came to him through the open casement. "I believe the Spring has come at last," said the Giant; and he jumped out of bed and looked out.

What did he see?

He saw a most wonderful sight. Through a little hole in the wall the children had crept in, and they were sitting in the branches of the trees. In every tree that he could see there was a little child. And the trees were so glad to have the children back again that they had covered themselves with blossoms, and were waving their arms gently above the children's heads. The birds were flying about and twittering with delight, and the flowers were looking up through the green grass and laughing. It was a lovely scene, only in one corner it was still winter. It was the farthest corner of the garden, and in it was standing a little boy. He was so small that he could not reach up to the branches of the tree, and he was wandering all around it, crying bitterly. The poor tree was still quite covered with frost and snow, and the North Wind was blowing and roaring above it. "Climb up! little boy," said the Tree, and it bent its branches down as low as it could; but the boy was too tiny.

And the Giant's heart melted as he looked out. "How selfish I have been!" he said; "now I know why the Spring would not come here. I will put that poor little boy on the top of the tree, and then I will knock down the wall, and my garden shall be the children's playground forever and ever." He was really very sorry for what he had done.

So he crept downstairs and opened the front door quite softly, and went out into the garden. But when the children saw him they were so frightened that they all ran away, and the garden became Winter again. Only the little boy did not run, for his eyes were so full of tears that he did not see the Giant coming. And the Giant stole up behind him and took him gently in his hand, and put him up into the tree. And the tree broke at once into blossom, and the birds came and sang on it, and the little boy stretched out his two arms and flung them around the Giant's neck, and kissed him. And the other children, when they saw that the Giant was not wicked any longer, came running back, and with them came the Spring. "It is your garden now, little children," said the Giant, and he took a great ax and knocked down the wall. And when the people were going to market at twelve o'clock they found the Giant playing with the children in the most beautiful garden they had ever seen.

All day long they played, and in the evening they came to the Giant to bid him good-bye.

"But where is your little companion?" he said; "the boy I put into the tree." The Giant loved him the best because he had kissed him.

"We don't know," answered the children; "he has gone away."

"You must tell him to be sure and come here tomorrow," said the Giant. But the children said that they did not know where he lived, and had never seen him before; and the Giant felt very sad.

Every afternoon, when school was over, the children came and played with the Giant. But the little boy whom the Giant loved was never seen again. The Giant was very kind to all the children, yet he longed for his first little friend, and often spoke of him. "How I would like to see him!" he used to say.

Years went by, and the Giant grew very old and feeble. He could not play about anymore, so he sat in a huge armchair and watched the children at their games, and admired his garden. "I have many beautiful flowers," he said; "but the children are the most beautiful flowers of all."

One Winter morning he looked out of his window while he was dressing. He did not hate the Winter now, for he knew that it was merely the Spring asleep, and that the flowers were resting.

Suddenly he rubbed his eyes in wonder and looked and looked. It certainly was a marvelous sight. In the farthest corner of the garden was a tree quite covered with lovely white blossoms. Its branches were all golden, and silver fruit hung down from them, and underneath it stood the little boy he had loved.

Downstairs ran the Giant in great joy, and out into the garden. He hastened across the grass, and came near to the child. And when he came quite close his face grew red with anger, and he said, "Who hath dared to wound thee?" For on the palms of the child's hands were the prints of two nails, and the prints of two nails were on the little feet.

"Who hath dared to wound thee?" cried the Giant; "tell me, that I might take my big sword and slay him."

"Nay!" answered the child; "but these are the wounds of Love."

"Who art thou?" said the Giant, and a strange awe fell on him, and he knelt before the little child.

And the child smiled on the Giant, and said to him, "You let me play once in your garden, today you shall come with me to my garden, which is Paradise."

And when the children ran in that afternoon, they found the Giant lying dead under the tree, all covered with white blossoms.

CHAPTER EIGHT

Reach for the Stars

"Death isn't terrible. The universe is full of love—
and spring comes everywhere—and in death you open
and shut a door. . . ."

"I wish you—could take me right through that
door," whispered Emily [to her father].

"After a while you won't wish that. You have to
learn how kind time is. And life has something for
you—I feel it. Go forward and meet it fearlessly, dear. I
know you don't feel like that just now—but you will
remember my words by-and-by." [Emily's dying father
to Emily]

From *Emily of New Moon*
by L. M. MONTGOMERY

 We were almost finished with dinner when my daughter Gillea offered an idle comment about acid rain; she had made one of those incredible seven-year-old segues from too much vinegar (acid) in the salad dressing to the devastation of our forests due to "acid rain." My husband, who does not sympathize with environmental fretting, dismissed her point. In an exquisite confrontation, she raised her voice and fired back every fact she could remember; she was forceful and passionate, and though only about 50 per cent of what she said made real sense, she was utterly convincing. Touché, sweetie.

Passion, fire in the belly, a sense of righteousness and fearlessness: this is the raw stuff that needs to be challenged and directed but never, ever extinguished in our children's formations. And two childhood experiences: dinner-table arguments and reading time spent with heroes can help a child fight thousands of battles before he even begins junior high school.

Shakespeare warned, "Do not be afraid of greatness," but in our lifetime we struggle with something worse than the fear of it. We very nearly do not believe in greatness anymore. In the past three decades, the notion of individual greatness—real-life heroes—has suffered terribly. The burnout of the 1960s and 1970s made us think narrowly and concretely; when our generation threw idealism out, so also went an animating ennobled world view. We exchanged big dragons for little ones. We settled for rock stars and million-dollar sports figures as hero substitutes. No wonder Americans have a self-esteem problem!

Certainly we should disengage ourselves from this kind of cynicism, but we should also fight to protect our children from it; to do less would be a betrayal. Josiah Royce says, "If I have never been fascinated in childhood by my heroes and the wonders of life, it is harder to fascinate me later with the call of duty." In this regard, you have no better allies than the great works of literature from The *Iliad* to *Robin Hood* and Anne Frank's *Diary of a Young Girl*. An understanding of the history of man's deeds is crucial; it gives your child a connectedness, a context in which to understand his life role. Biographies are enormously inspiring to young children. Girls especially should be exposed to as many well-written works about strong females as you can find.

In every life of a great or accomplished individual, you read about the profound influence of family while growing up. You may or may not agree with their politics, but the Kennedy family spent their dinnertime arguing and discussing power, while Ralph Nader's family table centered its conversations on justice. Margaret Thatcher's family stressed achievement and service to others. These backgrounds reveal a lot about the individuals and what animated their core personalities. Sacrifice and a sense of citizenship and duty are not genetically endowed, they come from the family ethos.

Nurturing your child's core—indeed, his soul—is what great parenting is all about. Greatness is not about celebrity or the grand gesture, it is about a vital, considered existence, a life passionately lived. So many children when asked what they are going to do with their life reply that they "haven't found themselves yet." The individual is not an essence waiting to be discovered, it is an essence waiting to be created.

The literate child, the child who knows of the deep traditions from which he springs, is armed with the triumphs of many men and women. He has seen what tremendous lives have been created. In the pages that follow are just a few.

"The Monster Humbaba"
from Gilgamesh
by Bernarda Bryson

This is from a stunning version of the oldest epic known, first recorded in cuneiform almost three thousand years before Christ. Here Gilgamesh, our hero, takes on his great mission to conquer the monster Humbaba despite the enormous risks. His friend, Enkidu, is not so sure about this venture.

Perfect was the friendship of Gilgamesh and Enkidu. The wild man asked only to be the servant of the King, but Gilgamesh called him "my younger brother," and Ninsun, the queen, looked upon him almost as a son. Everywhere they went together and everywhere they were admired. They took part in feats of strength and daring, winning all prizes and all praise. And in all this Enkidu was content.

Not so Gilgamesh. On one occasion he said to his friend, "Day and night I dream of a great enterprise. Whenever I close my eyes, voices come to me and say: 'Arouse yourself, Gilgamesh, there are great things to be done!' "

Enkidu's mind was full of foreboding.

"You and I, Enkidu, we will climb the mountain and destroy the monster Humbaba!"

Enkidu's eyes filled with tears and he turned away.

"Why should you cry, O Enkidu? Are you not the bravest of men? Are you no longer my friend and brother whom I admire more than anyone at all?"

Enkidu spoke: "I knew the presence of Humbaba even when I was a wild man on the steppes and in the forest. I could hear the sighing of his voice rise over the sound of thunder and high wind. I could hear the beating of his heart and feel the heat of his breath at a distance of five hundred shar. I do not fear beast or mortal man, O Gilgamesh, but Humbaba is not mortal; he is the appointed servant of the gods, the guardian of the wild cows and the cedar forest. Whoever comes near him will grow weak. He will become paralyzed and will fail."

"The monster is an everlasting evil," said Gilgamesh. "It oppresses the people. Day and night it spreads fires and spews its ashes over the town. It is hated by great Shamash, constantly obscuring his face. O Enkidu, shall my life be as an empty wind? What am I, if I turn aside from the things I want to do? I am nothing, only someone waiting for death! But if I do this thing, O Enkidu, even though I should fail, then they will say, 'Gilgamesh died a hero's death! He died defending his people.' I will have made an everlasting name for myself and my life will not be as an empty wind!"

Still Enkidu turned away.

Gilgamesh then called in the armorers, the makers of spears and shields and axes. They cast for him swords of bronze inlaid with silver and gold. They made powerful longbows and arrows tipped with stone, and most beautiful of all, a spear with a handle of lapis lazuli and gold inset with many glittering jewels.

Gilgamesh called Enkidu and laid the weapons before him, hoping to tempt him with their beauty. And still Enkidu said no.

Gilgamesh was downcast. "My brother has grown soft and timid. He no longer loves daring; he has forgotten adventure; I will go alone!"

The elders of Uruk, who had long ago forgotten their hatred of the King, now came to him: "O Gilgamesh, do not undertake this thing. You are young; your heart has carried you away. Settle down, O King; take a bride to yourself; let your life be tranquil!"

Gilgamesh laughed. "Save your wise counsel for my friend, Enkidu. He'll listen. You waste your words on me, good fathers!"

The elders came in secret to Enkidu. "If the King stubbornly insists on doing this thing, risking danger and defying the gods, then Enkidu, you must accompany him!"

"Indeed, you must go ahead of him," a second elder said, "for it is known that whoever first encounters the cedar gate will be the first killed."

"Besides, it is you who knows the way, Enkidu. It is you who have trodden the road!"

"May Shamash stand beside you!"

"May he open the path for you!"

Enkidu went to Gilgamesh. "My head is bowed, O King. I am your brother and your servant; wherever you will go, I will go."

Tears came into the eyes of Gilgamesh; his faith in Enkidu was restored. "Now, my brother, we will go to Ninsun; we will tell our plans and ask her to petition the gods for our success!"

Pale as she was, Ninsun turned more pale. But since she could not dissuade her son, she merely kissed him, giving him her blessing. To Enkidu she said, "Even though you are not my son, O Enkidu, you are like a son to me, and I shall petition the gods for you as for Gilgamesh. But remember, please, that as a man protects his own person, so must he guard the life of his companion!"

The people of Uruk walked with the two friends through the streets admiring their weapons and praising their bold plan: "Praise be to Gilgamesh, who dares everything! Praise be to Enkidu, who will safeguard his companion!" But Harim the priestess mourned, "May your feet carry you back safely to the city, Enkidu!" And thus they set out.

Ninsun dressed herself in her finest garments. She attached the golden pendants to her ears and set the divine tiara upon her head. She anointed herself with perfumes and carried in her hand an incense that would carry its pleasant odors into the sky. Mounting with stately grace to the roof of her palace, she raised her voice to its highest pitch and called out, "O Shamash, listen to me!" Then waiting a little for her voice to reach the ears of the god, she went on: "O Shamash, why have you given my son Gilgamesh such a restless heart? Why have you made him so eager for adventure? Now he has gone up to fight with the indestructible monster Humbaba. Why have you sent him, O Shamash, to wipe out the evil that you abhor? It is all your plan! It is you who have planted the idea in his head! May you not sleep, O Shamash, until Gilgamesh and his friend Enkidu return to Uruk. If they fail, may you never sleep again!"

Ninsun extinguished the small blaze from under the incense and descended from the roof of the palace.

Gilgamesh and Enkidu walked toward the mountain of the cedar forest. At a distance of twenty double-hours they sat down beside the path and ate a small amount of food. At a distance of thirty double-hours, they lay down to sleep, covering themselves with their garments. On the following day they walked a distance of fifty double-hours. Within three days' time, they covered a distance that it would have taken ordinary men some fifteen days to cover. They reached the mountain and saw before them a towering and magnificent gate of cedar wood.

"Here," said Gilgamesh, "we must pour meal upon the earth, for that will gain us the goodwill of the gods; it will persuade them to reveal their purpose in our dreams!"

They poured meal on the ground and lay down to sleep. After some time Gilgamesh wakened his friend. "Enkidu, I have had a dream; it went like this: We were standing in a deep gorge beside a mountain. Compared to it, we were the size of flies! Before our very eyes the mountain collapsed; it fell in a heap!"

"The meaning of that seems very clear," said Enkidu. "It means that Humbaba is the mountain and that he will fall before us!"

They closed their eyes again and slept. After some time, Gilgamesh again awakened his friend. "I've had another dream, Enkidu. I saw the same mountain this time, and again it fell, but it fell on me. However, as I lay struggling, a beautiful personage appeared. He took me by my feet and dragged me out from under the mountain. Now I wonder what this means? Is it that you will rescue me from the monster, or will someone else come along?"

They pondered a little and went back to sleep. Next Enkidu wakened his brother, Gilgamesh. "Has a cold shower passed over us? Did the lightning strike fires, and was there a rain of ashes?"

"The earth is dry and clean," said Gilgamesh. "You must have dreamed!" But since neither of them could understand the meaning of this dream, they fell asleep again, and soon the day came.

They approached the magnificent gate. "Let's open it, Enkidu! Let's be on our way!"

For a last time, Enkidu tried to persuade his friend to turn back.

But since the King would not listen, it was he who went first and placed his hand against the gate to push it open. Enkidu was thrown backward with such violence that he fell to the earth. He rose to his feet. "Gilgamesh, wait! My hand is paralyzed!"

"Put it on my arm, Enkidu! It will take strength from my arm because I am not afraid."

When the two friends threw their weight against the gate, however, it swung inward.

They walked up the mountainside through the sacred trees. And these became closer and thicker until the sky was blotted out. They could hear the giant heartbeat of Humbaba and smell the smoke from his lungs.

To show his daring, Gilgamesh cut one of the cedar trees. The blows of his ax rang out, and from afar the terrible Humbaba heard the sound.

With a crashing of timbers and a rolling of loose stones, Humbaba came down upon them. His face loomed among the treetops, creased and grooved like some ancient rock. The breath he breathed withered the boughs of cedar and set small fires everywhere.

Enkidu's fears now vanished and the two heroes stood side by side as the monster advanced. He loomed over them, his arms swinging out like the masts of a ship. He was almost upon them when suddenly the friends stepped apart. The giant demon lurched through the trees, stumbled, and fell flat. He rose to his feet bellowing like a bull and charged upon Enkidu. But the King brought down his ax on the toe of Humbaba so that he whirled about roaring with pain. He grasped Gilgamesh by his flowing hair, swung him around and around as if to hurl him through the treetops, but now Enkidu saw his giant ribs exposed and he thrust his sword into the monster's side. Liquid fire gushed from the wound and ran in small streams down the mountainside. Gilgamesh fell to the earth and lay still, trying to breathe. But meanwhile Humbaba grasped the horns of Enkidu and began to flail his body against a tree. Surely the wild man would have died, but now Gilgamesh roused himself. He lanced into the air his long spear with its handle of lapis lazuli and gold. The spear caught Humbaba in the throat and remained there poised and glittering among the fires that had ignited everywhere.

The giant loosened his hold on Enkidu; he cried out. The earth reverberated with the sound, and distant mountains shook.

Gilgamesh felt pity in his heart. He withdrew his sword and put down his ax, while the monster Humbaba crept toward him groveling and wailing for help. Now Enkidu perceived that the monster drew in a long breath in order to spew forth his last weapon—the searing fire that would consume the King. He leapt on the demon and with many sword thrusts released the fire, so that it bubbled harmlessly among the stones.

Humbaba was dead; the two heroes, black with soot and dirt, were still alive. They hugged each other; they leapt about; and singing and shouting, they descended the mountainside. Gentle rains fell around them and the land was forever free from the curse of the giant Humbaba.

"Be Like the Bird"

by Victor Hugo

Be like the bird who,
Halting in his flight
On limb too slight,
Feels it give way beneath him,
Yet sings
Knowing he has wings.

"The Legend of William Tell"

Anonymous

This is the story of a man who wanted more than survival under a cranky despotic government. He wanted to be free. One of the great legends about the human spirit, courage, and the love of freedom, William Tell still embodies for us the height of citizenship.

Many years ago the free and sturdy people who lived in the quaint little villages among the mountains of Switzerland were ground down beneath the heel of the emperor of Austria and governed by Austrian bailiffs with the greatest cruelty and oppression. The most devoted patriots of the four forest cantons of Switzerland met, therefore, and determined to rise up and strike for their freedom. One moonlit night of October, 1307, a little band of these faithful men met on the Rutli, a small plateau overlooking the gleaming waters of the beautiful Lake of Lucerne. Beneath the open sky and in sight of the glistening snow-capped peaks that loom up about the lake, the three leaders of that little band clasped hands, raised three fingers to heaven, and solemnly swore to shake off the yoke of Austria.

Among the patriots who took the oath upon Rutli was a young man named William Tell, who was noted far and wide for his skill with the crossbow and arrows. Strong and surefooted was Tell, and he delighted in pursuing the chamois over almost inaccessible heights, or plucking the snowy flower of the edelweiss from the edge of some dangerous precipice. With his wife and two little sons Tell lived in a cozy chalet at Burglen in the canton of Uri.

About this time it came to pass that Gessler, an Austrian bailiff, determined to ascertain by a clever device how many men in Uri were loyal to his master. He therefore set up a pole in the quaint old marketplace of the village of Altdorf. On this pole he hung a hat—the emblem of Austrian power—and he bade a herald proclaim that all who passed must do homage to that hat under penalty of death or lifelong imprisonment. The freemen of Uri were justly incensed when they heard this decree and by common consent avoided passing through the square. Those who must go that way made use of every possible excuse to avoid bending their heads to the hat.

Now, at this time Tell, living in his quiet chalet at some distance from Altdorf, was ignorant of all that had recently happened there. One day he came down to the village bearing his crossbow over his shoulder and holding his little son by his hand. Unconscious alike of pole, hat, and guards he strolled across the square and was greatly surprised when suddenly a throng of soldiers surrounded him and placed him under arrest, crying out that he had defied the orders of Gessler. While Tell was protesting his innocence and striving to make the guards release him, he saw Gessler himself approaching on horseback around one of the quaintly painted houses that bordered the square. Going at once to the bailiff, Tell loudly demanded justice. In the midst of a gathering crowd, the bailiff listened, sneering.

It happened, however, that Gessler had often heard men praise the remarkable skill of Tell as a marksman and he had long desired to see how well the man could shoot. Moreover, he wished to punish Tell for his neglect of the hat in as cruel a way as he could devise, in order to make him an example to the other rebellious inhabitants of Altdorf. Therefore he thundered forth: "You shall be free on one condition only—if you shoot an apple from the head of your son at a distance of one hundred and fifty paces!"

The people who stood about gasped, and a murmur of indignation went up from all the crowd, but so great was the fear that Gessler had inspired in them all that no one dared interfere. Tell himself, a moment before so confident and self-possessed, seemed suddenly to collapse at hearing the bailiff's words. Gessler could have thought of nothing more cruel than thus to insist that the father must shoot at his own little son.

"Place any other punishment upon me!" cried Tell. "What if the boy should move? What if my hand should tremble?"

"Say no more!" cried Gessler. "Shoot!"

Tell was in despair, but the little lad, his face bright with perfect trust, ran and stood against a linden tree at one end of the square.

"Shoot, Father!" he cried. "Shoot! I know you can hit the apple!"

The boy's absolute and fearless confidence determined Tell. Yet he still trembled as he selected two arrows from his quiver, while a soldier took an apple from a fruit vendor who stood near and placed it on the boy's head. One arrow Tell thrust hastily into his belt, the other he carefully adjusted in his crossbow. For a moment his eyes followed the distant line of the snow-capped mountains, resting to gather strength on their calm and quiet peaks. Then his hand grew steady and he took aim.

Twang! went the bow. The arrow whistled through the air. All noise in the square was stilled and everyone held his breath. But lo! the arrow struck the apple squarely in the center, split it, and carried it away! The boy had not moved a hairsbreadth! A mighty shout went up from the crowd! But as Tell was turning away, Gessler pointed to the second arrow which the marksman had stuck in his belt.

"Fellow," cried he, "what did you mean to do with that arrow?"

"Tyrant," was Tell's proud answer, "that second arrow was for you if I had struck my child."

Beside himself with rage at these bold words, Gessler angrily bade his guards to bind Tell fast and convey him down to his waiting boat at Fluhlen, whence he should be carried across the lake and cast into the foulest of dungeons. Friends led the little boy away, but in the train of the tyrant, Tell was marched in chains down to the edge of the Lake of Lucerne. Placed in the boat with fast-bound hands and feet, his useless weapons beside him, Tell despairingly watched the bailiff embark and the shore near Altdorf slowly recede. Soon, however, clouds began to hide the sun and roll down over the pure white peaks. The ripples in the water grew into waves, the sky grew darker and darker. At last there broke a mighty storm on the little boat. Thunder crashed, the water heaved and dashed in angry foam, and lightning streaked from shore to shore. In vain did the Austrians try to guide the boat through the tempest. They were not well enough acquainted with the lake. Then the boatsmen, knowing well that Tell was the most clever steersman in the canton of Uri, began to implore Gessler to let him be unbound in order to help them. In a voice that could scarcely be heard above the shriek of the storm, Gessler cried, "Unloose the prisoner's chains. Let him take the helm!"

Accordingly, Tell was unbound. He seized the helm and the boat went plunging forward. With a strong arm and fearless gaze he directed it straight toward a narrow ledge of rock which forms a natural landing place in the mighty cliffs that at this point rise up sheer from the lake. The water there is seven hundred feet deep, but as the boat drew near and a sudden flash of lightning revealed the spot, Tell suddenly let go of the rudder and with one mighty leap sprang from the pitching boat across the seething waves to the shore. There were angry cries from the lake, but Gessler's boat went drifting off into the darkness again, hurled back, wildly tossing among the waves.

Tell made his way straight around the lake to a spot that Gessler would have to pass on his way home after his landing. There, crouching in the bushes on the steep bank, he waited patiently to see whether the tyrant would escape the storm. At length the bailiff appeared, riding proudly at the head of his troops. Then Tell took his second arrow, the arrow that he had meant should wipe out tyranny from Switzerland. As Gessler passed by, he let the arrow fly, and true to its mark it sped. Gessler fell and with him Austria's reign of tyranny. For the Swiss people, encouraged at hearing what Tell had done, threw off the fear that had bound them, rose up, and Switzerland once more was free.

"Timo and the Princess Vendla"

by James Cloyd Bowman and Margery Bianco

This is a Finnish folktale about a suitor who will go to any length to gain his love.

There was once a proud King who had an only daughter named Vendla. He said, "My daughter shall be different from any other woman in the world. I want her to be wiser than anyone else, in order that she will do me honor."

So he sent for all the most famous teachers, and told them to teach his daughter every language in the world. After Vendla had learned French and English and German and Spanish and Greek and Latin and Chinese and all the other languages as well, so that she could talk to the courtiers of the world each in his own tongue, the King called his heralds and said, "Go forth throughout the whole kingdom, and say to the people: 'The King will give the Princess Vendla in marriage to the man who can speak a new tongue that she does not understand. But let everyone beware, for any man who dares to woo the Princess without speaking a new tongue shall be flung into the Baltic Sea.' "

It happened that there dwelt in the kingdom a young shepherd lad named Timo. Timo was a dreamer who spent his time wandering about the deep wild forest talking to the birds and the beasts. And by talking to them he had learned to understand their language, and they his.

When Timo heard the King's proclamation he laughed.

"It shouldn't be so hard to win the Princess Vendla. There are many tongues in the world. Even the wisest men and women cannot understand them all."

So he started on his way to the King's castle. Before he had gone very far he met a sparrow.

"Where are you going with such a happy face, Timo?" the sparrow chirped.

"I am going to marry the Princess Vendla. Come with me and I'll give you a ride in my fine leather pouch."

"Surely I'll go with you," said the sparrow. And he hopped into the pouch, while Timo went his way.

Presently Timo met a squirrel that sat under his fluffy tail and nibbled at a hazelnut.

"Where are you going with such a happy face, Timo?" chattered the squirrel.

"I am going to marry the learned Princess Vendla."

"How wonderful!"

"Come with me and I'll give you a ride in my fine leather pouch."

The squirrel hopped into the pouch, and Timo strode gaily onward. Soon he met a crow, then a raven, then an owl. Each in turn asked him where he was going, and each in turn hopped into Timo's leather pouch to keep him company. On he strode, and before he knew it he came to the gates of the King's castle.

"Halt! Who are you?" boomed one of the King's soldiers.

"I am Timo, and I've come to woo the fair and learned Princess Vendla."

"Why, you're only a shepherd boy," cried the guard. "What's more, you're a fool as well."

"You must be in a hurry to taste the Baltic Sea!" laughed another of the soldiers.

"You can't even speak your own tongue properly, let alone others," cried a third soldier. "Where you come from, the people all talk as if they had a hot potato in their mouth!"

"You'd better run along back to your flocks while you've still got a chance," added the first soldier.

But Timo stood his ground.

"I come to woo the most beautiful and learned Princess Vendla," he said again. "Open the gates and let me in, for I can speak a dozen tongues that the Princess has never even heard."

"Well, remember we warned you," said the guard as he slowly

opened the gates. "Next thing you know, we'll be giving you a ride to the Baltic Sea!"

Vendla was seated beside her father on a high golden throne. Her hair was decked with jewels and her face was so beautiful that when Timo saw her he fell on his knees.

"Is it true, most beautiful and learned Princess, that you will marry the man who can speak a language you do not understand?"

"This must be a brave man," thought the Princess as she looked at Timo standing there with his leather pouch across his shoulder.

"Yes," she said, "it is true."

"Do you know what will happen to you if you dare to woo the Princess, and fail to speak this unknown tongue you talk about?" thundered the King.

"I would swim a dozen seas bigger than the Baltic for such a Princess," cried Timo as he looked into Vendla's blue eyes.

"Then let us hear this fine language of yours," said the King.

Timo turned to the Princess.

"Listen, most beautiful Princess, and tell me if you understand."

As he spoke Timo thrust his hand into the leather pouch, and touched the sparrow softly. The bird woke up and chirped, "Tshiu, tshiu, tshiu, tshiu! What do you want, Timo?"

"What tongue is that?" Timo asked.

"Truly," said the Princess, "it is a language I have never heard."

"So you don't understand all the tongues in the world!" Timo laughed. He touched the squirrel's tail.

"Rak-rak-rak! Rak-rak! Ka-ka-ka-ka-ka-ka! Leave me alone!" chattered the squirrel.

"Do you understand that?" Timo asked.

"I do not," said the Princess meekly.

Then Timo touched the crow.

"Vaak, vaak, vaak-ak-ak! Don't disturb me!" cawed the crow.

The Princess shook her head in amazement. Neither could she understand the "thiuu, thiuu, thiuu" of the owl, nor the "kronk, kronk, kronk" of the raven.

"It is all most strange," said the Princess. "I cannot understand why my teachers never taught me these words!"

"You see, there are many languages that even the wisest men on earth do not know," said Timo, smiling.

"Vendla, I thought you the most learned woman in the world," cried the King furiously, "yet you let a country lad make fools of us both!"

"O King, this is not so," Timo pleaded. "Vendla is still the most learned lady in the land, for she has admitted her ignorance, and truly the greatest wisdom is to know that one does not know everything."

The Princess was pleased with Timo's honest eyes and his understanding words. She was glad that he had won her hand.

"O King," asked Timo, "will you now keep your bargain with me?"

"Take Vendla for your bride," answered the King. "You have won her, and with her I give you half of my kingdom. May you always be as wise in the future as you have shown yourself today!"

Then the Princess climbed down from her high throne, and Timo took her in his arms and kissed her cheek.

The King proclaimed a glorious holiday with feasting throughout the land, and Timo and Vendla lived happily ever after.

"If"

by Rudyard Kipling

If you can keep your head when all about you
Are losing theirs and blaming it on you;
If you can trust yourself when all men doubt you,
But make allowance for their doubting too;
If you can wait and not be tired by waiting,
Or, being lied about, don't deal in lies,
Or, being hated, don't give way to hating,
And yet don't look too good, nor talk too wise;

If you can dream—and not make dreams your master;
If you can think—and not make thoughts your aim;
If you can meet with triumph and disaster
And treat those two imposters just the same;
If you can bear to hear the truth you've spoken
Twisted by knaves to make a trap for fools,
Or watch the things you gave your life to broken,
And stoop and build 'em up with worn-out tools;

If you can make one heap of all your winnings
And risk it on one turn of pitch-and-toss,
And lose, and start again at your beginnings
And never breathe a word about your loss;
If you can force your heart and nerve and sinew
To serve your turn long after they are gone,
And hold on when there is nothing in you
Except the Will which says to them: "Hold on";

If you can talk with crowds and keep your virtue,
Or walk with kings—nor lose the common touch;
If neither foes nor loving friends can hurt you;

If all men count with you, but none too much;
If you can fill the unforgiving minute
With sixty seconds' worth of distance run—
Yours is the Earth and everything that's in it,
And—which is more—you'll be a Man, my son.

CHAPTER NINE

Count Your Blessings

"Everything gets over, and nothing is ever enough. Except the part you carry with you. It's the same as going on a vacation. Some people spend all their time on a vacation taking pictures so that when they get home they can show their friends evidence that they had a good time. They don't pause and let the vacation enter inside of them and take that home." [Mrs. Basil E. Frankweiler]

From *From the Mixed-up Files of Mrs. Basil E. Frankweiler* by E. L. KONIGSBURG

One afternoon I peeked in on my girls, who were dressed in ballet attire and dancing to Mozart. The sun was streaming into their pink bedroom, and they were lost in the music. After a few minutes, Gillea, the eldest, slowly pulled back from her sisters and began to watch.

"Come here," she said, motioning me to her side. "When I watch them dancing, I get butterflies." She leaned into my ear and whispered, "I think this is the greatest moment of our lives."

It was Gillea's remark that gave me butterflies that afternoon. In a moment of light, a seven-year-old knew: it doesn't get any better than this.

Some people in life know how to poeticize it and drink its grandeur, while others view it as something to get through, daily. If their world view is essentially one of gratitude, families seem to have the capacity to ride out every adventure life deals them. Families who are grateful have a sense of the deepest realities; it is not whether a glass is half empty or half full, it is more that we have a glass at all, a simple clear cylinder created by rock and heated into forms we can use.

This chapter is about blessings. Children who have a basic understanding that the love of parents and family and friends is a grace, and that their bodies and minds and this universe are all occasions for wonder, have the bulk of the wisdom they will need in this life. Gratitude is not a virtue, per se, but an awareness. It is an awareness of God.

A grateful heart enables the child to appreciate his own talents and the talents of others; it allows him to mature from being the centerpiece of a family to an animated member of his world; it engenders a kind of humility that allows him to truly love.

Gratitude also means understanding history, the sacrifice of grandparents and great-grandparents, and the millions of human beings who came before us. It means not taking things for granted.

Parents inculcate the lion's share of their child's sense of gratitude. Children need to have it pointed out to them: money doesn't grow on trees, dinner doesn't just happen, a ride to piano lessons comes at a cost. The parent who teaches his children how things grow or how electricity works—all with a sense of appreciation and interest—develops gratitude. Making a thank-you call or writing a thank-you note helps the child acknowledge that a present was chosen and wrapped and mailed with care.

Life is so hurried and planned these days. The grateful family slows it all down to a lyrical, simple pace that supports a child's natural sense of wonder. Wonder is what we seem to pound out of our children. Clumsy fingers poking a hill of ants, little backs melting into grass watching the clouds on a curved blue sky, a cold nose pressing on a windowpane against the racing raindrops, this is a world view that leaves us as we age—yet at no time in our lives do we see more perfectly.

"John and Barbara's Story"
from Mary Poppins
by P. L. Travers

Reading Mary Poppins *is even more fun than watching the movie. Everything in the English nanny's world is magical, and only children can understand it. This is a little interlude in the book, where the two baby twins, John and Barbara, are resting in the nursery while Mary Poppins busies about, talking with the birds. Mary Poppins is discussing how babies can understand the language of birds until they are one year old—and then they lose their knowledge. We unlearn so much!*

Jane and Michael had gone off to a party, wearing their best clothes and looking, as Ellen the housemaid said when she saw them, "just like a shop window."

All the afternoon the house was very quiet and still, as though it were thinking its own thoughts, or dreaming perhaps.

Down in the kitchen Mrs. Brill was reading the paper with her spectacles perched on her nose. Robertson Ay was sitting in the garden busily doing nothing. Mrs. Banks was on the drawing-room sofa with her feet up. And the house stood very quietly around them all, dreaming its own dreams, or thinking perhaps.

Upstairs in the nursery Mary Poppins was airing the clothes by the fire, and the sunlight poured in at the window, flickering on the white walls, dancing over the cots where the babies were lying.

"I say, move over! You're right in my eyes," said John in a loud voice.

"Sorry!" said the sunlight, "but I can't help it. I've got to get across this room somehow. Orders is orders. I must move from east to west in a day and my way lies through this nursery. Sorry! Shut your eyes and you won't notice me."

The gold shaft of sunlight lengthened across the room. It was obviously moving as quickly as it could in order to oblige John.

"How soft, how sweet you are! I love you," said Barbara, holding out her hands to its shining warmth.

"Good girl," said the sunlight approvingly, and moved up over her cheeks and into her hair with a light, caressing movement. "Do you like the feel of me?" it said, as though it loved being praised.

"Dee-licious!" said Barbara, with a happy sigh.

"Chatter, chatter, chatter! I never heard such a place for chatter. There's always somebody talking in this room," said a shrill voice at the window.

John and Barbara looked up.

It was Starling, who lived on the top of the chimney.

"I like that," said Mary Poppins, turning around quickly. "What about yourself? All day long—yes, and half the night, too, on the roofs and telegraph poles. Roaring and screaming and shouting—you'd talk the leg off a chair, you would. Worse than any sparrer, and that's the truth."

The Starling cocked his head on one side and looked down at her from his perch on the window frame.

"Well," he said, "I have my business to attend to. Consultations, discussions, arguments, bargaining. And that, of course, necessitates a certain amount of—er—quiet conversation—"

"Quiet!" exclaimed John, laughing heartily.

"And I wasn't talking to you, young man," said the Starling, hopping down on the windowsill. "And you needn't talk anyway. I heard you for several hours on end last Saturday week. Goodness. I thought you'd never stop—you kept me awake all night."

"That wasn't talking," said John. "I was—" He paused. "I mean, I had a pain."

"Humph!" said the Starling, and hopped onto the railing of Barbara's cot. He sidled along it until he came to the head of the cot. Then he said in a soft, wheedling voice, "Well, Barbara B., anything for the old fellow today, eh?"

Barbara pulled herself into a sitting position by holding on to one of the bars of her cot.

"There's the other half of my arrowroot biscuit," she said, and held it out in her round, fat fist.

The Starling swooped down, plucked it out of her hand, and flew back to the windowsill. He began nibbling it greedily.

"Thank you!" said Mary Poppins meaningly, but the Starling was too busy eating to notice the rebuke.

"I said 'Thank you!' " said Mary Poppins a little louder.

The Starling looked up.

"Eh—what? Oh, get along, girl, get along. I've no time for such frills and furbelows." And he gobbled up the last of his biscuit.

The room was very quiet.

John, drowsing in the sunlight, put the toes of his right foot into his mouth and ran them along the place where his teeth were just beginning to come through.

"Why do you bother to do that?" said Barbara, in her soft, amused voice that seemed always to be full of laughter. "There's nobody to see you."

"I know," said John, playing a tune on his toes. "But I like to keep in practice. It does so amuse the Grown-ups. Did you notice that Aunt Flossie nearly went mad with delight when I did it yesterday? 'The Darling, the Clever, the Marvel, the Creature!'—didn't you hear her saying all that?" And John threw his foot from him and roared with laughter as he thought of Aunt Flossie.

"She liked my trick, too," said Barbara complacently. "I took off both my socks and she said I was so sweet she would like to eat me. Isn't it funny—when I say I'd like to eat something I really mean it. Biscuits and rusks and the knobs of beds and so on. But Grown-ups never mean what they say, it seems to me. She couldn't have really wanted to eat me, could she?"

"No. It's only the idiotic way they have of talking," said John. "I don't believe I'll ever understand Grown-ups. They all seem so stupid. And even Jane and Michael are stupid sometimes."

"Um," agreed Barbara, thoughtfully pulling off her socks and putting them on again.

"For instance," John went on, "they don't understand a single thing we say. But, worse than that, they don't understand what other things say. Why, only last Monday I heard Jane remark that she wished she knew what language the Wind spoke."

"I know," said Barbara. "It's astonishing. And Michael always insists—haven't you heard him?—that the Starling says 'Wee-Tweee--ee!' He seems not to know that the Starling says nothing of the kind, but speaks exactly the same language as we do. Of course, one doesn't expect Mother and Father to know about it—they don't know anything, though they are such darlings—but you'd think Jane and Michael would—"

"They did once," said Mary Poppins, folding up one of Jane's nightgowns.

"What?" said John and Barbara together in very surprised voices. "Really? You mean they understood the Starling and the Wind and—"

"And what the trees say and the language of the sunlight and the stars—of course they did! Once," said Mary Poppins.

"But—but how is it that they've forgotten it all?" said John, wrinkling up his forehead and trying to understand.

"Aha!" said the Starling knowingly, looking up from the remains of his biscuit. "Wouldn't you like to know?"

"Because they've grown older," explained Mary Poppins. "Barbara, put on your socks at once, please."

"That's a silly reason," said John, looking sternly at her.

"It's the true one, then," Mary Poppins said, tying Barbara's socks firmly around her ankles.

"Well, it's Jane and Michael who are silly," John continued. "I know I shan't forget when I get older."

"Nor I," said Barbara, contentedly sucking her finger.

"Yes, you will," said Mary Poppins firmly.

The Twins sat up and looked at her.

"Huh!" said the Starling contemptuously. "Look at 'em! They think they're the World's Wonders, Little Miracles—I don't think! Of course you'll forget—same as Jane and Michael."

"We won't," said the Twins, looking at the Starling as if they would like to murder him.

The Starling jeered.

"I say you will," he insisted. "It isn't your fault, of course," he added more kindly. "You'll forget because you just can't help it. There never was a human being that remembered after the age of one—at the very latest—except, of course, Her." And he jerked his head over his shoulder at Mary Poppins.

"But why can she remember and not us?" said John.

"A-a-a-h! She's different. She's the Great Exception. Can't go by her," said the Starling, grinning at them both.

John and Barbara were silent.

The Starling went on explaining.

"She's something special, you see. Not in the matter of looks, of course. One of my own day-old chicks is handsomer than Mary P. ever was—"

"Here, you impertinence!" said Mary Poppins crossly, making a dart at him and flicking her apron in his direction. But the Starling leapt aside and flew up to the window frame, whistling wickedly, well out of reach. He jeered and shook his wing feathers at her.

Mary Poppins snorted.

The sunlight moved on through the room, drawing its long gold shaft after it. Outside a light wind had sprung up and was whispering gently to the cherry-trees in the Lane.

"Listen, listen, the wind's talking," said John, tilting his head on one side. "Do you really mean we won't be able to hear that when we're older, Mary Poppins?"

"You'll hear all right," said Mary Poppins, "but you won't understand." At that Barbara began to weep gently. There were tears in John's eyes, too. "Well, it can't be helped. It's how things happen," said Mary Poppins sensibly.

"Look at them, just look at them!" jeered the Starling. "Crying fit to kill themselves! Why, a starling in the egg's got more sense. Look at them!"

For John and Barbara were now crying piteously in their cots—long-drawn sobs of deep unhappiness.

Suddenly the door opened and in came Mrs. Banks.

"I thought I heard the babies," she said. Then she ran to the Twins. "What is it, my darlings? Oh, my Treasures, my Sweets, my Lovebirds, what is it? Why are they crying so, Mary Poppins? They've been so quiet all the afternoon—not a sound out of them. What can be the matter?"

"Getting their teeth, ma'am," said Mary Poppins, deliberately not looking in the direction of the Starling.

"Oh, of course—that must be it," said Mrs. Banks brightly.

"I don't want teeth if they make me forget all the things I like best," wailed John, tossing about in his cot.

"Neither do I," wept Barbara, burying her face in her pillow.

"My poor ones, my pets—it will be all right when the naughty old teeth come through," said Mrs. Banks soothingly, going from one cot to another.

"You don't understand!" roared John furiously. "I don't want teeth."

"It won't be all right, it will be all wrong!" wailed Barbara to her pillow.

"Yes . . . yes. There . . . there. Mother knows . . . Mother understands. It will be all right when the teeth come through," crooned Mrs. Banks tenderly.

A faint noise came from the window. It was the Starling hurriedly swallowing a laugh. Mary Poppins gave him one look. That sobered him, and he continued to regard the scene without the hint of a smile.

Mrs. Banks was patting her children gently, first one and then the other, and murmuring words that were meant to be reassuring. Suddenly John stopped crying. He had very good manners, and he was fond of his mother and remembered what was due to her. It was not her fault, poor woman, that she always said the wrong thing. It was just, he reflected, that she did not understand. So, to show that he forgave her, he turned over on his back, and very dolefully, sniffing back his tears, he picked up his right foot in both hands and ran his toes along his open mouth.

"Clever One, oh, Clever One," said his mother admiringly. He did it again and she was very pleased.

Then Barbara, not to be outdone in courtesy, came out of her pillow and with her tears still wet on her face, sat up and plucked off both her socks.

"Wonderful Girl," said Mrs. Banks proudly, and kissed her.

"There, you see, Mary Poppins! They're quite good again. I can always comfort them. Quite good, quite good," said Mrs. Banks, as though she were singing a lullaby. "And the teeth will soon be through."

"Yes, ma'am," said Mary Poppins quietly; and smiling to the Twins, Mrs. Banks went out and closed the door.

The moment she had disappeared the Starling burst into a peal of rude laughter.

"Excuse me smiling!" he cried. "But really—I can't help it. What a scene! What a scene!"

John took no notice of him. He pushed his face through the bars of his cot and called softly and fiercely to Barbara, "I won't be like the others. I tell you I won't. They," he jerked his head toward the Starling and Mary Poppins, "can say what they like. I'll never forget, never!"

Mary Poppins smiled, a secret, I-know-better-than-you sort of smile, all to herself.

"Nor I," answered Barbara. "Ever."

"Bless my tail-feathers—listen to them!" shrieked the Starling, as he put his wings on his hips and roared with mirth. "As if they could help forgetting! Why, in a month or two—three at the most—they won't even know what my name is—silly cuckoos! Silly, half-grown, featherless cuckoos! Ha! Ha! Ha!" And with another loud peal of laughter he spread his speckled wings and flew out of the window. . . .

It was not very long afterward that the teeth, after much trouble, came through as all teeth must, and the Twins had their first birthday.

The day after the birthday party the Starling, who had been away on holiday at Bournemouth, came back to Number Seventeen, Cherry-Tree Lane.

"Hullo, hullo, hullo! Here we are again!" he screamed joyfully, landing with a little wobble upon the windowsill.

"Well, how's the girl?" he enquired cheekily of Mary Poppins, cocking his little head on one side and regarding her with bright, amused, twinkling eyes.

"None the better for your asking," said Mary Poppins, tossing her head.

The Starling laughed.

"Same old Mary P.," he said. "No change out of you! How are the other ones—the cuckoos?" he asked, and looked across at Barbara's cot.

"Well, Barbarina," he began in his soft, wheedling voice, "anything for the old fellow today?"

"Be-lah-belah-belah-belah!" said Barbara, crooning gently as she continued to eat her arrowroot biscuit.

The Starling, with a start of surprise, hopped a little nearer.

"I said," he repeated more distinctly, "is there anything for the old fellow today, Barbie dear?"

"Ba-loo—ba-loo—ba-loo," murmured Barbara, staring at the ceiling as she swallowed the last sweet crumb.

The Starling stared at her.

"Ha!" he said suddenly, and turned and looked enquiringly at Mary Poppins. Her quiet glance met his in a long look.

Then with a darting movement the Starling flew over to John's cot and alighted on the rail. John had a large woolly lamb hugged close in his arms.

"What's my name? What's my name? What's my name?" cried the Starling in a shrill, anxious voice.

"Er-umph!" said John, opening his mouth and putting the leg of the woolly lamb into it.

With a little shake of the head the Starling turned away.

"So—it's happened," he said quietly to Mary Poppins.

She nodded.

The Starling gazed dejectedly for a moment at the Twins. Then he shrugged his speckled shoulders.

"Oh, well—I knew it would. Always told 'em so. But they

wouldn't believe it." He remained silent for a little while, staring into the cots. Then he shook himself vigorously.

"Well, well. I must be off. Back to my chimney. It will need a spring cleaning. I'll be bound." He flew to the windowsill and paused, looking back over his shoulder.

"It'll seem funny without them, though. Always liked talking to them—so I did. I shall miss them."

He brushed his wing quickly across his eyes.

"Crying?" jeered Mary Poppins. The Starling drew himself up.

"Crying? Certainly not. I have—er—a slight cold caught on my return journey—that's all. Yes, a slight cold. Nothing serious." He darted up to the windowpane, brushed down his breast-feathers with his beak and then, "Cheerio!" he said perkily and spread his wings and was gone. . . .

"The Golden Touch"

by Nathaniel Hawthorne

This is probably the most obvious and wonderful tale ever told about one who learned to count his blessings the hard way.

Once upon a time there lived a very rich King whose name was Midas. He was fonder of gold than of anything else in the whole world. But he loved dearly, also, his little daughter who played so merrily around the palace.

The more Midas loved his daughter, the more he wished to be rich for her sake. This foolish man thought that the best thing he could do for his child was to leave her the biggest pile of glittering gold that had ever been heaped together since the world began. So he gave himself up to dreams of gold.

When his little daughter ran to him with her hands full of buttercups and dandelions, he used to say, "Ah, child, if only these flowers had been made of real gold, they would have been worth gathering!"

He had been fond of gardening once, but now if he looked at his roses at all, it was only to calculate how much the garden would be worth if each rose petal were a thin plate of gold. At length he could hardly bear to see or touch anything that was not made of gold.

He made it his custom, therefore, to spend a large part of each day in a dreary basement dungeon with his bags of golden coin, bars of gold, and vases and statues, all of gold. Sometimes he would carry a boxful of gold dust from the dark corner where it lay and he would look at the shiny heap by the light that came from a tiny window.

To Midas's greedy eyes there never seemed to be half enough. He was quite discontented. "How happy I would be," he said one day, "if only the whole world were made of gold and if it all belonged to me!"

Just then a shadow fell over his gold. Midas looked up with a start to see a young man with a cheerful, rosy face standing in the narrow strip of sunlight that came through the window. Midas was sure he had carefully locked the door before he opened his treasures, so he knew his visitor must be other than mortal to get into the room.

The stranger seemed so friendly and pleasant that Midas felt he must surely have come to do him a favor.

"You are a rich man, friend Midas," said the visitor. "I doubt if any other room in this whole world has as much gold in it as this."

"I've done fairly well," said Midas in a discontented voice. "But I wish it were much more. No one lifetime is long enough, though. If only I could live for a thousand years, then I might become really rich."

"What?" exclaimed the stranger. "What would satisfy you?"

Midas looked at his visitor for a moment, and then said, "I am tired of having to take so much trouble to get money. I wish everything I touched might turn to gold."

The stranger smiled, and his smile seemed to fill the room like a flood of sunshine.

"The golden touch!" he exclaimed. "But are you quite sure, Midas, that this would make you happy?"

"Quite sure," said Midas. "I ask nothing more to make me perfectly happy."

"Be it as you wish, then," said the stranger. "From tomorrow at sunrise you will have your desire—everything you touch will be changed to gold."

The figure of the stranger grew brighter and brighter so that Midas had to close his eyes. When he opened them again, he saw only one yellow sunbeam in the room, and all around him the glittering precious gold he had spent his life in hoarding up.

Midas could scarcely sleep that night. How he longed for the dawn! As soon as the night began to fade, he reached out eagerly and touched a chair by his bed. When he saw that nothing happened, he nearly cried. The chair remained just as it was. The stranger had failed him, thought Midas. Or had the whole thing been only a dream? His spirits sank.

But just then the sun rose. Its first rays fell on the brocaded cover of his bed, which gleamed in the golden rays.

Midas sat up and looked more closely. To his delight he saw that the bedcovers on which his hands rested had become a cloth of purest and brightest gold. The golden touch had come to King Midas with the first sunbeam!

Midas leapt up in a frenzy of joy and ran about touching everything. He caught hold of the bedpost. Instantly it became a golden pillar. He pulled aside the window curtain and the tassel he pulled it by became a heavy mass of gold! He picked up a book from a table, and at first touch it became a bundle of gold pages with nothing to read on them. His clothes became magnificent robes of gold cloth.

Midas had to admit that all these golden things were somewhat heavy. Nevertheless he was delighted with his good fortune. He took his spectacles from his pocket and put them on, so that he might see more distinctly what he was about. To his surprise he could not see through the spectacles at all. The clear glass had turned to gold, and though they were worth a great deal of money, they were useless as spectacles.

Midas found this inconvenient, but surely, he thought, the golden touch was worth the sacrifice of a pair of spectacles. His spirits rose as he went down the palace stairs and saw the railing become a bar of shining gold as he rested his hand on it!

The garden was very lovely. In the old days Midas had been fond of flowers and had spared no effort in getting rare trees and plants to make his garden even more beautiful. But since he had become so fond of gold, he had lost all pleasure in his garden. He did not even see how lovely it was this morning.

He was thinking only of the wonderful gift the stranger had granted him and he was sure he could make the garden of far more value than it had ever been. So he went from bush to bush, touching the flowers. And the beautiful colors faded from them and the petals became stiff glittering flakes of gold—gold glistening so brightly in the sunshine that Midas had to shade his eyes from the glare of them.

However, he was quite satisfied with the morning's work and went back to the palace feeling very happy and with a hearty appetite for breakfast.

Just then he heard his little daughter sobbing as if her heart would break. "Look, Father," she said as she came running toward him holding out one of the golden roses. "All the beautiful blossoms that smelled so sweetly are spoiled. They have grown stiff and yellow and ugly, and they have no fragrance at all. What can be the matter?" And she cried bitterly.

Midas was ashamed to confess that he had caused her unhappiness, so he said, "Pooh, my dear, don't cry about it. Sit down and eat your bread and milk."

They sat down at the table. The King was very hungry and poured himself a cup of coffee. But the moment he lifted the cup to his lips the coffee turned to molten gold and then hardened into a solid lump.

"Oh, dear me!" exclaimed the King, rather surprised.

"What's the matter, Father?" asked his little daughter.

"Nothing, child, nothing," Midas answered. "Eat your bread and milk."

Then he looked at the nice little fish on his plate, and gently touched its tail with his finger. It was immediately changed into gold.

He took one of the smoking hot cakes and had scarcely broken it when the white flour turned into golden crumbs that gleamed like grains of hard sea sand.

"I do not see how I am going to get any breakfast," he exclaimed peevishly. And he looked with envy at his little daughter who had dried her tears and was eating her bread and milk eagerly. "I wonder whether it will be the same at dinner," he thought, "and if so, how am I going to live if all my food is turned to gold?"

Midas began to grow very anxious and to think about many things that he had never thought of before. Here was the richest breakfast that could be set before a King, and yet there was nothing he could eat! The poorest laborer sitting down to a crust of bread and cup of water was far better off than King Midas, whose delicate food was really worth its weight in gold.

He began to wonder whether, after all, gold was the only good thing in the world. Yet the glitter of the yellow metal so fascinated him that he would still have refused to give up the golden touch just for some breakfast. But he was so hungry that he could not help groaning.

His little daughter had noticed that her father ate nothing, and at first she sat still, gazing at him and trying to find out what it was that troubled him. Then she got down from her chair, and ran with outstretched arms to her father.

Midas bent down and kissed her. As he did so, he suddenly knew that his child's love was a thousand times more precious than all the gold he had gained since the stranger had visited him. "My precious, precious little girl!" he cried.

But there was no answer. Alas, what had he done? The moment his lips had touched his child's forehead, her sweet rosy face, so full of love and happiness, hardened and became a glittering yellow. Her beautiful brown curls hung like golden wires around her head. And her soft tender little figure grew stiff in his arms.

It had always been a favorite saying of Midas that his little girl was worth her weight in gold to him.

Midas began to wring his hands. He wished he were the poorest man in the world if the loss of all his wealth could bring back the flush of life and color to his dear child's face.

In his grief and despair, he suddenly saw a stranger standing near the door.

"Well, friend Midas," said the stranger, "pray how are you enjoying your new power?"

Midas shook his head. "I am very miserable," he replied.

"Very miserable, are you?" exclaimed the stranger. "How does that happen?"

"Gold is not everything," answered Midas, "and I have lost all that my heart really cared for."

"Ah! So you have made some discoveries since yesterday? Tell me truly, which of these things do you really think is worth more—a cup of clear cold water and a crust of bread, or the power of turning everything you touch into gold? Your own little girl, alive and loving, or the statue of solid gold your child has now become?"

"Oh, my little daughter, my dear child!" sobbed Midas, wringing his hands. "I would not have given that small dimple in her chin for the power of changing this whole big Earth into gold. And I would give all I own for a cup of cold water and a crust of bread."

"You are wiser than you were, King Midas," said the stranger. "Tell me, now, do you really wish to get rid of your fatal gift?"

"Oh, yes! exclaimed Midas. "It is hateful to me."

"Go, then," said the stranger, "and plunge into the river that flows at the bottom of your garden. Take a pitcher of that same water and sprinkle it over anything you wish to change back again from gold to its former substance."

King Midas bowed low. When he lifted his head the stranger was gone.

Midas lost no time in snatching up a big earthen pitcher. Immediately it turned to gold. Then he ran toward the river and plunged in without waiting even to take off his royal shoes.

"How delightful!" he said, as he came out with his hair dripping.

Then he dipped the pitcher into the water. How happy he was to see it change from gold into the same earthen pitcher it had been five minutes ago, before he had touched it!

Now he also began to feel a change within himself. A cold heavy weight seemed to have lifted from his heart, and he felt light and happy and human once more. Maybe his heart had been changing into gold, too, and had now softened again and become gentle.

Midas saw a violet growing by the river bank. He touched it and was overjoyed to find that the delicate flower kept its purple hue instead of turning to solid gold.

He hurried back to the palace with his pitcher of water and the first thing he did was to sprinkle it by handfuls over the stiff golden figure of his daughter. At once the rosy color came back to her cheeks and she began to sneeze and cough. And how amazed the little girl was to find herself dripping wet and her father throwing water over her!

You see, she did not know she had been a little golden statue, for she could not remember anything from the moment when she ran with outstretched arms to comfort her poor father.

The King then led his little girl into the garden, where he sprinkled all the rest of the water over the rose bushes and the grass and the trees. In a moment they were blooming as freshly as ever, and the air was filled with the scent of flowers.

There were only two things left which kept on reminding King Midas of the stranger's fatal gift. One was that from then on the sands at the bottom of the river always sparkled like gold. The other was that his daughter's curls were no longer brown. They had a golden tinge that had not been there before the King had received the fatal gift of the golden touch and his kiss had changed the precious curls into gold. These two things served to remind King Midas, as long as he lived, that nothing could be worse than the curse of gold.

"The Foolish Man"

by Virginia Tashjian

Only the fool doesn't count the blessings that stare him in the face. A wise Armenian folktale you will appreciate.

Once there was and was not in ancient Armenia a poor man who worked and toiled hard from morn till night, but nevertheless remained poor.

Finally one day he became so discouraged that he decided to go in search of God in order to ask Him how long he must endure such poverty—and to beg of Him a favor.

On his way, the man met a wolf.

"Good day, brother man," asked the wolf. "Where are you bound in such a hurry?"

"I go in search of God," replied the man. "I have a complaint to lodge with Him."

"Well," said the wolf, "would you do me a kindness? When you find God, will you complain to Him for me, too? Tell Him you met a half-starved wolf who searches the woods and fields for food from morning till night—and though he works hard and long, still finds nothing to eat. Ask God why He does not provide for wolves, since He created them?"

"I will tell Him of your complaint," agreed the poor man, and continued on his way.

As he hurried over the hills and through the valleys, he chanced to meet a beautiful maid.

"Where do you go in such a hurry, my brother?" asked the maid.

"I go in search of God," replied the man.

"Oh, kind friend, when you find God, would you ask Him something for me? Tell Him you met a maid on your way. Tell Him she is young and fair and very rich—but very unhappy. Ask God why she

266

cannot know happiness. What will become of her? Ask God why He will not help her to be happy."

"I will tell Him of your trouble," promised the poor man, and continued on his way.

Soon he met a tree which seemed all dried up and dying even though it grew by the side of a river.

"Where do you go in such a hurry, O traveler?" called the dry tree.

"I go in search of God," answered the man. "I have a complaint to lodge with Him."

"Wait a moment, O traveler," begged the tree. "I, too, have a question for God.

"Please ask Him why I am dry both in summer and winter. Though I live by this wet river, my leaves do not turn green. Ask God how long I must suffer. Ask Him that for me, good friend," said the tree.

The man listened to the tree's complaint, promised to tell God, and continued once again upon his way.

Finally, the poor man reached the end of his journey. He found God seated beneath the ledge of a cliff.

"Good day," said the man as he approached God.

"Welcome, traveler," God returned his greeting. "Why have you journeyed so far? What is your trouble?"

"Well, I want to know why there is injustice in the world. Is it fair that I toil and labor from morn till night—and yet never seem to earn enough for a full stomach, while many who do not work half as hard as I live and eat as rich men do?"

"Go then," replied God. "I present you the Gift of Luck. Go find it and enjoy it to the end of your days."

"I have yet another complaint, my Lord," continued the man—and he proceeded to list the complaints and requests of the starved wolf, the beautiful maid, and the parched tree.

God gave appropriate answers to each of the three complaints, whereupon the poor man thanked Him and started on his way homeward.

Soon he came upon the dry, parched tree.

"What message did God have for me?" asked the tree.

"He said that beneath your trunk there lies a pot of gold which prevents the water from seeping up your trunk to your leaves. God said your branches will never turn green until the pot of gold is removed."

"Well, what are you waiting for, foolish man!" exclaimed the tree. "Dig up that pot of gold. It will make you rich—and permit me to turn green and live again!"

"Oh, no," protested the man. "I have no time to dig up a pot of gold. God has given me the Gift of Luck. I must hurry and search for it." And he hurried on his way.

Presently, he met the beautiful maid who was waiting for him. "Oh, kind friend, what message did God have for me?"

"God said that you will soon meet a kind man who will prove to be a good life's companion to you. No longer will you be lonely. Happiness and contentment will come to you," reported the poor man.

"In that case, what are you waiting for, foolish man?" exclaimed the maid. "Why don't you stay here and be my life's companion?"

"Oh, no! I have no time to stay with you. God has given me the Gift of Luck. I must hurry and search for it." And the man hurried on his way.

Some distance away, the starving wolf impatiently awaited the man's coming, and hailed him with a shout.

"Well, what did God say? What message did He send to me?"

"Brother wolf, so many things have happened since I saw you last," said the man. "I hardly know where to begin. On my way to seek God, I met a beautiful maid who begged me to ask God the reason for her unhappiness. And I met a parched tree who wanted God to explain the dryness of its branches even though it stood by a wet river.

"I told God about these matters. He bade me tell the maid to seek a life's companion in order to find happiness. He bade me warn the tree about a pot of gold buried near its trunk which must be removed before the branches can receive nourishment from the earth.

"On my return, I brought God's answers to the maid and to the tree. The maid asked me to stay and be her life's companion, while the tree asked me to dig up the pot of gold.

"Of course, I had to refuse both since God gave me the Gift of Luck—and I must hurry along to search for it!"

"Ahhh, brother man, and what was God's reply to me?" asked the starving wolf.

"As for you," replied the man, "God said that you would remain hungry until you met a silly and foolish man whom you could eat up. Only then, said God, would your hunger be satisfied."

"Hmmmmmm," mused the wolf, "where in the world will I find a man more silly and stupid than you?"

And he ate up the foolish man.

"The Tiger"

by William Blake

Tiger! Tiger! burning bright
In the forests of the night,
What immortal hand or eye
Could frame thy fearful symmetry?

In what distant deeps or skies
Burnt the fire of thine eyes?
On what wings dare he aspire?
What the hand dare seize the fire?

And what shoulder, and what art,
Could twist the sinews of thy heart?
And when thy heart began to beat,
What dread hand? and what dread feet?

What the hammer? What the chain?
In what furnace was thy brain?
What the anvil? What dread grasp
Dare its deadly terrors clasp?

When the stars threw down their spears,
And watered heaven with their tears,
Did He smile His work to see?
Did He who made the Lamb make thee?

Tiger! Tiger! burning bright
In the forests of the night,
What immortal hand or eye
Dare frame thy fearful symmetry?

From "Song of Myself" [Sec. 31]
from Leaves of Grass
by Walt Whitman

I believe a leaf of grass is no less than the
    journey-work of the stars,
And the pismire is equally perfect, and a grain of
    sand, and the egg of the wren,
And the tree-toad is a chef-d'oeuvre for the
    highest,
And the running blackberry would adorn the parlors
    of heaven,
And the narrowest hinge in my hand puts to scorn
    all machinery,
And the cow crunching with depressed head surpasses
    any statue,
And a mouse is miracle enough to stagger
    sextillions of infidels.

"Home Folks"
from The Prairie Town Boy
by Carl Sandburg

This is from a wonderful autobiography; I hope this sliver of it gets you started on the entire book. Here Mr. Sandburg's appreciation of his parents and their migration to America is depicted in a straightforward and powerful excerpt.

Of the house where I was born I remember nothing—a three-room frame house on Third Street, the second house east of the Chicago, Burlington & Quincy Railroad tracks, in Galesburg, Illinois. The date was January 6, 1878, a little after midnight. The first baby, some three years earlier, was my sister Mary. They wanted a boy. I was a welcome man-child.

Mary once pointed to the cradle in later years and said, "When they took me out they put him in." The cradle stood on three legs at each end, and Mother told Mary that Father had made it. A year and a half later they took me out to put Mart in.

I was born on a cornhusk mattress. Until I was past ten or more years, when we became a family of nine, the mattresses were bedticking filled with cornhusks. As we all slept well on cornhusks and never knew the feel of feather beds till far later years, we were in favor of what we had. Of the slats on which the mattress rested, we sometimes murmured. One would break, then another, till finally the mattress crashed to the floor—and we were suspicious of the new slats.

We moved to another three-room one-story house, on the north side of South Street, three doors west of Pearl. Here I wore dresses and watched my father spade a garden and plant and dig potatoes and carrots. I liked the feel of potatoes and carrots as my fingers brushed the black loam off them and I threw them into baskets. Here we had the mare Dolly—a small bay, old, fat, and slow—kept in a shed at the end of the lot. Dolly pulled us in a four-wheeled, two-seater wagon out from the town streets and houses to where we saw for the first time the open country, rolling prairie and timber, miles of zigzag rail fences, fields of corn and oats, cows, sheep, and horses feeding in pastures. Grazing animals in the open had wonder for me.

We were regulars at Swedish Lutheran Church services, though about once a month of a Sunday morning Father would throw the harness on old Dolly and the word was, "We are going to the Kranses." Out seven miles near a small coal mine crossroads with a post office named Soperville, on a thirty-acre farm, lived John and his wife Lena Krans. Lena was a cousin of my mother. Those four Swedish-born Americans had warm kinship. Their faces lighted on seeing each other, and their talk ran warm and pleasant. They were all strong for work, liked it, and talked it in those years of their thirties. The Swedish language was hurled back and forth, too swift for us children to be sure what they were saying. But when they talked of the steerage trip from Sweden, six to ten weeks on a sailing ship, their food only the black bread and cheese and baloney they brought along, we knew it was rugged going. Often we heard from Father and Mother, "In the old country we had white bread only at Easter and Christmas. Here in America we have white bread every day in the year!"

The Kranses were the nearest kinfolk we had in America except for the Holmes family in Galesburg. When John and Lena Krans bought their farm in the early 1870s, they worked from daylight to dark eight or nine months of the year till at last the mortgages were paid off. They had help from neighbors in getting in their crops and in turn helped the neighbors. The Kranses became part of the land they owned. Their feet wore paths that didn't change over the years—in the cow pasture with a small creek winding over it, the corn and oat fields, the vegetable garden, the potato patch. John Krans was a landsman, his thoughts never far from his land, the animals, the crops. He could talk about *hastarna*, meaning "horses," so to my mind he seemed part horse.

He was a medium-size man but he had a loose, easy way of carrying his shoulders with his head flung back so he gave the impression of being a big man. His eyes had a gleam and his lips had a smile you could see through the beard. Even amid the four walls of a room his head, hair, and beard seemed to be in a high wind. When I sat on his knee and ran my five-year-old hand around his beard, he called me *min lille goose* ("my little boy") and there was a ripple of laughter and love in it. He read his Bible and sometimes a newspaper, though most often he liked to read the land and the sky, the ways of horses and corn. He wasn't an arguing man except that with a plow he could argue against stubborn land and with strong hands on leather reins he could argue with runaway horses.

Not often on Sunday did he miss hitching a horse to a light wagon and taking the family to the Lutheran church a mile or two away. I doubt whether he ever listened to a preacher who had less fear and more faith than he had. I have sometimes thought that John Krans pictured God as a Farmer whose chores were endless and inconceivable, that in this world and in worlds beyond God planted and tended and reaped His crops in mysterious ways past human understanding.

The Kranses had a wooden barn with a dirt floor and three horses and four cows that were driven to and from the nearby pasture night and morning. Here we saw hands at udders and milk steaming into pails. The pails were carried up a slope to the house thirty yards away, where the cellar had a clean, hard dirt floor and plank shelves with a long line of crocks into which the milk was poured. We saw the yellow cream at the top of the crocks and once saw cream churned into butter. Here for the first time we drank milk from cows we saw give the milk and ate fried eggs having seen the hens that laid the eggs.

When I was about four we moved two blocks over to Berrien Street and a ten-room house with a roomy third-story garret running the length of the house and a four-room cellar that had floors in the two front rooms. A two-compartment privy had a henhouse back of it. The lot was three times the size of the South Street place and had a big garden with several gooseberry bushes, a front yard with five tall soft-maple trees, a picket fence, a brick sidewalk, and a ditch in front. It was really two houses and lots. Two sign numbers said we lived at 622 and 624 East Berrien Street. Here the emigrant Swede August Sandburg set himself up, with due humility and constant anxiety, as a landlord. The two east rooms of the first floor, along with the two cellar rooms under them, were rented to different families across the years, never vacant for more than a day or two. And the large upstairs east rooms always had a renter.

My father had never learned to write. His schooling had only taught him to read when his father and mother died in Sweden and he went to work as a chore boy in a distillery. He became a teamster at the distillery and laid by enough money for steerage passage to America. Arriving in New York, Swedes who had kinfolk at Herkimer, New York, sent him to a job in a cheese factory there. After a few months at cheese-making he read a letter from his cousin in Galesburg, Illinois, Magnus Holmes, who wrote that the chances were all good out there. Magnus Holmes had arrived by rail in 1854, the first year the C.B.&Q. reached Galesburg, and joined a gang that built a bridge over the Rock River. He was nineteen. Had he stayed two years longer in Sweden he would have had to serve two years in the Swedish army. His father had spent all his years after he was twenty-one in the Swedish army, till he was retired. And Magnus Holmes had seen army life close up, didn't want to be a soldier, and at nineteen skipped Sweden, took steerage passage for New York on a sailing vessel that buffeted stormy seas for ten weeks and, blown off its course, landed at Quebec.

He reached Albany, took the Erie Canal to Buffalo, and railroads to Chicago and Galesburg. There in Galesburg he kept his name of Magnus and changed Holm to Holmes because Holm sounded Swedish and Holmes sounded English. He worked with a railroad construction gang out of Hannibal, Missouri. At a Methodist camp meeting he fell in love with a Swedish girl, a housemaid living with a family that kept slaves. She moved from Hannibal to Galesburg, and Holmes used to call on her when she worked at the Ladies' Dormitory of Lombard College and he had a job in the Q. blacksmith shop forging and hammering bolts. He was interested that she was not merely good-looking and handy as a cook but that she owned a book she was reading, a translation of Faust. They were married.

They went to the Knox College campus the afternoon of October 7, 1858, and stood for three hours in a cold northwest wind, in a crowd of twenty thousand, listening to Abraham Lincoln and Stephen Douglas debate. Magnus Holmes voted for Lincoln, but refused to answer Lincoln's call for troops because he hated war and had a conscience about it. So because Holmes hated military service and left Sweden early, to end up at work in a C.B.&Q. Railroad shop, he was there to advise a newcomer cousin to come out West and get a job. The first job my father had was on the Q. Railroad with a construction gang at a dollar a day. They lived in bunk cars, cooked their own meals, did their own washing, worked six days a week, ten hours a day.

My mother—young Clara Mathilda Anderson who married my father—told of her mother dying early and her father marrying again. Her mother was a gooseherd in Appuna, and she helped her mother in working with geese and ducks in two ponds on their place. When her stepmother came, "We didn't get along so good. I left Sweden because she was so different from my mother. Letters came from Swedes in America about how things were better there and I managed to save the money to come over and do my best. There was a chum, like you say, a good friend of mine, came with me and I wasn't lonely."

How my father and mother happened to meet I heard only from my mother. I had asked her how they came to marry and she said, "I was working in a hotel in Bushnell [Illinois], making the beds and helping in the kitchen. He came to Bushnell with the railroad gang. He came to the hotel and saw me and we talked and he said he wanted to marry me. I saw it was my chance and soon went to Galesburg and the Reverend Lindahl married us and we started housekeeping." A smile spread over her face half bashful and a bright light came to her eyes as she said, "I saw it was my chance." She was saying this years after the wedding and there had been hard work always, tough luck at times, and she had not one regret that she had jumped at her "chance" when she saw it.

My father's hair was straight and black and his eyes, black with a hint of brown, were deep-set in the bone, the skin around them crinkling with his smile or laugh. He was below medium height, weighed about a hundred and forty-eight, was well muscled, and the skin of his chest showed a pale white against the grime when his collar was turned down. No sports interested him, though he did make a genuine sport of work that needed to be done. He was at the C.B.&Q. blacksmith shop, rated as "a helper," the year round, with no vacations. He left home at six forty-five in the morning, walked to arrive at the Q. shop at seven, and was never late. He mauled away at engine and car parts till twelve, then walked home, ate the noon "dinner," walked back to the shop to begin work at one and go on till the six o'clock whistle, when he stood sledge alongside anvil and walked home.

It would take him ten or fifteen minutes to get the grime off hands, face, and neck before supper. He poured the cistern rainwater from a pail into a tin basin on a washstand, twice throwing the used water into another pail on the floor before the final delicious rinsing at a third basin of the water that had run off the roof into the cistern. The calluses inside his hands were intricate with hollows and fissures. To dig out the black grit from the deep cracks took longer than any part of the washing, and still black lines of smudge failed to come out.

In late spring, summer, and early fall, he would often work in the garden till after dark, more than one night in October picking tomatoes and digging potatoes by the light of a moon. In the colder months he always found something to fix or improve. He liked to sew patches on his jeans pants or his work coat and had his own strong thread and large needle for replacing lost buttons. In those early years he read a weekly paper from Chicago—*Hemlandet*, Swedish for "homeland." Regularly he or Mother read aloud, to each other and the children, from the Swedish Bible.

My mother had fair hair, between blond and brown—the color of oat straw just before the sun tans it—eyes light-blue, skin white as fresh linen by candlelight, the mouth for smiling. She had ten smiles for us to one from our father. Her nose was retroussé, not snub. She was five feet five inches high and weighed perhaps one hundred and forty. She had tireless muscles on her bones and was tireless about her housework. She did the cooking, washing, sewing, bedmaking, and housecleaning for her family of nine. At six in the morning she was up to get breakfast for her man and later breakfast for the children. There were meals for all again at noon and at evening. Always there were clothes to be patched, the boys sometimes wearing out a third seat of trousers. As we got into long pants, the knees usually needed patching. Playing marbles in the spring, wrestling, and scuffling, we wore holes at the knees, which went bare till "Mama" patched the holes. That was always our name for her when we spoke to her or of her in the family circle.

My father had respect and affection for Magnus Holmes, older by fifteen years, and his close friend and adviser. He was well Americanized when August Sandburg arrived at the Holmes house in the early 1870s. He had been in Galesburg more than fifteen years; the men he worked with were mostly Irish and English, and he and Mrs. Holmes learned English so well that they made it the one language spoken in their house. So their four sons never learned to speak Swedish and their daughter Lily learned her Swedish speech by going one summer to the Swedish Lutheran parish school.

From Magnus Holmes, August Sandburg learned many simple and important English words he needed. And this cousin explained where to go and what papers to sign in order to become an American citizen. For years the Holmeses came to the Sandburgs for Thanksgiving dinner and the Sandburgs went to the Holmeses on New Year's Day. Once in our house on Thanksgiving I heard Mr. Holmes talk on the Declaration of Independence and then make clear to my father the Constitution of the United States.

In the Sandburg family the first three children, Mary, Carl August, and Martin Godfrey, learned Swedish fairly well. I am sure that while I was still in dresses, I used only Swedish words to tell what I was wanting. But while the two boys, Emil and Fred, and the two girls, Esther and Martha, who came later knew that *mjolk* was milk, they couldn't count to six in Swedish.

Among the younger church members later there were grumblings and mutterings. "Why must we listen to sermons in Swedish when we can't understand what the preacher is telling us?" After a time there were occasional sermons in English, and changes went on in many churches till all the preaching was in English. This didn't come easy for gray-bearded old-timers who could remember when they sat in their pews two hours with their ears drinking in the beloved syllables of the speech of the homeland that still had its hold over them.

278

For all that was unjust in living conditions in Sweden that had sent them to America, my father and mother kept a warmth of feeling, a genuine affection, for Swedish people and the language of *gamla hemlandet* (the old country). It stayed deep in their hearts. But they told us little about the Old Country. In their first years in America they had their minds set on making a go of it in the New Country. Then as the years passed they spoke the language of the new land and made many friends and acquaintances who spoke no Swedish, their own later children speaking only English. They became part of the new land.

From The Sword in the Stone
by T. H. White

This is one of my very favorite books. It is, of course, about young Wart, who is tutored by Merlin, and becomes King Arthur. The Sword in the Stone is about Wart's education as a young boy, before he becomes king. It is clear that Wart could not have drawn the sword from the stone if he had not been truly prepared for it, educated in a way that he might truly fulfill his destiny.

In a way, all the stories in Teach Your Children Well *are gifts from many Merlins. In this final excerpt, Wart follows Merlin's advice and meets with the badger. The child has studied animals and birds and fish, and now he is ready to learn about Man.*

"So, Merlyn sent you to me," said the badger, "to finish off your education. Well, I can only teach you two things: to dig, and to love your home. These are the true end of philosophy."

"Would you show me your home?"

"Certainly," said the badger, "though, of course, I don't use it at all. It's a rambling old place, much too big for a single man. I suppose some parts of it may be a thousand years old. There are about four families of us in it, here and there, take it by and large, from cellar to attics, and sometimes we don't meet for months. A crazy old place, I suppose it must seem to you modern people, but there, it's cozy."

He went ambling off down the corridors, rolling from leg to leg with that queer badger paddle, his white mask with its black stripes looking ghostly in the gloom.

"It's along that passage," he said, "if you want to wash your hands."

Badgers are not like foxes. They have a special midden where they put out their used bones and rubbish, proper earth closets, and bedrooms whose bedding they turn out frequently, to keep it clean. The Wart was enchanted with all he saw. He admired the Great Hall most, for this was the central room of the whole fortification—it was difficult to know whether to think of it as a fortification or as a palace—and all the various suites and bold holes radiated outward from it. It was a bit cobwebby, owing to being a sort of common room instead of being looked after by one particular family, but it was decidedly solemn. Badger called it the Combination Room. All around the paneled walls there were ancient paintings of departed badgers, famous in their day for scholarship or godliness, lit up from above by shaded glowworms. There were stately chairs with the badger arms stamped in gold upon their Spanish leather seats—the leather was coming off—and a portrait of the Founder over the fireplace. The chairs were arranged in a semi-circle to the top. Some black gowns hung in the passage outside, and all was extremely ancient.

"I'm a bachelor at the moment," said the badger apologetically, when they got back to his own snug room with the flowered wallpaper, "so I'm afraid there is only one chair. You will have to sit on the bed. Make yourself at home, my dear, while I brew some punch, and tell me how things are going on in the wide world."

"Oh, they go on much the same. Merlyn is very well, and Kay is to be made a knight next week."

"An interesting ceremony," commented the badger, stirring the spirits with a big spoon.

"What enormous arms you have got," remarked the Wart, watching him. "So have I, for that matter." And he looked down at his own bandy-legged muscles. He was really just a tight chest holding together a pair of forearms, mighty as thighs.

"It's to dig with," said the badger complacently. "Mole and I, I suppose you would have to dig pretty quick to match with us."

"I met a hedgehog outside," said the Wart.

"Did you now? They say nowadays that hedgehogs can carry swine fever and foot-and-mouth disease."

"I thought he was rather nice."

"They do have a sort of pathetic appeal," said the badger sadly, "but I'm afraid I generally just munch them up. There is something irresistible about pork crackling.

"The Egyptians," he added, and by this he meant the gypsies, "are fond of them for eating, too."

"Mine wouldn't uncurl."

"You should have pushed him into some water," said the badger, "and then he'd have shown you his poor legs quick enough. Come, the punch is ready. Sit you down by the fire and take your ease."

"It's nice to sit here with the snow and wind outside."

"It is nice. Let us drink good luck to Kay in his knighthood."

"Good luck to Kay, then."

"Good luck."

"Well," said the badger, setting down his glass again with a sigh. "Now what could have possessed Merlyn to send you to me?"

"He was talking about learning," said the Wart.

"Ah, well, if it's learning you are after, you have come to the right shop. But don't you find learning rather dull?"

"Sometimes I do," said the Wart, "and sometimes I don't. On the whole I can bear a good deal of learning if it's about natural history."

"I am writing a treatise just now," said the badger, coughing diffidently to show that he was absolutely set upon explaining it, "which is to point out why Man has become the master of all the animals. Perhaps you would like to hear that?

"It's for my D.Litt., you know," added the badger hastily, before Wart could protest. He got so few chances of reading his treatises to anybody, that he could not bear to let this priceless opportunity slip by.

"Thank you very much," said the Wart.

"It will be good for you, you know," explained the badger in a humble tone. "It's just the thing to top off your education. Study birds and fish and animals: then finish off with Man. How fortunate you came. Now where the devil did I put that manuscript?"

The old gentleman hurriedly scratched about with his great claws until he had turned up a dirty old bundle of papers, one corner of which had been used for lighting something. Then he sat down in his leather armchair, which had a deep depression in the middle of it; put on his velvet smoking-cap with the tassel; and produced a pair of tarantula spectacles, which he balanced on the end of his nose.

"Hem," said the badger.

He immediately became completely paralyzed with shyness, and sat blushing at his papers, unable to begin.

"Go on," said the Wart.

"It's not very good," explained the badger coyly. "It's just a rough draft, you know. I shall alter a lot before I send it in."

"I am sure it must be interesting," said the Wart.

"Oh, no, it isn't a bit interesting. It's just an old thing I threw off in an odd half-hour, just to pass the odd time, you know. But still, this is how it begins."

"Hem!" said the badger. Then he put on an impossibly high falsetto voice and began to read as fast as possible.

"People often ask as an idle question whether the process of evolution began with the chicken or the egg. Was there an egg out of which the first chicken came, or did a chicken lay the first egg? I am in a position to state that the first thing created was the egg.

"When God had manufactured all the eggs out of which the fishes and the serpents and the birds and the mammals and even the duck-billed platypus would eventually emerge, he called the embryos before him, and saw that they were good.

"Perhaps I ought to explain," added the badger, lowering his papers nervously and looking at the Wart over the top of them, "that all embryos look very much the same. They are what you are before you are born, and whether you are going to be a tadpole or a peacock or a camelopard or a man, when you are an embryo you just look like a peculiarly repulsive and helpless human being. I continue as follows:

"The embryos stood up in front of God, with their feeble hands clasped politely over their stomachs and their heavy heads hanging down respectfully, and God addressed them.

"He said, 'Now, you embryos, here you are, all looking exactly the same, and We are going to give you the choice of what you are going to be. When you grow up you will get bigger anyway, but We are pleased to grant you another gift as well. You may alter any parts of yourselves into anything which you think would be useful to you in after life. For instance, at the moment you can't dig. Anybody who would like to turn his hands into a pair of spades or garden forks is allowed to do so. Or, to put it another way, at present you can only use your mouths for eating with. Anybody who would like to use his mouth as an offensive weapon, can change it by asking, and be a corkindrill or a saber-toothed tiger. Now then, step up and choose your tools, but remember that what you choose you will grow into, and will have to stick to.'

"All the embryos thought the matter over politely, and then, one by one, they stepped up before the eternal throne. They were allowed two or three specializations, so that some chose to use their arms as flying machines and their mouths as weapons, or crackers, or drillers, or spoons, while others selected to use their bodies as boats and their hands as oars. We badgers thought very hard and decided to ask three boons. We wanted to change our skins for shields, our mouths for weapons, and our arms for garden forks. These boons were granted to us. Everybody specialized in one way or another, and some of us in very queer ones. For instance, one of the lizards decided to swap his whole body for blotting paper, and one of the toads who lived in the antipodes decided simply to be a water bottle.

"The asking and granting took up two long days—they were the fifth and sixth, so far as I remember—and at the very end of the sixth day, just before it was time to knock off for Sunday, they had got through all the little embryos except one. This embryo was Man.

" 'Well, Our little Man,' said God. 'You have waited till the last, and slept on your decision, and We are sure you have been thinking hard all the time. What can We do for you?'

" 'Please, God,' said the embryo, 'I think that You made me in the shape which I now have for reasons best known to Yourselves, and that it would be rude to change. If I am to have my choice I will stay just as I am. I will not alter any of the parts which You gave to me, for other and doubtless inferior tools, and I will stay a defenseless embryo all my life, doing my best to make unto myself a few feeble implements out of the wood, iron, and other materials which you have seen fit to put before me. If I want a boat I will endeavor to construct it out of trees, and if I want to fly I will put together a chariot to do it for me. Probably I have been very silly in refusing to take advantage of Your kind offer, but I have done my best to think it over carefully, and now hope that the feeble decision of this small innocent will find favor with Yourselves.'

" 'Well done,' exclaimed the Creator in delighted tones. 'Here, all you embryos, come here with your beaks and whatnots to look upon Our first Man. He is the only one who has guessed Our riddle, out of all of you, and We have great pleasure in conferring upon him the Order of Dominion over the Fowls of the Air, and the Beasts of the Earth, and the Fishes of the Sea. Now let the rest of you get along, and love and multiply, for it is time to knock off for the weekend. As for you, Man, you will be a naked tool all your life, though a user of tools: you will look like an embryo till they bury you, but all others will be embryos before your might; eternally undeveloped, you will always remain potentially in Our image, able to see some of Our sorrows and to feel some of Our joys. We are partly sorry for you, Man, and partly happy, but always proud. Run along then, Man, and do your best. And listen, Man, before you go . . .'

" 'Well?' asked Adam, turning back from his dismissal.

" 'We were only going to say,' said God shyly, twisting Their hands together. 'Well, We were just going to say, God bless you.' "

Highly Recommended Reading

This is an eclectic, utterly opinionated survey of children's books that I have read myself and recommend without hesitation. They are either fiercely grounded in basic Western philosophy, or just plain fun to read. I think you and your children will love them.

The books are primarily for six- to twelve-year-olds. Obviously, this covers a lot of ground and I have indicated when a book is clearly for older readers. There are some holes here. I have not included books that rely on illustration to make them work. Nor have I included "information books," though it is assumed that a steady diet of nonfiction, especially history and science, is crucial for the educated child. I have grouped the books into three categories: fiction, biographies, and fairy tales.

You will note that I am partial to classics, modern and not-so-modern. "Lite" books don't get a mention; from time to time your child will probably gravitate to them without encouragement anyway. And because authors are the core of it all, my list runs alphabetically, by author. I am sure I have missed dozens, no, hundreds of wonderful books, but these at least have been pioneered for you by a thoughtful eye.

Fiction

Alcott, Louisa May, *Little Women; Little Men*: These are available in myriad editions, and they are still beloved by children. The writing is fresh and the characters still engaging.

Alexander, Lloyd, *The Book of Three*, Henry Holt & Co., 1964: Taran, the pig-keeper, is fated to become king. A fast-paced fantasy novel that boys will love; well written and imaginative.

Armstrong, William H., *Sounder* (illustrated by James Barkley), Harper & Row, 1969: Sounder, a great coon dog, and his master are wounded and doomed to a shared and terrible destiny. A classic tale about a young boy who must struggle with poverty and the trappings of sharecropper life. An exceptional read.

Avi, *Bright Shadow*, Aladdin Books, Macmillan, 1985: A philosophical thriller. Morwenna is the lowliest servant in the palace and leads a dull life, until she accidentally is entrusted with the last five wishes in the kingdom. This book investigates choices and responsibilities. Great for middle and older readers.

Babbitt, Natalie, *Tuck Everlasting*, Farrar, Straus and Giroux, 1975: This is for older children but one to keep on your list. It is a character study of Winnie Foster, an eleven-year old who discovers a secret stream; anyone who drinks from it will live forever. This book poses a philosophical question about the worth of eternal life, and so causes the reader to examine his own life. Beautiful.

Barrie, J. M., *Peter Pan*: Most of us know the cut-off version of *Peter Pan*. The book actually takes Wendy into her adulthood and has Wendy's daughter caring for Peter. A wonderful read-aloud. Available in various editions.

Baum, L. Frank, *The Wizard of Oz*: There is a whole family of Oz books, and they are highly recommended and fun (see excerpt, pages 29–35). This may be one of the first "series" books.

Burnett, Frances Hodgson, *The Secret Garden* (many editions): This classic is a must-read in the eight-and-up category. About the self-absorbed little girl who joins an indulged, sickly boy to learn about life.

Burnford, Sheila, *The Incredible Journey* (illustrated by Carl Berger), Little, Brown, 1961: A seven-hankie book based on actual events about two dogs and a cat who share a truly, well, incredible journey. This book embodies the idea of devotion and loyalty and love.

Carrick, Carol, *Stay Away from Simon* (illustrated by Donald Carrick), Clarion, 1985: Marion Geller, who taught Gillea in first grade, introduced me to the world of Carrick books, and it is a wonderful world indeed. This is the story of Simon, a retarded child, who is feared by his neighborhood until he becomes a hero to Lucy and her brother.

Carroll, Lewis, *Alice's Adventures in Wonderland* (drawings by Sir John Tenniel), St. Martin's, 1977: This is like introducing you to apple juice, right? But have your children actually read the book? It's an incredible read, and extremely sophisticated. Best for slightly older children; six-year-olds won't be able to revel in the wit.

Cleary, Beverly, *Ramona the Pest* (illustrated by Louis Darling), William Morrow, 1968: Young girls seem to enjoy all of the Ramona books; they are almost too obvious to mention but I'll do it anyway. They are great fun and wonderfully detailed. Reluctant readers seem to get a jolt from them. Cleary also has an appealing series about a little boy called Henry Huggins.

Cleaver, Vera and Bill, *Where the Lilies Bloom*, Lippincott, 1969: When I read this book aloud to my children, they were too young to appreciate the poetry of the description or the melody of the dialogue. I, however, was in heaven. I highly recommend this story about Mary Call, who at fourteen must do whatever she can to keep her brothers and sisters from being separated and sent off to foster care now that their father is dead. Mary Call is one of the admirable female heroines in literature. A must for readers nine and up.

de Angeli, Marguerite, *The Door in the Wall*, Doubleday, 1949: Robin, the crippled son of a great lord, proves his courage and wins his King's recognition. Great book. Girls won't pick this up without some encouragement, but give it a shot. Girls have to learn how to be gentlemen too.

Enright, Elizabeth, *The Saturdays*, Dell, 1941: Writer Joyce Harris mailed me a box of Elizabeth Enright books when she heard about this book project, introducing me to the Melendy Family. It's a delightful series (includes *The Four-Story Mistake, Then There Were Five, Spiderweb for Two*), but it is also admirable for its handling of friendships, family, and respect for older people. It was written fifty years ago, but it still speaks to children, especially girls.

Estes, Eleanor, *The Hundred Dresses* (illustrated by Louis Slobodkin), Harcourt, 1944: This is a great one to hand to the second-grader who is beginning to enter into the world of girl cliques. It's about a poor Polish child named Wanda, who wears a ragged dress each day but boasts that she has a hundred dresses at home. The "group" is merciless and Maddie, who knows better, fails to come to poor Wanda's defense. An excellent book for second- and third-grade girls. Also recommended is *The Moffats* by Eleanor Estes. Tales of four lively children; a modern classic.

Farley, Walter, *The Black Stallion,* Random House, 1941: Another of the series books; it is good storytelling about the adventures of a young boy and a horse. You probably saw the movie. The book is even better.

Fisher, Dorothy Canfield, *Understood Betsy,* Henry Holt & Co., 1945: The story of a sheltered girl named Elizabeth Ann, who at the book's beginning is helpless and overprotected. Her adventures lead her to a new sense of herself and life—and even a new name—Betsy.

Fitzgerald, John D., *The Great Brain* (illustrated by Mercer Mayer), Dial, 1967: This is an extremely witty, well-written series, which I recommend for slightly older children. (Six- and seven-year-olds won't get it.) The Great Brain is a scheming smart kid who solves mysteries and helps people. His brother narrates the series from a fond distance. Funny, wise books.

Fitzhugh, Louise, *Harriet the Spy,* Harper & Row, 1964: Harriet is a precocious, isolated young girl who keeps copious, rather mean-spirited notes on her family and friends. Her notebook is discovered; and Harriet makes some discoveries of her own about life.

George, Jean C., *My Side of the Mountain,* Dutton, 1959: Sam Gribley is chiseling out his own identity by going back to the land of his forebears and spending a year as a mountain boy near the Catskill Mountains. It is a year of adventures and a special kind of survival. Outdoors lovers will especially enjoy.

Gipson, Fred, *Old Yeller,* Harper & Row, 1964: The storybook is as moving as the moving picture. Why not read it aloud?

Godden, Rumer, *The Story of Holly and Ivy,* Viking Penguin: Puffin, 1986: If your daughter likes dolls, she will find a literary companion in Rumer Godden, who wrote numerous lovely "doll" tales. They are all well-told stories, and many are beautifully illustrated.

Grahame, Kenneth, *The Wind in the Willows* (illustrated by Ernest H. Shepard), Scribner's, 1908: Life in the Wild Wood, the story of rodents and reptiles living in inspired harmony. This book is great fare for seven or eight and up.

Henry, Marguerite, *Misty of Chincoteague* (illustrated by Wesley Dennis), Rand McNally, 1947: For younger readers (and an excellent read-aloud); it is basically about two children who love a wild pony on Chincoteague Island. For horse fans, especially. If it appeals, go on to *Sea Star*.

Holm, Anne, *North to Freedom*, Harcourt Brace Jovanovich, 1965: David, a twelve-year-old, escapes from an Eastern European concentration camp where he has lived most of his life. Alone he traverses the European continent on foot. American children, who cannot imagine life without freedom, benefit enormously from reading about those who must pursue it at all costs. It is for an older reader, and it is magnificent.

Kelly, Eric P., *The Trumpeter of Krakow* (illustrated by Janina Domanska), Macmillan, 1966: A tale of medieval Poland, this book is a beautiful tale of courage and justice. For older readers.

Kipling, Rudyard, *The Jungle Book*: The Disney generation is often not aware that there actually is a *book* about Mowgli, the boy raised in the jungle by marvelous witty and wise beasts! Available in many versions.

Konigsburg, E. L., *From the Mixed-up Files of Mrs. Basil E. Frankweiler*, Atheneum, 1967: Claudia runs away . . . to the Metropolitan Museum of Art. 'Nuff said. A wonderful read.

LeGuin, Ursula, *The Wizard of Earthsea* (illustrated by Ruth Robbins), Parnassus, 1968: A fantasy book, this is the story of Ged and the great lessons he learns about good and evil.

L'Engle, Madeleine, *A Wrinkle in Time*, Farrar, Straus and Giroux, 1962: Madeleine L'Engle is my idol. This book is the story of Meg and her quest to save her missing father; her journey takes her into another dimension in time where success depends on the power of love. Madeleine L'Engle writes fantasy books, but even children who are not fantasy lovers per se will be swept away by this magnificent storyteller. Ms. L'Engle deserves a national shrine; her books are exciting, poetic, and wise (see excerpt, pages 182–193).

Lewis, C. S., The Narnia Chronicles: If you are only going to read one book to your child in His Entire Life it should be *The Lion, the Witch and the Wardrobe* (Macmillan, 1951), one of the Narnia Chronicles. It is one of the finest tales ever told. Nine-year-olds and up will enjoy reading the Chronicles privately, but it would be *much* better if you were involved (see excerpt, pages 62–71).

Little, Jean: *One to Grow On*, Little, Brown & Co., 1969: About an interminable liar who comes to terms with her family, her friends, and herself. Chatty writing. Girls will enjoy. Jean Little has written numerous other books, many of which address the difficulties of being "different." (Ms. Little is blind and is particularly sensitive to children with disabilities.) Other choices include *Mine for Keeps, Listen for the Singing* and *From Anna,* to name a few.

London, Jack, *The Call of the Wild* (illustrated by Karel Kezer), Macmillan, 1966: Buck, part St. Bernard, part shepherd dog, is snatched from a sheltered life in California and thrust into the Klondike to live the life of a sled dog. A classic tale to be read aloud—especially if you missed it the first time.

Lord, Bette Bao, *In the Year of the Boar and Jackie Robinson* (illustrated by Marc Simont), Harper & Row, 1984: The story of a little girl who leaves China and resettles with her parents in Brooklyn. A warm account of a difficult situation.

MacDonald, George, *At the Back of the North Wind*, David R. Goodine, 1988: This is a mystical fantasy about a little boy named Diamond and his friend, a beautiful and terrible lady called the North Wind. She carries the good child on adventures, flying in the cradle of her long tresses. A story about unforgettable worlds. For older readers. Extraordinary.

MacLachlan, Patricia, *Sarah, Plain and Tall*, Harper & Row, 1985: I found this story charming. It's about a family who advertises for a wife and mother, and the woman who responds: Sarah, who is both plain and tall but is filled with inner light and beauty. She comes into the life of two children and their father, and changes them forever.

Manes, Stephen, *Be a Perfect Person in Just Three Days!* (illustrated by Tom Huffman), Clarion, 1982: I like the message in this silly book. Milo dreams of being "perfect" and comes up with the panacea à la Dr. K. Pinkerton Silverfish's advice. A worthy revelation comes about.

Milne, A. A., *When We Were Very Young* (illustrated by E. H. Shepard), Dutton, 1924: I mention this classic collection of poems only in the remote event of someone from Pluto picking up this list. Also, of course: *Winnie-the-Pooh* and *Now We Are Six.*

Montgomery, L. M. *Anne of Green Gables*, Buccaneer Books, 1908: A classic story about an orphaned girl who finds a new life with a new family. A series book, which is excellent, though I am a greater fan of the Emily series; try *Emily of New Moon* and see if you don't agree.

Nesbit, E., *The Five Children and It* (illustrations by H. R. Millar), Puffin, 1959: Written at the turn of the century, this series is about (surprise) five children and a sand fairy. For older children, it is high quality, engaging literature.

O'Dell, Scott, *Island of the Blue Dolphins*, Houghton Mifflin, 1960: The story of a young Indian girl, Karana, struggling to make it on a deserted island off the coast of California. A tale of nature and courage and resourcefulness. Excellent.

Paterson, Katherine, *The Bridge to Terabithia*, Crowell, 1977: This is a love story about a country boy and a city girl, the imaginary world they create together, and then the girl's accidental death. An extraordinary book about friendship and loss, for older children.

Pearce, Philippa, *Tom's Midnight Garden*, Lippincott, 1958: A good tale, well told about young Tom, who while staying at his aunt's house takes a trip back in time. A complex thriller, this should be saved for older readers.

Rawls, Wilson, *Where the Red Fern Grows*, The Curtis Publishing Company, 1961: A story about a boy and two dogs and things sacred. It is for an older reader—ten and up—or to be read aloud to a patient audience (it's long). Magical storytelling.

Robinson, Barbara, *The Best Christmas Pageant Ever*, Harper & Row, 1972: This book will crack your children up. Wonderful holiday book.

Rodowsky, Colby, *What About Me,* Franklin Watts, 1976: I cried through this whole book, and I'm glad I read it privately. It's a love story about a girl whose brother has Down syndrome. It's not like having a normal brother, whom you can "hate." This is a tough read—the little boy dies in the end—and the sister is sort of left with her contradictory feelings hanging. It is a masterfully written book, however, for a very mature child—or adult.

Sandburg, Carl, *Abe Lincoln Grows Up,* Harcourt, 1926: Why not go to the master? For older children, this biography of Lincoln is a classic.

Singer, Isaac Bashevis, *Stories for Children,* Farrar, Straus and Giroux (paper): This is a delightful, warm, and powerful collection of short stories for children by the sainted I. B. Singer. Over thirty stories in all. For children and adults as well (see excerpt on pages 73–78).

Smith, Robert K., *Chocolate Fever,* Dell, 1978: This is the chocolate version of King Midas. Children love it.

Sorenson, Virginia, *Plain Girl,* Harcourt, 1955: This is a quaint and lyrically written book about an Amish girl, who was "home-schooled" until she was ten years old and then forced by Pennsylvania school authorities to attend public school. The book tracks her and her brother Dan's travails and choices.

Spyri, Johanna, *Heidi*: The orphan Heidi transforms the heart and mind of her grandfather and then a crippled child. For nine- to twelve-year-olds and available in many editions.

Steig, William, *The Real Thief,* Farrar, Straus and Giroux. A thief, burdened by guilt, aims to set everything straight—and discovers how hard it is to right a wrong. A wonderful tale of justice and injustice, this is a kiddy crash course on ethics without preaching a word. Mr. Steig is one of the best storytellers your children will ever read. Other masterpieces of his to borrow or buy (but not steal): *Amos and Boris, Abel's Island, Dominic, Brave Irene.* Get them all.

Taylor, Sydney, *All-of-a-Kind Family,* Dell, 1966: This is a lovable series about a Jewish family who lives during the turn of the century in New York; five girls, lots of fun. My daughter loves these books.

Tolkien, J.R.R., *The Hobbit* (illustrated by Michael Hague), Houghton Mifflin, 1984: For fantasy lovers, the ultimate tale of elves and trolls and little ghosts. An unforgettable read for older children.

Travers, P. L., *Mary Poppins* (illustrated by Mary Shepard) Voyage/ Harcourt, 1985: A magic nanny for children of all ages and all time. The book is splendidly written and children nine to twelve will love it (see pages 250–258 for excerpt).

Twain, Mark, *The Adventures of Tom Sawyer*: For children ten and older, this is brilliant writing, funny and wise and exciting (see pages 14–28 for excerpt). It goes without saying that *Adventures of Huckleberry Finn* should be read as well.

White, E. B., *Charlotte's Web* (illustrated by Garth Williams), Harper & Row, 1952. When a spider saves a pig's life, you've got a classic. No one should get out of childhood without reading this wonder.

Wilder, Laura Ingalls, *Little House on the Prairie* (illustrated by Garth Williams), Harper & Row, 1935: This is another one to make sure your child gets a chance to read. If she or he gets hooked, there's a slew of "Little House" books to read. All of the pioneer values of commitment, sacrifice, adventure, and stamina are portrayed here.

Yep, Laurence, *Dragonwings*, Harper Trophy 1975: The story of Moon Shadow, an eight-year-old boy who leaves China to join his father in San Francisco. Not only is the country and its customs all new, but Moon Shadow has never met his father before. With Moon Shadow's help, his father builds a flying machine. A literary celebration of courage and the human spirit. (I also recommend Yep's *The Rainbow People*, a collection of Chinese-American folklore.)

Biographies and Profiles

Aliki, *A Weed Is a Flower: The Life of George Washington Carver*, Simon and Schuster, 1988. This book is a wonderful beginner biography about Mr. Carver, who was born a slave and became a noted scientist devoted to helping the South improve its agriculture. For the very beginning reader.

Bragdon, Lillian, *Meet the Remarkable Adams Family,* Atheneum, 1967: A spirited biography of this extraordinary family, good for older readers.

Brink, Carol Ryrie, *Caddie Woodlawn,* Macmillan, 1935: This is one you might remember reading when you were a child; it is based on a true story of a pioneer family in 1864. Caddie is a feisty eleven-year-old tomboy, an excellent model for girls and lots of fun to read.

Cleary, Beverly, *A Girl from Yamhill: A Memoir,* Dell, 1989. This is an autobiography by one of America's favorite children's authors, who recalls her childhood in Portland, Oregon. Probably best for the child nine years or older.

Dahl, Roald, *Boy: Tales of Childhood,* Puffin, 1984: The true stories behind the twisted humor of one of the best-loved children's authors.

Dalgliesh, Alice, *The Courage of Sarah Noble,* Macmillan: In this fictionalized account, a little girl travels with her father to their new homestead and then is left with a group of Indians while her father goes back for the rest of the family. For grades one through four, wonderful especially for girls.

d'Aulaire, Ingri and Edgar Parin, *Columbus; Benjamin Franklin; Abraham Lincoln; Pocahontas; George Washington,* Doubleday. Some of the best beginner biographies available, these oversized picture books have large, bright illustrations and simple, engaging text. They are ideal for grades K through four.

Davidson, Margaret, *Helen Keller,* Scholastic, 1969: An easy-to-read version of Helen Keller's remarkable life, Scholastic also includes a Braille alphabet on the back cover. Related additional reading: Margaret Davidson's *Helen Keller's Teacher,* the biography of Annie Sullivan, Scholastic, 1972; Edith Fisher Hunter's *Child of the Silent Night,* Dell, 1963, the story of Laura Bridgman, who was also deaf and blind. She studied with Samuel Gridley Howe, the first director of the Perkins School for the Blind; her education paved the way for Helen Keller. (For beginners, grades two to four); Margaret Davidson's *Louis Braille: The Boy Who Invented Books for the Blind,*

Scholastic, 1971 (grades K to three); and *The Story of My Life* by Helen Keller (grades seven and up).

Forbes, Esther, *Johnny Tremain* (illustrated by Lynd Ward), Dell Yearling/ Laurel Leaf, 1969: A wonderful historical novel for older children (ten to twelve). This book has excited thousands of children about history, and is highly recommended.

Frank, Anne, *The Diary of a Young Girl*, Doubleday, 1967: This is so obvious, but must not be forgotten. An important book for all educated children to read and discuss.

Fritz, Jean, *Traitor: The Case of Benedict Arnold*, Putnam Publishing Group, 1981: I wish Jean Fritz had been writing biographies when I was a young girl. She writes powerful, readable, real accounts that bring historical characters alive. You can't go wrong with this biographer and historian, who has written a multitude of books about famous people, including Pocahontas, Sam Houston, King George, and Stonewall Jackson.

Killilea, Marie, *Karen*, Dell, 1952: Marie Killilea writes of the trials and triumphs in the life of her daughter, Karen, who was born in 1940 with cerebral palsy. An exquisite book about the human spirit. Also *With Love from Karen* from Dell.

Little, Jean, *Little by Little: A Writer's Childhood*, Viking, 1988: Jean Little's biographies are riveting. This book chronicles her own childhood in Canada, the difficulties growing up visually impaired, and her aspirations to become a writer in spite of it all. Marvelous.

Meigs, Cornelia, *Invincible Louisa: The Story of Louisa May Alcott*, Scholastic, 1987: For grades six and up, this is an award-winning biography of the beloved children's author.

Peet, Bill, *Bill Peet: An Autobiography*, Houghton Mifflin, 1989: has illustrated jillions of picture books and in this book he tells the story of his boyhood in Indiana, art school, his work at Disney Studios (his illustrations of Dumbo were based on his own infant son) and more. I think anyone who has read his stories will enjoy this book. For grades three and up.

Petry, Ann, *Harriet Tubman: Conductor on the Underground Railroad*, HarperCollins, 1955: For grades five and up, an excellent biography of the remarkable woman who was born a slave and escaped to freedom on the Underground Railroad and spent her life helping others along the dangerous route North. Also *Freedom Train: The Story of Harriet Tubman*, Scholastic, 1987: For grades four through six.

Stanley, Diane and Peter Vennema, *Good Queen Bess: The Story of Elizabeth I of England*, Macmillan, 1990: Simple text and lots of illustrations make this story of Elizabeth I accessible to younger readers, grades one through four.

Fairy Tales, Folktales, Legends

Andersen, Hans Christian: Here is an obvious master, and I mention him only because I want to underscore the importance of fairy tales. This book contains a few fairy tales, but to be truly educated a child should have a working knowledge of the "greats," from Andersen, the Brothers Grimm, Perrault, and others. *Dulac's the Snow Queen: And Other Stories*, published by Doubleday, is a fine collection for starters. Also, I recommend *The Little Mermaid*, illustrated by Katie Thamer Treherne, published by Harcourt, Brace, Jovanovich.

Courlander, Harold, *The Crest and the Hide and Other African Stories of Heroes, Chiefs, Bards, Hunters, Sorcerers and Common People* (illustrated by Monica Vachula), Putnam, 1982: Mr. Courlander is an immensely gifted folklorist (see pages 106–109 for "The Fire on the Mountain"). He recreates his tales with poetry and authenticity— and only after having done meticulous research. I recommend any and all of his work.

d'Aulaire, Ingri and Edgar Parin, *d'Aulaires' Norse Gods and Giants*, Doubleday, 1967: This book is a classic on the classics. Children love the illustrations as well as the stories. A crucial introduction to mythology, this book is highly recommended. (Also look for the d'Aulaires' book on Greek mythology.)

dePaola, Tomie, *The Clown of God*, Harcourt, Brace, Jovanovich, 1978:

This is one of my all-time favorite books, and can be read to persons of all ages. It is a folktale retold about the dying juggler who performs his best act before a stone statue of the Mother and Child, miraculously transforming the child's expression from a stern stare to a smile. The message is that "everything sings to the glory of God—even juggling." Anything Tomie dePaola does sings to the glory of God, and is worth the purchase or the loan. Discover him for your six- to nine-year-old now.

Evslin, Bernard, *The Green Hero: The Early Adventures of Finn McCool*, Four Winds Press, 1975: I have a great admiration for this writer, whose retelling of myths and folktales is unsurpassed. Finn Mc-Cool is an utterly lovable Irish hero with lots of warts and a wonderful heart (see pages 162–173 for excerpt). Please seek out all of Evslin's works, including *The Adventures of Ulysses.*

Garner, Alan, *Alan Garner's Book of British Fairy Tales* (illustrated by Derek Collard), Delacorte, 1985: This man can write. The stories are for children, of course, but the writing is so superb I wonder if only adults can truly appreciate it. A lovely collection of twenty-one tales.

Hamilton, Virginia, *The People Could Fly: American Black Folktales* (illustrated by Leo and Diane Dillon), Knopf, 1985: This is a marvelous collection of retold tales, including many classical characters like Br'er Rabbit, John de Conquer, and some you've never heard of.

Hodges, Margaret, *Saint George and the Dragon* (illustrated by Trinia Schart Hyman), Little, Brown, 1984: The legend of St. George's heroics in slaying the dragon that has been menacing the countryside. A beautiful book. Also, for the younger reader, I recommend *Saint Jerome and the Lion*, which is a simple, beautiful tale children of any age will enjoy.

Jarrell, Randall, *Snow White and the Seven Dwarfs* (illustrated by Nancy E. Burkert), Farrar, Straus and Giroux, 1972: This book was given to Gillea by a passionate editor, Jeffrey Schaire, a few days after she was born. It was the first children's book in our library and it signaled an entry into the world of literature that has transformed our entire family. An exquisitely illustrated, beautifully penned translation, this book should be in your library as well.

Keats, Ezra Jack, *John Henry, An American Legend,* Pantheon, 1965: This is a wonderfully illustrated version of the famous tale of John Henry geared especially for younger children. The writing is superb and poetic. My girls loved this book and wanted it read to them over and over again.

McKinley, Robin, *Beauty: A Retelling of the Story of Beauty and the Beast,* Harper & Row, 1978: An exquisite, powerful version not to be missed.

Yolen, Jane, *Favorite Folktales from Around the World,* Pantheon, 1986: A fabulous collection of folktales by a much-loved author. A good choice for your personal library.

Epilogue

Babar finally drops off to sleep,
his sleep is restless and soon *he dreams*:
He hears a knocking on his door,
    Tap! Tap! Tap!
then a voice says to him:
"It is I, Misfortune,
with some of my companions,
come to pay you a visit."
Babar looks out of the window,
and sees a frightful old woman
surrounded by flabby ugly beasts
(anger, stupidity, sickness, indolence,
discouragement, cowardice, laziness,
ignorance, despair, fear).
He opens his mouth to shout:
"Ugh! Faugh! Go away quickly!"
But he stops to listen
to a very faint noise:
    Frr! Frr! Frr!
as of birds
flying in a flock,
and he sees coming toward him . . .
. . . graceful winged elephants
(goodness, hope, intelligence,
work, patience, courage, perseverance,
learning, joy, health, happiness, love)
who chase Misfortune

away from Celesteville
and bring back Happiness.
At this point he awakes,
and feels ever so much better.

from *Babar the King*
by Jean de Brunhoff

INDEX